About this Book

Uri Davis has been at the forefront of the defence of human rights in Israel since the mid-1960s, as well as being at the cutting edge of critical research on Israel and the Israeli–Palestinian conflict.

In this book, a sequel to *Israel: An Apartheid State* (Zed Books, 1987), Uri Davis provides a critical insight into how it came about that Jewish people, including the victims of Nazi genocide in the Second World War, subjected the Palestinian people, beginning with the 1948–49 war, to such criminal policies as mass deportation, population transfers and ethnic cleansing; prolonged military government (with curfews, roadblocks, so-called security fences and the like); and economic, social, cultural, civil and political strangulation, punctuated by house demolitions and Apache helicopters strafing civilians and their homes.

Since its establishment in 1948 Israel has acted in blatant violation of most UN Security Council and General Assembly resolutions, including amassing weapons of mass destruction in violation of international law. How is it then possible for this country, its apartheid legislation notwithstanding, still to maintain its reputation in the West as 'the only democracy in the Middle East' and effectively to veil the apartheid cruelty it has perpetrated against the Palestinian people?

In the course of outlining answers to these questions, Uri Davis traces the departure of the Palestine Liberation Organization (PLO) from its declared political programme; its steep decline beginning with the Oslo 'peace process'; and the struggle within Israel against Israeli apartheid.

The object of this book is to contribute to a moral understanding, political framework and climate of opinion in the West that will support international sanctions against the rogue government of Israel, with the aim of dismantling the state's apartheid structures as a state for Jews only, and assisting in the establishment of a democratic (whether confederal, federal or unitary) state of Palestine in conformity with the values of the Universal Declaration of Human Rights and the standards of international law.

Other books by Uri Davis

Documents from Israel (co-ed.), Ithaca Press, London, 1975

Dissent and Ideology in Israel (co-ed.), Ithaca Press, London, 1975

Israel and the Palestinians (co-ed.), Ithaca Press, London, 1975

Israel: Utopia Incorporated, Zed Books, London, 1977

Palestinian Arabs in Israel: Two Case Studies (co-author), Ithaca Press, London, 1977

Towards a Socialist Republic of Palestine (co-ed.), Ithaca Press, London and Miftah, Kefar Shemaryahu, 1978 (Arabic edition Miftah, Kefar Shemaryahu, 1978)

Debate on Palestine (co-ed.), Ithaca Press, London, 1981

Golan Heights under Israeli Occupation, Centre for Middle Eastern and Islamic Studies, University of Durham, 1983

Israel: An Apartheid State, Zed Books, London, 1987 (abridged edition Media Review Network, Laudium, 2001)

The Jewish National Fund (associate author), Kegan Paul International, London, 1988

The State of Palestine, Ithaca Press, Reading, 1991

Crossing the Border: A Political Autobiography, Books & Books, London, 1995 (Hebrew edition, Breirot, Tel Aviv, 1994)

Citizenship and the State: A Comparative Study of Citizenship Legislation in Israel, Jordan, Palestine, Syria and Lebanon, Ithaca Press, Reading, 1997

Citizenship and the State in the Middle East: Approaches and Applications (co-ed.), Syracuse University Press, 2000

APARTHEID ISRAEL
Possibilities for the struggle within

URI DAVIS

PRETORIA

Zed Books
LONDON · NEW YORK

Apartheid Israel: Possibilities for the struggle within was first published by Zed Books Ltd, 7 Cynthia Street, London N1 9JF, UK and Room 400, 175 Fifth Avenue, New York, NY 10010, USA in 2003.

www.zedbooks.co.uk

Published in South Africa by Media Review Network, PO Box 14391, Laudium, Pretoria 0037

www.mediareviewnet.com

Cover designed by Andrew Corbett
Set in Monotype Dante by Ewan Smith, London
Printed and bound in Malta by Gutenberg Ltd

Distributed in the USA exclusively by Palgrave Macmillan, a division of St Martin's Press, LLC, 175 Fifth Avenue, New York, NY 10010

A catalogue record for this book is available from the British Library.

Library of Congress cataloging-in-publication data has been applied for.

ISBN 1 84277 338 0 cased
ISBN 1 84277 339 9 limp

Contents

Acknowledgements

I wish to thank the Institute for Middle Eastern and Islamic Studies (IMEIS), University of Durham, notably Professor Anoushiravan Ehteshami and Dr Paul Starkey, for provision of an academic home for me as senior research fellow and making available to me valuable research facilities; the Institute of Arab and Islamic Studies (IAIS), University of Exeter, for library assistance; *Haaretz* daily newspaper archive for their service; AL-BEIT: Association for the Defence of Human Rights in Israel of 'Ar'ara and the Media Review Network (MRN) of Laudium, for their research grants; Karl Brandt and System Solutions of London for IT support; Adrian Brown of London, Walia Kani of Durham, Tosje Maks and Mike Garton of Exeter, Judith Perera of Berkhamsted and Fathi Mahamid of Qatzir for their hospitality; Zed Books for their publishing and editorial support; George Wilson, Hazel Simons and Yeshaayahu Toma Sik for initial proofreading; Advocates Tawfiq Jabarin and Siddiq Nassar for assistance with legal references; Ataliyah Boymel and Susan Nathan for assistance with research; the American Jewish Alternatives to Zionism (AJAZ); the Association of American Arab University Graduates (AAUG); the Center for Policy Analysis on Palestine (CPAP); the Council for the Advancement of Arab British Understanding (CAABU); Croom Helm; Al-Hayat Publishing Co. Ltd, UK; the Institute of Palestine Studies (IPS); the International Organization for the Elimination of All Forms of Racism and Racial Discrimination (EAFORD); Ithaca Press; the *Journal of Palestine Studies*, Melisende Press; the Norwegian Trade Union Federation, International Department; PASSIA: Palestinian Academic Society for the Study of International Affairs; *SAIS Review*: A Journal of International Affairs, Paul H. Nitze School of Advanced International Studies, Johns Hopkins University; United Nations Organization (UN); and Zed Books for their permission to quote from and draw upon the material acknowledged below in date order:

Uri Davis and Walter Lehn, 'And the Fund Still Lives: The Role of the Jewish National Fund in the Determination of Israel's Land Policies', *Journal of Palestine Studies*, Vol. VII, no. 4 (Issue 28, Summer 1978).

Havah ha-Levi, 'The Taste of Mulberries' in Fouzi el-Asmar, Uri Davis and Naim Khader (eds), *Debate on Palestine* (Ithaca Press, London

1981), pp. 56–61 and 'The Female Snake' in Uri Davis, *Israel: An Apartheid State*, Zed Books, London 1987, pp. 97–8.

Uri Davis, 'The Israeli Invasion of Lebanon: Regional and Global Implications', address to the Association of American Arab University Graduates (AAUG) Fifteenth Annual Convention, Panel One: 'What Made It Happen – The Israeli Factor', Montreal, Quebec, Canada, 22–24 October 1982.

Uri Davis, 'Israel's Zionist Society: Consequences for Internal Opposition and the Necessity for External Intervention', paper submitted before the American Jewish Alternatives to Zionism (AJAZ) and the International Organization for the Elimination of All Forms of Racism and Racial Discrimination (EAFORD), conference on Judaism or Zionism: What Difference for the Middle East – A Conference for Understanding and Peace, Madison Hotel, Washington, DC, 6–7 May 1983.

'Palestine at the UN: Dr Uri Davis and Felicia Langer, Supporters of the Palestinian Rights, Address the International Conference on the Question of Palestine, Geneva, 29 August–7 September 1983' (Views from Abroad), *Journal of Palestine Studies*, Vol. XIII, no. 2 (Issue 50, Winter 1984), pp. 192–4.

Uri Davis, 'Assessing the Dangers of Palestinian Defeat in the Current Peace Negotiations', address before the CAABU Monthly Meeting, House of Commons, 29 June 1993.

Uri Davis, 'Re-Examining History: Israel and the Holocaust', paper presented before the Third International Sabeel Conference, 'The Challenge of Jubilee: What Does God Require?', Bethlehem University, 10–15 February 1998 and published in Naim Ateek and Michael Prior (eds), *Holy Land, Hollow Jubilee*, Melisende, London, 1999, pp. 97–104.

Uri Davis, 'The Story of Qatzir' and 'That's One Small Step for Adil and Iman Qaadan and One Giant Leap Towards the Democratization of the State of Israel', *Al-Hayat*, 24 March 2000.

Uri Davis, 'Who is a Hebrew: A Reading of an Identity Construction: Palestinian Hebrew Anti-Zionist Jew of Dual Israeli and British Citizenship', *SAIS Review: A Journal of International Affairs*, Paul H. Nitze School of Advanced International Studies, Johns Hopkins University, Vol. XX, no. 1, Winter/Spring 2000, pp. 107–16.

Uri Davis, '*Histadrut*: Continuity and Change', paper submitted to the Norwegian Trade Union Federation, International Department, January 1999; Israel: State, Society and Politics, PASSIA: Palestinian Academic Society for the Study of International Affairs, Jerusalem, 2000.

'The Movement Against Israeli Apartheid in Palestine', *Information Briefs*, Center for Policy Analysis on Palestine, Washington, DC, 4 June 2002.

Appendix 1: Vladimir Jabotinsky, 'The Iron Wall' (excerpts), first published in Russian under the title 'O Zheleznoi Stene' in *Rassvyet*, 4 November 1923; published in English in *Jewish Herald* (South Africa), 26 November 1937; reprinted here from Lenni Brenner, *The Iron Wall: Zionist Revisionism from Jabotinsky to Shamir*, Zed Books, London, 1984, pp. 73–5.

Appendix 2: David Ben-Gurion, Statement of Introduction of the Law of Return Before the Knesset (3 July 1950) (excerpts) is reprinted from Akiva Orr, *The UnJewish State: The Politics of Jewish Identity in Israel*, Ithaca Press, London, 1983, pp. 27–30.

Appendix 3: Naim Khader, PLO Representative to Belgium and the European Economic Community (EEC), The Democratic State and Armed Struggle in 'An Initial Response to Dr Emil Tuma and His Comments on the Socialist Republic of Palestine', Fouzi el-Asmar, Uri Davis and Naim Khader, *Debate on Palestine*, Ithaca Press, London, 1981, pp. 85–92.

Appendix 5: The Palestinian Declaration of Independence reprinted from *The Palestinian–Israeli Peace Agreement: A Documentary Record*, Institute of Palestine Studies, Washington, DC, 1994, pp. 268–72.

Unless otherwise indicated, all translations from original Hebrew sources are the author's own.

Words and phrases bounded by square brackets inside a quote represent additions inserted by the author.

Abbreviations and Acronyms

ACRI	Association for Civil Rights in Israel
ALA	Arab Liberation Army
AL-BEIT	Association for the Defence of Human Rights in Israel
CAABU	Council for the Advancement of Arab–British Understanding
CEC	Central Elections Committee
DFPE/*Jabha*	Democratic Front for Peace and Equality (*Al-Jabha al-Dimuqratiyya li-al-Salam wa-al-Musawa*)
DOP	Declaration of Principles on Interim Self-Government Arrangements
GSS/SHABAK	General Security Service (*Sherut Bitahon Kelali*)
IDF/ZAHAL	Israel Defence Forces (*Tzeva Haganah le-Israel*)
ILA	Israel Lands Administration
IZL	National Military Organization (*Irgun Tzevai Leumi*)
JA	Jewish Agency
JNF	Jewish National Fund
LEHI	Israel Freedom Fighters (*Lohamei Herut Yisrael*)
MAIAP	Movement Against Israeli Apartheid in Palestine
MAKI	Israeli Communist Party (*Mifalgah Comunistit Ysraelit*)
MAPAI	*Eretz Israel* Workers' Party (*Mifleget Po'alei Eretz Yisrael*)
MAPAM	United Workers' Party (*Mifleget Po'aim Meuhedet*)
MERETZ	Alignment of MAPAM, RATZ (the Citizens' Rights Movement) and a faction of Shinui
MK	member of the Knesset
NDA/BALAD	National Democratic Assembly (*Al-Tajammu al-Watani al-Dimuqrati*)
NGO	non-governmental organization
PA	Palestinian Authority
PADI	Judgments of the Supreme Court (*Pisqei Din shel Beit ha-Mishpat ha-Elyon*)
PISGA	Palestinian Interim Self-Governing Authority
PLO	Palestine Liberation Organization

PNC	Palestine National Council
RAKAH	New Communist List (*Reshimah Qomunistit Hadashah*)
RASSCO	Rural and Suburban Settlement Company
SHAS	Sephardi Torah Guardians
SHELI	Israel Left (*Semol Yisraeli*)
Shinui	Democratic Movement for Change
TA'AL	Arab Movement for Change (*Al-Haraka al-Arabiyya li-al-Taghyir*)
UAK	United Arab Kingdom (speculative)
UDHR	Universal Declaration of Human Rights
UNGA	United Nations General Assembly
UNRWA	United Nations Relief and Works Agency for Palestine Refugees in the Near East
WCAR	United Nations World Conference Against Racism
WZO	World Zionist Organization

Foreword

Since the first publication of *Israel: An Apartheid State* by Zed Books in 1987, the legal system regulating apartheid in Israel has evolved and changed in a number of significant ways, notably with the passage by the Israeli Parliament (the Knesset) in 1992 of the two Basic Laws, Basic Law: Human Dignity and Liberty and Basic Law: Freedom of Occupation.

Since the passage by the Knesset of the said two Basic Laws, the State of Israel is legally defined as 'a Jewish and democratic state'. This writer, an anthropologist with a keen interest in law, hopes to demonstrate convincingly that the said legal definition of the State of Israel is an oxymoron. Apartheid, namely institutionalized racism legislated by Acts of Parliament, does not sit very well with democratic values, notably the values of the Universal Declaration of Human Rights.

Also, in the years that have elapsed since the publication of the first edition of *Israel: An Apartheid State*, the PLO has significantly evolved and changed. In September 1993 in Washington, DC the PLO and the Government of Israel signed the Declaration of Principles on Interim Self-Government Arrangements (DOP) negotiated in Oslo.

The DOP and the so-called subsequent Oslo peace process undercut the Palestinian Declaration of Independence of 1988 and the political programmes developed by successive Palestine National Councils. Rather than representing a victory for the Palestinian struggle led by the PLO since its establishment in 1964, the DOP and the subsequent 'Oslo peace process' represent a strategic defeat for the PLO, and cast a serious question on its potential as an alternative to Israeli apartheid.

These and related significant changes are reflected in this work – notably, while *Israel: An Apartheid State* had a chapter entitled 'The Alternative: The PLO', this work has a chapter entitled 'Possibilities for the Struggle Within', which is also the subtitle of this book.

Sakhnin, 2003

To Sirkku and our children,
Daniel and Iris

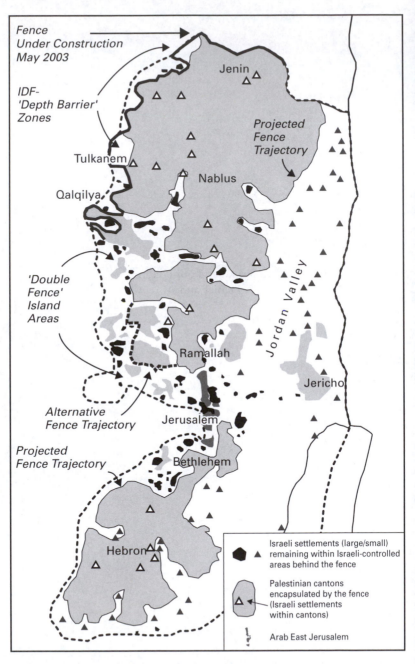

The *Apartheid Wall* (for more information see: http://www.pengon.org/
wall/newmaps.html)

Preface

This volume represents a sequel to *Israel: An Apartheid State*, first published by Zed Books, London, 1987 (second impression 1990) and the abridged edition published by the Media Review Network, Laudium, 2001.

The first edition of *Israel: An Apartheid State* as well as the second impression were structured in three chapters preceded by an introduction and supplemented by appendices, bibliography and an afterword. Chapter 1: State, Citizenship, Land; Chapter 2: Political Repression in Israel; and Chapter 3: The Alternative: The PLO.

This work, *Apartheid Israel: Possibilities for the Struggle Within*, is a new book. All the texts have been rewritten and Chapter 3: The Alternative: The PLO replaced with a new Chapter 5: Possibilities for the Struggle Within.

The vision underpinning the publication of *Israel: An Apartheid State*, as well as the publication of this book, is a vision of justice: the desire to make a contribution to the removal of the institutions of apartheid, colonization, dispossession and occupation imposed by Israel on the native indigenous Palestinian Arab people, and the replacement of these institutions with a better and more just social and political order. The value orientation informing this vision is secular legal Kantianism: the insistence that justice, as institutionalized in a future better social and political order, be based on the categorical imperative of equality of individual and collective, economic, social, cultural, civil, political and national rights for all – both the formerly colonized and the former colonizer peoples – without distinction or discrimination with regard to religion, culture, nationality, language, tribal affiliation, descent, sex or any other social status. In other words, the value orientation informing this vision is represented in the text of the UN Universal Declaration of Human Rights of 1948.

This volume is a political treatise bringing together a significant part of my work written over the past two-odd decades (1980–2002), hence, perhaps, a certain amount of repetitiveness. The various facets of this treatise are informed by the political distinction between the country of geographical Palestine (as defined for the British Mandate by the

Council of the League of Nations in 1922 between the River Jordan and the Mediterranean sea) versus the sovereign polity of the State of Israel. The object of this book is to contribute to the development of a moral understanding, a political framework and a climate of opinion in the West that will be able to countenance, in politically responsible terms, the prospects of the dismantlement of the State of Israel as a Jewish state in the political Zionist sense of the term, an apartheid state, and its replacement with a democratic Palestine.

This work is, thus, intended to contribute to the development in the West of an anti-Zionist moral understanding, political framework and a climate of opinion as the best practical option to secure the welfare of both the Arab and the Hebrew peoples of Palestine as equal future Palestinian Arab and Palestinian Hebrew citizens in a democratic (confederal, federal or unitary) state for all of its citizens and Palestine refugees (all current Hebrew and Arab citizens of Israel, all residents and refugees of the post-1967 occupied territories and all 1948 Palestine refugees and their descendants). It is the hope of the author that this political treatise will establish convincingly the falsehood of the political Zionist tenet that in order to be a 'good Jew' it is somehow necessary to be 'pro-Zionist' and that to be anti-Zionist is somehow tantamount to being 'anti-Jewish', namely, 'anti-Semitic'.

Political Zionism, founded at the First Zionist Congress convened in Basle in August 1897, is the dominant and hegemonic mainstream school within the World Zionist Organization (WZO). The political Zionist school of thought and practice is committed to the normative statement that it is a good idea to establish and consolidate in the country of Palestine a sovereign state, a Jewish state, that attempts to guarantee in law (e.g., Absentees' Property Law of 1950) and in practice (e.g., the mass expulsion, under the cover of the 1948–49 war, of the native indigenous Palestinian Arab people) a demographic majority of the Jewish tribes in the territories under its control. In other words, another form of apartheid.

The first political programme of the World Zionist Organization, known as the 'Basle Programme', was formulated at the First Zionist Congress in 1897 as follows:

> Zionism seeks to establish a home for the Jewish people in Palestine secured under public law. The Congress contemplates the following means to the attainment of this end:
>
> 1. The promotion by appropriate means of the settlement in Palestine of Jewish farmers, artisans, and manufacturers;
> 2. The organization and uniting of the whole of Jewry by means of

appropriate institutions, both local and international, in accordance with the laws of each country;

3. The strengthening and fostering of Jewish national sentiment and national consciousness;

4. Preparatory steps toward obtaining the consent of governments, where necessary, in order to reach the goal of Zionism.

It has since been revised a number of times (see Chapter 1, below).

Since the American and the French Revolutions in 1776 and 1789 respectively, the democratic political systems of most west European states, let alone the United States of America, are predicated on the principles of separation of religion from the state and separation of tribalism from the state, as well as on the values of the Universal Declaration of Human Rights.

Given the above, those committed to such principles and these universal values would have good reasons to conclude that the idea of political Zionism, the idea of a Jewish state, is a bad idea and that positing the 'centrality of Israel in Jewish life' cannot sit very well with the principle of separation of religion from the state.

It is, thus, of some interest to explore why and in what way it was possible for the State of Israel, an apartheid state, informed by the ideology of political Zionism, to project itself in the West as the 'only democracy in the Middle East' and effectively veil from critical scrutiny, let alone prosecution before international war crimes tribunals, the crime against humanity of the mass expulsion of the native indigenous Palestinian Arab people perpetrated by the Israeli army under the cover of the 1948–49 war as well as the war crimes perpetrated subsequent to the said war.

It took the UN far too long to realize that Zionism is a form of racism, representing a blatant violation of the norms of the Universal Declaration of Human Rights and the standards of international law. It was only in the wake of the 1967 war and the consequent war crimes perpetrated by the Israeli occupation forces, challenged by the renewed resistance of the Palestinian Arab people led by the PLO, that the UN corrected its record and passed General Assembly Resolution 3379 of November 1975 determining that 'Zionism is a form of racism and racial discrimination'. And it is, indeed, most regrettable that in the wake of the Middle East Peace Conference convened in Madrid in October 1991, co-sponsored by the USA and the former USSR, the General Assembly muddied its record again by passing Resolution 46/86 of December 1991, revoking Resolution 3379.

Let us all hope that following the UN World Conference Against

Racism (WCAR) in Durban, South Africa, August–September 2001 as well as the World Summit on Sustainable Development (WSSD) in Johannesburg, South Africa, August–September 2002, and predicated on the clear and firm distinction between Judaism as a confessional statement that strictly belongs to the private realm of the individuals concerned versus Zionism as a political programme that, like all political programmes, ought to be critically attended to and judged by the extent that they are compatible with the values of the Universal Declaration of Human Rights and the standards of international law – all those committed to the values of the Universal Declaration of Human Rights and the consistent application of the standards of international law worldwide will coordinate their efforts with the view to motivate the UN to recognize that Zionism is another form of apartheid.

There is little doubt that, as in the case of the dismantlement of the apartheid legislation in South Africa, the UN is able to play a critical role, mutually beneficial to all parties concerned, by applying to the State of Israel suitably corresponding sanctions with the view to suggest to the Government of the State of Israel that just as the international community would not tolerate apartheid in South Africa, it would not tolerate apartheid in Palestine.

All parties involved with the Israeli–Palestinian conflict, first and foremost the State of Israel, the colonial occupation party, as well as the PLO, the anti-colonial resistance party, could do worse than remember that the Universal Declaration of Human Rights and international law frame universal norms for the removal of injustice in such terms as secure the human rights and fundamental freedoms of everyone, including those of the former colonizer and those of the former colonized; those of the former occupier and those of the former occupied.

During the heyday of the apartheid regime in South Africa the Dutch Reformed Church educated its constituents, almost exclusively classified as 'White' in the apartheid legal system, and their supporters in the West and beyond, that to oppose the political programme of apartheid, to be anti-apartheid, was somehow tantamount to being 'anti-Christian', and thus, 'pro-Devil', or worse, 'pro-communist'.

In a similar way, under the dominance of political Zionist ideology and practice, Zionist and Israeli educational and information establishments educate their constituents, almost exclusively classified as 'Jews' in the Zionist legal system, and their supporters in the West and beyond, that to oppose the political programme of Zionism, to be anti-Zionist, is somehow tantamount to being 'anti-Jewish', and thus, 'anti-Semitic', or worse, 'pro-Nazi'.

It took many decades of protracted struggle, including armed struggle, by the native indigenous ('non-White') peoples of South Africa under the leadership of the African National Congress (ANC), supported by international solidarity and culminating in UN sanctions, before the criminal education of equating Christianity with apartheid and being a 'good Christian' with being 'pro-apartheid' was effectively challenged. In the new South Africa today, where in 1994 the apartheid legal system was dismantled and replaced with a democratic constitution, one would be hard put to find anyone admitting that they were ever pro-apartheid.

The distinct minority of South African citizens classified as 'White' in the apartheid legal system, who recognized apartheid to be what it was: an abomination in terms of the Universal Declaration of Human Rights and a crime under the standards of international law, and who crossed the political lines to join the struggle for democracy in South Africa, have made significant educational and other contributions to this process.

And it will hopefully not take decades of protracted struggle, including armed struggle, by the native indigenous ('non-Jewish') peoples of Palestine under a leadership of similar quality to the leadership of the ANC, supported by international solidarity and culminating in UN sanctions, before the criminal education of equating Judaism with Zionism and being a 'good Jew' with being 'pro-Zionist' is effectively challenged, so that in the new Palestine of tomorrow one would be hard put to find anyone admitting that they were ever pro-Zionist.

The distinct minority of Israeli citizens classified as 'Jews' in the Zionist legal system, who have recognized political Zionism to be what it is: an abomination in terms of the Universal Declaration of Human Rights and a crime under the standards of international law, and who crossed the political lines to join the struggle for democracy in Palestine, have made and will continue to make significant educational and other contributions to this process.

In other words, it is the hope of this author that this political treatise will establish convincingly the viability of the contrary tenet to the Zionist political tenet above, namely, that in order to be a 'good Jew' it is necessary to be anti-Zionist in the same sense that under the apartheid regime in South Africa, in order to be a 'good Christian' it was necessary to be anti-apartheid.

1 · Zionism

Anti-Semitism and the holocaust

The *Encyclopaedia Hebraica* defines 'Zionism' as a Jewish national movement emerging at the end of the nineteenth century with the object of returning the people of Israel to their historical homeland in the land of Israel, drawing its inspiration from the vision of return to Zion (a synonym for Jerusalem), which has impacted the history of Israel throughout the centuries of its exile (*Encyclopaedia Hebraica*, 1976, Vol. 28, p. 592).

The above definition embraces a number of schools of thought and practice, of which political Zionism, founded by Theodor Herzl, became the hegemonic and dominant mainstream. As defined in the Preface above, the political Zionist school of thought and practice is committed to the normative statement that it is a good idea to establish and consolidate in the country of Palestine a sovereign state, a Jewish state, that attempts to guarantee in law and in practice a demographic majority of the Jewish tribes in the territories under its control.

Until the establishment of the State of Israel in 1948, the primary opposition to political Zionism inside the Zionist movement came from the school of spiritual Zionism led by Asher Ginsberg (Ahad ha-Am), which was roundly opposed to the idea of a Jewish state. The efforts to establish a Jewish state were led by political Zionists. The efforts to establish the Hebrew University in Jerusalem were led by spiritual Zionists.

Following his visit to Palestine (26 February–17 May 1891) Ahad ha-Am published his seminal critique of political Zionism under the title 'Truth from *Eretz Israel*', first published as a series of articles in the Hebrew daily newspaper *Ha-Melitz* (St Petersburg) 19–30 June 1891.

From abroad, we are accustomed to believe that *Eretz Israel* is presently almost totally desolate, an uncultivated desert, and that anyone wishing to buy land there can come and buy all he wants. But in truth this is not so. In the entire land, it is hard to find a tillable land that is not already tilled; only sandy fields and stony hills, suitable at best for planting trees or vine and, even that, after considerable work and expense in clearing and preparing them ... (Ahad ha-Am, 'Truth from *Eretz Israel*', translated by Alan Dowty, *Israel Studies*, Vol. 5, No. 2, Fall 2000, pp. 161–2)

It is the view of this writer that political Zionism, like all political organizations, ought to be attended to critically in terms of the values of the Universal Declaration of Human Rights, and assessed by the standard of its approximation (or otherwise) to the implementation of these universal values in its political programme and practice. The critical question with reference to political Zionism is not whether political Zionism represents the national liberation movement of the 'Jewish people' or whether it is a settler colonial movement. Rather, the critical question is what actions and/or omissions adherents of political Zionism justify in the name of Zionism.

The mass expulsion of a native indigenous people is clearly incompatible with the values of the Universal Declaration of Human Rights and is defined as a crime against humanity in international law. It is clearly irrelevant that the crime was and remains perpetrated in the name of 'the national liberation of the Jewish people'. Decent people would want to have nothing to do with a 'national liberation movement' that attempts to justify war crimes and crimes against humanity such as ethnic cleansing.

I further suggest that in the same way decent people would want to have nothing to do with a divinity who according to a text alleged to be 'holy', namely, the Old Testament, claimed by some to be the living word of God, promises 'his people', the Israelite tribes, a land, the land of Canaan, that is to be made vacant by the genocide of its native indigenous peoples ('When the Lord your God exterminates the nations whose lands he is giving you, and you take their place and settle in their cities and houses ...'; Deuteronomy, 19:1), and orders 'his' anointed king, King Saul, to fall upon his enemy, the Amalekites, destroy them; put their property under ban; and 'spare no one; put them all to death, men, women, children and babes in arms, herds and flocks, camels and asses' (First Book of Samuel, 15:3).

As Nur Masalha points out, citing an article by Rabbi Israel Hess, former campus rabbi of Bar Ilan University, entitled 'The Commandment of Genocide in the Torah', the biblical commandment to 'blot out the memory of the Amalekites from under heaven' (Deuteronomy, 25: 19) is given an actual contemporary relevance in the conflict between Israelis and Palestinians in political messianic Zionism, where the Palestinians are identified as the 'Amalekites of today' (Masalha 1997: 208). Similarly, Rabbi Menachem Froman, the rabbi of the Jewish settlement of Teqo'a, south of Bethlehem in the occupied West Bank, an advocate of Jewish–Muslim dialogue, made public his view that 'the Palestinian murder network, cursed be its name, and all of its extensions, should be regarded as Amalek, and we are commanded to fight and attack Amalek until they are annihilated' (quoted in *Haaretz*, 19 July 2002).

Heathens, worshippers of idols, are as human as those worshipping a monotheistic divinity. A divinity that does not recognize all human beings as being entitled to equal human rights is suspect. And a 'national liberation movement' that claims the right to dispossess and expel a native indigenous people in the name of the genocidal conquest of a claimed patrimony perpetrated by a claimed ancestry and ordered by the alleged living words of God in a book that is claimed to be holy is plainly a criminal 'national liberation movement' that ought to be resisted and defeated.

Political Zionism emerged against the backdrop of European industrialization and the capitalist transformation of the feudal European social order, which prompted the secularization of reason and morality, and gave rise to the two paradigmatic mainstream traditions of modern Western thought: enlightenment and racism.

For Jewish communities in Europe, enlightenment brought emancipation and legal equality of civil rights. In parallel, a newly secular racism manifested itself in the form of anti-Jewish persecution, which culminated in repeated pogroms, mass murder and, under the Nazi occupation of Europe, mass annihilation.

Those in the Jewish communities who opted for secularism and enlightenment lent their support, in one capacity or another, to liberal democratic, socialist or revolutionary political organizations in the countries of their residence. Those who opted for secularism and racism turned, in one capacity or another, to political Zionism. Thus, for instance, in 1934, the late Rabbi Joachim Prinz in his treatise *Wir Juden*, considered perhaps his most important work of that period, could write as follows:

> The significance of the German revolution (1933) for the German people will ultimately be revealed only to those who have undertaken to achieve it, and have themselves shaped its form. Its significance for us [Jews] will be stated here: the liberal option has been lost for ever, [liberalism] the only political way of life which Jewish assimilationism was prepared to promote has sunk away for good. How long it will survive in disparate individual countries only prophets can venture to determine. But the dispassionate, cool observer of world affairs can determine the following facts: everywhere throughout the world symptoms develop which spell

doom to the cornerstone values of liberalism. Parliament and democracy are increasingly shattered; the exaggerated and harmful emphasis on the value of the individual is recognized to be mistaken; the concept and reality of the nation and the people are, to our happiness, gaining more and more ground. The last and most powerful and sublime formulation of national rights and the rejection of internationalism are found in the demands of socialism that it be found exclusively on the unique character of every nation and the special demands of every nation, namely national socialism.

The collapse of Jewish anonymity is now clear to everyone. Jews are now torn away from the last hiding place: their aspirations for conversion to Christianity and mixed marriages. Thereby some of us have been made despondent [but] we consider this necessity an opportunity for a courageous and unequivocal statement in favour of standing amongst our own, alone. We also see the fulfilment of our most sublime aspirations. In vain did we struggle against imitation, conversion and mixed marriages. And now more powerful forces have come to our aid and have redeemed us. The time has come to draw the conclusions and not to destroy our lives in miserable indecision and spiritual sorrow over the destruction of something good. The theory of assimilation has been destroyed. There is no longer any hiding place for us under the negation which protected it. We want to posit instead of assimilation something new: undertaking the yoke of joining the Jewish people and the Jewish race. *Only a state based on the principle of the purity of the nation and the race can possibly endow dignity and honour on [and only on] those Jews who themselves subscribe to this principle.* The state cannot desire any other Jews except those who subscribe to this principle amongst their own people. It cannot desire to have sycophantic Jews. It must demand from us recognition of our absolute uniqueness and qualities, since only those who give full honour to their own uniqueness, their own blood, could gain the respect and honour which are bestowed by similarly inspired nations subscribing to the same principle. (1934: 150–4, 155–6; emphasis added)[1]

The complex interrelationship between political Zionist philosophy and practice and modern secular racism – specifically, anti-Jewish racism (anti-Semitism) – has been extensively reviewed in post-Second World War writings on political science, history and philosophy, Zionist and anti-Zionist. Sartre's *Anti-Semite and Jew* and Hannah Arendt's *Eichmann in Jerusalem* are now recognized as classic works in this context.

There is nothing coincidental about the practical convergence of political Zionism and anti-Jewish racism (anti-Semitism). Political Zionism and secular anti-Jewish racism share a common view on the existential status of Jewish minority communities in non-Jewish ('Gentile') societies. Both the political Zionist and the anti-Jewish racist believe that, given the fundamental racial incompatibility of non-Jews and Jews, Jews, as individuals and as minority communities, cannot, by definition, be – nor can they be expected to be – equal citizens and free minority communities in a non-Jewish society and polity.

Consider, for instance, the seminal ideological political Zionist essay by Leo Pinsker, *Auto-Emancipation*, published in 1882:

> Judeophobia is a form of demonopathy with the distinction that the Jewish ghost has become known to the whole race of mankind, not merely to certain races, and that it is not disembodied, like other ghosts, but is a being of flesh and blood, and suffers the most excruciating pain from the wounds inflicted upon it by the fearful mob who imagine it threatens them.
>
> Judeophobia is a psychic aberration. As a psychic aberration, *it is hereditary; as a disease transmitted for two thousand years it is incurable.*
> (Pinsker, *Auto-Emancipation*, quoted in Hertzberg 1973: 185; emphasis added)

For the anti-Jewish racist it follows, therefore, that Jewish society must be segregated outside the body of 'Gentile' society; hence evacuation and, if necessary, annihilation. For the political Zionist, Jewish society must also be segregated outside the body of 'Gentile' society, in this case in Palestine, redefined and reified in Zionist ideology as the Land of Israel (*Eretz Israel*): the locus of concentration ('ingathering') of Jewish tribes.

Given the moral and ideological convergence of political Zionism and anti-Jewish racism, the Zionist movement, as represented in the official institutions of the World Zionist Organization, has, at critical junctures, opted for collaboration rather than conflict with anti-Jewish racists, even when that racism has taken the form of pogrom and genocide. Ben Hecht (1962) and Lenni Brenner (1983) offer detailed documentation on this subject.

With the outbreak of the Second World War in 1939 the convergence between political Zionist and Nazi anti-Jewish racism took a particular turn. But before progressing further it is in order to emphasize and emphasize again at least two fundamental distinctions, moral and conceptual, that underpin this work.

First, the distinction between Judaism (a confessional preference) versus Zionism (a political programme). Judaism is not Zionism. Judaism, as a confessional preference, should be strictly an individual matter, and, generally speaking, like other individual preferences (such as musical, culinary or sexual preferences) should not be the concern of the law.

Zionism, as a political programme, is a matter of public debate. As noted already more than once above, the political Zionist school of thought and practice is committed to the normative statement that it is a good idea to establish and consolidate in the country of Palestine a sovereign state, a Jewish state, that attempts to guarantee in law and in practice a demographic majority of the Jewish tribes in the territories under its control.

Such individuals and bodies as are, for instance, committed to the values of open society, democracy and the separation of religion from the state; who, therefore, disagree with the political aims of this particular political programme; and who regard this programme to be a negative political programme, are anti-Zionist in the same sense that those who for many decades opposed the political programme of apartheid in South Africa (which ended in 1994) were, and it is to be hoped remain, anti-apartheid.

Second, the distinction between guilt and responsibility. There is no collective guilt. Children are not guilty of the crimes of their parents; Germans in general are not guilty of the crimes of the Nazi occupation of Europe; western Christians in general are not guilty of the genocide of the holocaust; and Europe in general is not guilty of crimes against humanity perpetrated against Jews. Only anti-Jewish racists are guilty of what they did and continue to do to Jews.

And, by the same token, children of Zionist settlers in geographical Palestine are also not guilty of the crimes perpetrated by their parents.

Responsibility is, however, a different matter. While children of Zionist settlers in geographical Palestine are not collectively guilty of the crimes perpetrated by their parents against the native indigenous Palestinian Arab people, citizens of the State of Israel have a responsibility, a duty, which citizens of other states do not have in the same way, to raise their voices against these crimes, act in defence of the victims of these crimes and work for due reparations, compensation and return of the dispossessed and expelled Palestinian Arabs. This is the case not because children of Zionist settlers are collectively guilty of these crimes, but because these crimes were committed and continue to be committed by the successive governments of the State of Israel in their name.

Many of those who have spent a good part of their lives in defence of human rights – defence of the weak against the abuses of the powerful, defence of humankind against cruelty, and, in this connection, who are involved with the defence of the Palestinian people against the violation of their fundamental rights, against the abuses of political Zionism, against the cruelty of the Israeli occupation – are often required to address on the basis of truth and integrity the fallacious, misplaced and misleadingly simple question of 'How was it possible for a people, the Jewish people, victims of Nazi genocide during the occupation of Europe in the Second World War by the Third German Reich, to subject the Palestinian people to war criminal policies of mass deportation, transfer and ethnic cleansing during and around the 1948–49 war?'

Occupation is occupation. Occupation is the military presence of a state on the territory of another state with the result that all or part of the territory comes under its control. Occupying armies and occupation governments can commit terrible crimes against the population. Not all occupation governments commit the same war crimes under the cover of war, and the governments of the State of Israel have clearly not committed the crime of mass murder of the Palestinian people in death camps in the same way as the Nazi government of the Third German Reich, where two-thirds of the Jewish people, one-half of the Gypsy people, and untold tens of thousands of Slav people, German and non-German homosexual people, mentally challenged people and more were mass murdered by the Nazi annihilation machinery.

So when the British ambassador to Israel, Mr Sherard Cowper-Coles, after a tour of the West Bank that he is said to have found shocking, describes the Palestinian territories as 'the largest detention camp in the world' (*Daily Telegraph*, 15 October 2002), he is not saying that the Government of the State of Israel is annihilating Palestinians in gas chambers and burning their bodies in mass crematoria.

But the Israeli occupation of 1948–49 of some 77 per cent of the territory of geographical Palestine clearly did entail the crime against humanity of mass ethnic cleansing of the Palestinian people, mass transfer resulting in the depopulation of nearly 85 per cent of the native indigenous Palestinian Arab population resident in the territories that came under Israeli control, dispossessing them of their vast rural and urban real estate and financial properties, illegally appropriating this huge wealth for the colonial settlement of Jews and only Jews, and stripping some three-quarters of a million Palestinian Arabs (today numbering over four million) of their right to citizenship in Israel, thereby manufacturing the 1948 Palestine refugee problem.

The Israeli mass ethnic cleansing operations under the cover of the 1948–49 war, and the manipulation of the 1948–49 war and Israel's alleged security concerns as a veil to cover the war crimes of the mass transfer of the Palestinian people from the territories that came under Israeli control, have been the subject of extensive re-examination by a range of Israeli scholars in the past two decades, and their work is now widely available.[2] Not as much critical work has been done on the Zionist and Israeli manipulation of the Nazi occupation of Europe and the holocaust to cover up and veil Israeli and Zionist war crimes against the Palestinian people in Palestine and beyond, although an additional breakthrough has taken place with the publication of Jim Allen's *Perdition: A Play in Two Acts* in 1987 and Norman Finkelstein's *The Holocaust Industry*, 13 years later in 2000.

I begin my enquiry into the intellectual as well as political interface of Zionism and anti-Semitism and its implications for the question of Palestine by quoting a letter.

I should note at the outset, however, that in order to be able to quote this letter here, a small band of people associated with the publication of *Perdition: A Play in Two Acts* had to defend themselves against libel proceedings in London and Tel Aviv for the entire decade of 1987 through 1997. That they won the case, as well as all of their costs (well over £40,000) was due to their courage, tenacity and per-severance, notably the tenacity and perseverance of David Wolton, the publisher of *Perdition* at Ithaca Press, London.

The letter I quote below was written by Nathan Schwalb (Dror), representative of the Zionist *He-Halutz* (the Pioneer) organization in Geneva and addressed to the Jewish rescue Working Group in Bratislava. It was sent in or about the autumn of 1942 in reply to the repeated and pressing appeals of the said Working Group for money to bribe senior Nazi officials with the view to delay, suspend or otherwise obstruct the Nazi mass transport of Czechoslovakia Jewry to Auschwitz and other centres of genocide. The original letter was lost in the war. A copy may exist in the classified archives of Nathan Schwalb (Dror). The text quoted here was reconstructed by one of the recipients of the original letter, Rabbi Michael Dov Weissmandel, a leading member of the Working Group, reputed to possess a retentive memory that, like a plastered cistern, did not lose a drop of its contents, in his book *Min ha-Metzar* ('From the Depth of Distress') as follows:

> [It was] written in a strange foreign language and at first I could not decipher at all which language it was, until I realized that it was Hebrew written in Roman letters, and written to Schwalb's friends ... It is still before my eyes, as if I had reviewed it a hundred and one times. This was the content of the letter:
>
> Since a messenger has been found he [Schwalb] writes to the Group

that they must always remember that the most urgent issue, the main issue which must always be in front of us, is that in the end the Allies will win. After the victory they will divide the world again among the nations as they did at the end of the First World War. Then they paved the way for us to take the first step.

Now, at the end of the war we must do everything so that Palestine will become the State of Israel. There have already been important steps made in this direction. And as for the outcry coming from our country, we should know that all the Allied nations are spilling much blood. If we shall not make sacrifices, with what shall we buy the right to sit at the table when the division of the nation and the countries takes place after the war?

And therefore it is nonsense and even impudent on our part to ask from the nations who are spilling their blood that they permit their money to be brought into the land of their enemy to defend our blood – because only in blood shall we have the land (*rak b'dam tihje lanu haaretz*).

This is as far as the community as a whole is concerned. As for your members of the Group, you take a walk (*atem tajlu*) [namely, escape] and for this purpose I provide you with money illegally by means of this messenger. (Weissmandel 1960: 92; Allen 1987: 62–3, 77)

Schwalb's letter is an accurate representation of mainstream political Zionism, notably Labour Zionist thinking at the time. Consider, for instance, the speech by the Labour Zionist leader Yitzhaq Gruenbaum, head of the Rescue Committee of the Zionist settler community in Palestine at the time at the meeting of the Zionist Executive on 18 February 1943:

Meanwhile a mood swept over *Eretz Israel* that I think is very dangerous to Zionism ... How is it possible that ... people will call: 'If you don't have enough money [for rescue] you should take it from *Keren Hayesod* [Zionist settlement foundation fund]' ... I thought it obligatory to stand before this wave ... When some asked me: 'Can't you give money from *Keren Hayesod* to save Jews in the Diaspora?' I said no! and again I say no! ... we have to stand before this wave that is putting Zionist activity into the second row ... Because of this people called me an anti-Semite and concluded that I am guilty, because we do not give priority to rescue ... I think it is necessary to say here: Zionism is above everything. (Gruenbaum 1946: 68–9 quoted in Brenner 1987: 78 and 2002: 211)

And David Ben-Gurion, addressing a meeting of MAPAI (precursor of the Labour Party) Centre on 7 December 1938, a bare few weeks after the notorious Nazi anti-Jewish pogroms of *Kristallnacht* throughout the German Reich in the night of 9–10 November 1938:

> If I knew it would be possible to save all the [Jewish] children in Germany by bringing them to England, and only half of them by transporting them to *Eretz Israel* [Palestine], then I would opt for the second alternative. For we must weigh not only the life of these children but also the history of the people of Israel. (Yoav Gelber, 'Zionist Policy and the Fate of European Jewry [1939–1942]', *Yad va-Shem Studies*, Vol. XIII, p. 199, quoted in Brenner 1983: 149 and 150 n23)[3]

In the light of these rather authoritative quotes, the answer to the question 'How was it possible for a people, the Jewish people, victims of Nazi genocide during the occupation of Europe in the Second World War by the Third German Reich, to subject the Palestinian people to war criminal policies of mass deportation, transfer and ethnic cleansing during and around the 1948–49 war?' emerges quite clearly.

Here it is: a political elite, the leadership of the Zionist movement, opted politically, intellectually, morally and emotionally to hold back and deny much of its financial and other resources from rescue actions of 'its own people', 'the Jewish people' under Nazi occupation, because they gave priority to political Zionism and Jewish state-building. Needless to say, Zionist political leaders who have made themselves accomplices by default, and sometimes by deliberate design, to the mass murder of Jews by the Nazi annihilation machinery would have little political, intellectual, moral and emotional hesitation in manufacturing by design and sometimes by default the mass 'transfer' of the people they considered an alien people, the majority of the native indigenous Palestinian Arab inhabitants of the country of Palestine, from the territories designated for the projected Jewish state.

In order to understand the question it is first necessary to correctly identify the players in this equation. It is not 'the Jews' in general who committed the war crime of mass expulsion of the Palestinian people under the cover of the 1948–49 war, nor 'the victims of the holocaust' in general – rather, it was identifiable officers and soldiers of the Israeli army and members of the Israeli provisional government who are guilty. These are the same people who, until 1948, constituted the leadership of the World Zionist Organization and the Jewish Agency for the Land of Israel, whose real choices in the face of the holocaust are reflected in the statements of Nathan Schwalb, Yitzhaq Gruenbaum and David Ben-Gurion above.

The mainstream of political Zionism, notably Labour Zionist leadership, having made criminal choices regarding 'its own people' in the name of Zionism and Jewish state-building, such as the choices illustrated in the quotes above, would not hesitate to make war criminal choices with regard to 'another people', the native indigenous Palestinian Arab people, for the same purpose.

The Zionist leader David Ben-Gurion and his like, who would opt to see half of the Jewish children in Germany murdered in order to have the surviving half transported to Palestine in the name of political Zionism, would have few moral qualms, as prime minister of the provisional government of the newly established State of Israel, to effect by design and by default the mass expulsion of the native indigenous Palestinian people from such territories as came under the control of the Israeli army in the course of the 1948–49 war.

The humanity of a people is like the humanity of all people, and a people under occupation, all peoples under occupation, by and large respond to occupation in terms of developing two basic alternatives, with many shades of grey in between: collaboration versus resistance. The Jewish people under the Nazi occupation of Europe in the Second World War, like the Gypsy people, like the Norwegian people, like homosexual people, responded to the Nazi occupation in similar ways: some among each people opted for resistance and some for collaboration.

The Jewish people under the Nazi occupation were not unique in this respect. Some Jews resisted and some collaborated. The official Zionist and Israeli master narrative that being classified as a 'Jew' under the Nazi occupation was uniquely different from being classified as a 'Gypsy' or 'homosexual' in that a Jew under the Nazi occupation of Europe, by virtue of being a member of a people uniquely designated for mass annihilation, could, by definition, not be a collaborator, is historically incorrect, morally false, intellectually bankrupt and politically a brazen lie, a denial of an important aspect of holocaust history.

As noted above, political Zionism and European anti-Jewish racism meet politically, intellectually, morally and emotionally at one crucial point: both political Zionism and European anti-Jewish racism, for different, overlapping or parallel reasons, believe that Jews have no place on an equal footing as minorities in predominantly non-Jewish ('Gentile') societies.

At this point of meeting, mainstream political Zionism has historically collaborated with anti-Jewish racism. By way of highlights one could mention the Transfer (*Haavarah*) agreements between the World Zionist Organization and the Nazi government of 1933; the case of Rudolf Kastner's collaboration with Adolf Eichmann in Nazi-occupied Hungary in 1944–45 (of which Allen's *Perdition* is a dramatization); and the Memorandum submitted by the dissident Zionist LEHI paramilitary organization to the Nazi officials in Lebanon in 1941 suggesting that

> The establishment of the historical Jewish state on a national and totalitarian basis, and bound by a Treaty with the German Reich, would be in the interest of a maintained and strengthened future German position of power in the Near East. (quoted in Yizraeli 1974: 315–17 and Brenner 1983: 267–8 and 2002: 300–3)

It should be noted that a former leading member of the LEHI (Stern group at the time), Yitzhak Shamir, was to become a prime minister in Israel, succeeding the late Menachem Begin, the former leader of IZL (the *Irgun*). It is also in order to note that it was the LEHI together with the IZL who were the primary perpetrators of the horrendous Deir Yasin massacre of some 250 men, women and children in April 1948 (the record of the *Haganah* being equally horrendous, as documented below).

I submit that it is only when we include these and related historical records in our narrative of the Israeli–Palestinian conflict that we are then able to understand the historical inter-relations between the Palestinian catastrophe, the *nakba*, on the one hand and the Jewish holocaust, the *Shoah*, under the Nazi occupation of Europe on the other, and begin to answer with a measure of truth and integrity the question 'How was it possible for a people, the Jewish people, victims of Nazi genocide during the occupation of Europe in the Second World War by the Third German Reich, to subject the Palestinian people to war criminal policies of mass deportation, transfer and ethnic cleansing during and around the 1948–49 war?' thereby making a modest contribution to preventing such a catastrophe or holocaust from befalling any people anywhere again.

It is to Hisham Sharabi that I owe the insight that though Israeli ethnic cleansing of 1948–49 and the Israeli occupation of 1967 are no less cruel than, for instance, the mass ethnic cleansing that had taken place in India and Pakistan at about the same time, or the French occupation of Algeria, the tragedy of the Palestinian Arab people is that their persecutor and occupier is identified in Western narrative not as a 'Zionist', nor as an 'Israeli', but as a 'Jew'. This, Sharabi pointed out further, unfortunately means that so long as the Israeli occupation does not mass transport the Palestinian people into death camps, annihilate them in gas chambers and dispose of their bodies in crematoria with columns of smoke curling out of the chimneys, the cruelty of the Israeli occupation and the truly horrific suffering of the Palestinian people remain invisible to enlightened public opinion in the West.

It is our responsibility to make this suffering visible.

Transfer and massacre

Over the years, since the establishment of the World Zionist Organization at the First Zionist Congress in Basle in 1897 and the consolidation of political Zionism as the mainstream of the Zionist movement, two broad political Zionist traditions have emerged: Labour Zionism and Revisionist Zionism.

Labour Zionism is an attempt to reconcile the basic tenets of political Zionist and colonial practice with the tenets of the Enlightenment. Since these two sets of values are mutually exclusive, Labour Zionist literature has been largely predicated upon the obfuscation of Zionist colonial practice, and upon mystification, ignorance and cultivated deception. Revisionist Zionism has largely escaped the Labour Zionist predicament of attempting to reconcile the irreconcilable. In contradistinction to Labour Zionism, it has attempted, with considerable success, to locate Zionism ideologically and practically inside the tradition of modern secular racism and imperial colonialism. (See Appendix 1 for excerpts from the classic Revisionist Zionist tract, Vladimir Jabotinsky, 'The Iron Wall'.)

Political Zionism claims to offer an allegedly valid solution to the question of anti-Jewish racism, namely, the transformation of the Arab country of Palestine, in whole or in part, into the Jewish Land of Israel (*Eretz Israel*), through the dispossession and mass transfer of the native indigenous Palestinian Arab population out of Palestine, the mass migration of Jews the world over into Palestine, and the establishment, through the Jewish colonization of Palestine, of a sovereign Jewish state, a state that would, in the words of Chaim Weizmann, subsequently first President of the State of Israel, 'be as Jewish as America is American or England is English'.[4]

In other words, the political Zionist solution to the question of anti-Jewish racism is predicated on the successful establishment and consolidation, through the Jewish colonization of the country of Palestine, of a sovereign state, a Jewish state, that attempts to guarantee in law and in practice a demographic majority of the Jewish tribes in the territories under its control.

The practical implications of political Zionist aspirations to make Palestine 'Jewish' were outlined clearly by one of the architects of the Zionist settlement, the late Joseph Weitz (1890–1973), deputy chairman of the Board of Directors of the Jewish National Fund (JNF) from 1951 to 1973.[5] In 1967, contributing to the Israeli daily *Davar* ('The Word'), Weitz proposed 'A solution to the refugee problem', as follows:

Any suggestion for the colonization of the liberated territories (the West

Bank and Gaza Strip) and the territories held under Israeli administration (the Sinai Peninsula and the Golan Heights) must be subjected necessarily to a definite policy which addresses and solves three fundamental problems rendered more acute by the Six-Day War: regional security, demographic security and the settlement of the refugees. The first problem is understood by all and needs no explanations. As to the demographical problem, there are some who believe that the non-Jewish population, even in a high percentage, within our borders will be more effectively under our surveillance; and there are some who believe the contrary, i.e., that it is easier to carry out surveillance over the activities of a neighbour than over those of a tenant. The author of these columns tends to support the latter view, and has an additional argument to support his position: the need to sustain the character of the state which will henceforth be Jewish, and obviously in the near future, by the majority of its inhabitants, with a non-Jewish minority limited to 15 percent. I had already reached this fundamental conclusion as early as 1940, concerning which it is entered in my diary as follows: 'Among ourselves it must be clear that there is no place in the country for both peoples together ... With the Arabs we shall not achieve our aim of being independent people in this country. The only solution is *Eretz Israel* [Palestine], at least the west part of *Eretz Israel*, without Arabs ... and *there is no other way but to transfer the Arabs from here to the neighbouring countries, transfer all of them, not one village or tribe should remain*, and the transfer must aim at Iraq, Syria and even Transjordan. For this purpose money will be found, much money; and only with this transfer could the country absorb millions of our brothers. There is no other alternative ... One should investigate now the neighbouring countries in order to determine their capacity to absorb the Arabs of *Eretz Israel*.' (Joseph Weitz, 'A Solution to the Refugee Problem', *Davar*, 29 September 1967, quoted in Davis and Mezvinsky 1975: 21; emphasis added)[6]

As Nur Masalha observes in his penetrating study of the concept of 'transfer' in Zionist political thought, by the time the 1948 war ended the borders of the new State of Israel had been extended through conquest from 55.5 per cent of the territory of British Mandate Palestine, allocated by the UN General Assembly Resolution 181(II) of 1947 for the 'Jewish state', to some 77 per cent, and the proportion of the Arab population in these territories reduced through mass expulsion, 'transfer' in Zionist parlance, from nearly 50 per cent to approximately 20 per cent of the total population of the new state. Not quite 'as Jewish as England was English', but 'close enough to satisfy the new state's leaders' (Masalha 1992: 199).

The role of massacre in bringing about what Weitz termed 'the only solution', namely, '*Eretz Israel* [Palestine], at least the west part of *Eretz Israel*, without Arabs' cannot be overestimated. Take, for instance, the massacre in the Palestinian Arab village of Deir Yasin in April 1948. Prior to its destruction in 1948, the village of Deir Yasin, on the western outskirts of Jerusalem, had a population of some 750 people. On 9 April 1948, the Revisionist Zionist National Military Organization (*Irgun Tzevai Leumi*, IZL or *Irgun*), led by the future prime minister Menachem Begin (now deceased), and the Fighters for the Freedom of Israel (*Lohamei Herut Israel*, LEHI or Stern group), led by Begin's successor, Yitzhak Shamir, attacked Deir Yasin with some 130 men and murdered approximately 250 men, women and children. Some of the survivors were then marched in blood-drenched clothes through the streets of Jerusalem. As Meir Pa'il[7] testified:

> It was noon when the battle ended and the shooting stopped. Things had become quiet, but the village had not surrendered. The IZL [*Irgun*] and LEHI [Stern group] irregulars left the places in which they had been hiding and started carrying out cleaning up operations in the houses. They fired with all the arms they had, and threw explosives into the houses. They also shot everyone they saw in the houses, including women and children – indeed the commanders made no attempt to check the disgraceful acts of slaughter. I myself and a number of inhabitants begged the commanders to give orders to their men to stop shooting, but our efforts were unsuccessful. In the meantime some twenty-five men had been brought out of the houses: they were loaded into a freight truck and led in a 'victory parade', like a Roman triumph, through the Mahaneh Yahudah and Zikhron Yosef quarters [of Jerusalem]. At the end of the parade they were taken to a stone quarry between Giv'at Shaul and Deir Yasin and shot in cold blood. The fighters then put the women and children who were still alive on a truck and took them to the Mandelbaum Gate. (Meir Pa'il, *Yediot Aharonot*, 4 April 1972, as quoted in Hirst 1977: 126–7)

Another testimony of the massacre at Deir Yasin was provided by Jacques de Reynier, head of the International Red Cross Delegation in Palestine at that time:

> [T]he Commander of the *Irgun* detachment [referred to below as 'the gang'] did not seem willing to receive me. At last he arrived, young, distinguished, and perfectly correct, but there was a peculiar glitter in his eyes, cold and cruel. According to him the *Irgun* had arrived 24 hours earlier and ordered the inhabitants by loudspeaker to evacuate all houses

and surrender: the time given to obey the order was a quarter of an hour. Some of these miserable people had come forward and were taken prisoner, to be released later in the direction of the Arab lines. The rest, not having obeyed the order, had met the fate they deserved. But there was no point in exaggerating things, there were only a few dead, and they would be buried as soon as the 'cleaning up' of the village was over. If I found any bodies, I could take them, but there were certainly no wounded. This account made my blood run cold.

I went back to the Jerusalem road and got an ambulance and a truck that I had alerted through the Red Shield ... I reached the village with my convoy, and the Arab firing stopped. The gang was wearing country uniforms with helmets. All of them were young, some even adolescents, men and women, armed to the teeth: revolvers, machine-guns, hand grenades, and also cutlasses in their hands, most of them still blood-stained. A beautiful young girl, with criminal eyes, showed me hers still dripping with blood; she displayed it like a trophy. This was the 'cleaning up' team, that was obviously performing its task very conscientiously.

I tried to go into a house. A dozen soldiers surrounded me, their machine-guns aimed at my body, and their officer forbade me to move. The dead, if any, would be brought to me, he said. I then flew into one of the most towering rages of my life, telling these criminals what I thought of their conduct, threatening them with everything I could think of, and then pushed them aside and went into the house.

The first room was dark, everything was in disorder, but there was no one. In the second, amid disembowelled furniture and covers and all sorts of debris, I found some bodies, cold. Here the 'cleaning up' had been done with machine-guns, then hand grenades. It had been finished off with knives, anyone could see that. The same thing in the next room, but as I was about to leave, I heard something like a sigh. I looked everywhere, turned over all the bodies, and eventually found a little foot, still warm. It was a little girl of ten, mutilated by a hand grenade, but still alive ... everywhere it was the same horrible sight ... there had been 400 people in this village; about fifty of them had escaped and were still alive. All the rest had been deliberately massacred in cold blood for, as I observed for myself, this gang was admirably disciplined and only acted under orders.

After another visit to Deir Yasin I went back to my office where I was visited by two gentlemen, well dressed in civilian clothes, who had been waiting for me for more than an hour. They were the commander of the *Irgun* detachment and his aide. They had prepared a paper that they wanted me to sign. It was a statement to the effect that I had been very courteously received by them, and obtained all the facilities I had requested, in the accomplishment of my mission, and thanking them for the help I had received. As I showed signs of hesitation and even started to argue with them, they said that if I valued my life, I had better sign immediately. The only course open to me was to convince them that I did not value my life in the least. (Jacques de Reynier, *A Jerusalem un Drapeau Flottait sur la Ligne de Feu*, pp. 71–6, as quoted in Hirst 1978: 127–8)

Today, on the ruins of the village of Deir Yasin, a new quarter named Qiryat Har Nof (the Township of the Scenic Mountain) has been constructed. For whatever reason the late Menachem Begin, former head of the IZL and subsequently prime minister of the State of Israel, chose a flat in Har Nof as his last residence as a semi-recluse. By the time he died there he was reported to have been clinically depressed.

The impact of the Deir Yasin massacre in 1948 was subsequently assessed by Israel Eldad (Scheib), who together with the future prime minister of Israel, Yitzhak Shamir and the late Nathan Yalin-Mor (Friedman), led the LEHI. As noted above, the LEHI and the IZL together both planned the attack and perpetrated the massacre at Deir Yasin. Speaking at a closed discussion in the summer of 1967, as subsequently transcribed and published in the influential journal *De'ot* ('Opinions') in the winter of the following year, Eldad commented:

I have always said that if the deepest and profoundest hope symbolizing redemption is the re-building of the [Jewish] Temple ... then it is obvious that those mosques [Dome of the Rock and al-Aqsa] will have, one way or another, to disappear one of these days ... Had it not been for Deir Yasin – half a million Arabs would be living in the State of Israel [in 1948]. The State of Israel would not have existed. We must not disregard this, with full awareness of the responsibility involved. All wars are cruel. There is no way out of that. This country will either be *Eretz Israel* with an absolute Jewish majority and a small Arab minority, or *Eretz Ishmael*, and Jewish emigration will begin again if we do not expel the Arabs one way or another. (Eldad, 'On the Spirit that was Revealed in the People', *De'ot*, Winter 1968; as quoted in Davis and Mezvinsky 1975: 186–7)

The Deir Yasin massacre, perpetrated by the irregular Revisionist Zionist underground organizations, the IZL and the LEHI, was not an isolated incident. The regular forces of the Israeli army, the Israel Defence Forces (*Tzeva Haganah le-Israel*, IDF or ZAHAL) perpetrated similar outrages, two of which, the Tantura massacre and the Duwayma massacre, are documented below.

As Theodor Katz revealed, in the course of his research work towards an MA degree at Haifa University, oral reports and documentary records suggest that the IDF war crime at Tantura in May 1948 was an atrocity of the order of the Deir Yasin massacre:

> The village of Tantura was occupied by the soldiers of the 33rd battalion of the Alexandroni brigade on the night of the 22–23 May 1948. Research carried out by Theodor Katz for his MA dissertation, based on testimonies of the refugees from the village, Alexandroni soldiers and documents located with the IDF archive establishes that that night a horrific massacre of the menfolk of the village took place. According to the testimonies, the men were shot in the streets, in their homes and in concentrated manner, in groups of six to ten at a time, at the cemetery of the village. Some of the men were forced to dig trenches which became their graves after they were shot. More than 200 bodies were counted there in the night of the conquest and subsequent days. The slain people were buried in mass graves in the area which is today the car park of the Dor beach. Only the arrival of residents from Zikhron Ya'aqov put a stop to the campaign of carnage carried out by the soldiers. (Amir Gilat, 'The Massacre in Tantura', *Maariv* Weekend Supplement, 21 January 2000)

With regard to the massacre at Duwayma, the following account of the massacre appeared in the now defunct *Davar*, the official Hebrew daily of the Labour Zionist-controlled *Histadrut* General Federation of Workers in the Land of Israel:

> We did not always successfully face the test of Jewish ethics, of which we were proud: the purity of arms. Recently I ran across a letter dated 8.11.1948, which reads as follows:
>
> 'I wish to submit to you an eyewitness report given to me by a soldier who was in al-Duwayma on the day following its occupation … The man is one of us [member of the United Workers' Party (MAPAM)] …
>
> 'He opened his heart to me because there are not many hearts these days that are willing to listen. He arrived in al-Duwayma immediately after its occupation. The conquering army was 89th battalion … They killed some 80–100 Arabs, women and children. The children were killed by smashing their skulls with clubs. There was not a single house without dead. The second wave of the army consisted of the battalion of the soldier who gave this eyewitness report … In the village there remained Arab men and women who were put in the houses without food or drink. Then the sappers came to blow up the houses. One officer ordered a sapper to put two old women into the house he was about

to blow up. The sapper refused, and said that he would obey only such orders as were handed down to him by his immediate commander. So the officer ordered his own soldiers to put the old women in, and the atrocity was carried out. Another soldier boasted that he had raped an Arab woman and then shot her. Another Arab woman with a day-old baby was employed in cleaning jobs in the yard ... She worked for one or two days in the service, and then she was shot, together with her baby ... Cultured and well mannered commanders who are considered good fellows ... have turned into low murderers, and this happened not in the storm of the battle and blind passion, but because of a system of expulsion and annihilation. The fewer Arabs remain the better.' (quoted in Eyal Kafkafi, 'A Ghetto Attitude in the Jewish State', *Davar*, 6 September 1979)[8]

Deir Yasin, prior to its destruction in 1948, was a prosperous ex-panding village of some 750 inhabitants, with one school for boys and another school for girls. On the site of the destroyed village the State of Israel Ministry of Health placed a hospital facility for the mentally ill, incorporating some of the houses that survived the mass destruction into the hospital compound. The official State of Israel holocaust memorial, *Yad va-Shem*, is situated on the lands of Deir Yasin, as is the city of Jerusalem western cemetery.

Tantura, prior to its destruction in 1948, had twice as many inhabitants as Deir Yasin, also one school for boys and another school for girls servicing 1,500 inhabitants. A spur linked it to the coastal highway and a train station serviced the costal railway line, giving it access to Haifa and other urban centres. In 1949 Moshav Dor was established on the site of the destroyed village of Tantura and settled by Jewish immigrants from Iraq and Greece.

Al-Duwayma, before its destruction in 1948, was a large Palestinian Arab village 17 kilometres west of Hebron, with a population of 2,700. In 1955 Kibbutz Amatziyah was established on the site settled by a nucleus of Israeli-born Jews and new Anglo-Saxon Jewish immigrants. The settlement has since altered its status to that of a cooperative smallholder *moshav*.

Recent work by Salman Abu Sitta, the foremost researcher on the question of the right of return of the 1948 Palestine refugees, records 34 reported massacres perpetrated by the IDF, IZL and the LEHI in and around the 1948–49 war (Salman Abu Sitta 1999: 27).

It is hardly surprising that refusal to recognize the basic human rights of the 1948 Palestine refugee to repatriation, compensation and return, in blatant disrespect for the Universal Declaration of Human

Rights ('Everyone has the right to freedom of movement and residence within the borders of each state; and everyone has the right to leave any country, including his own, and to return to his country', UDHR, Article 13) is common to all political Zionists, let alone recognition of the fundamental rights of the 1948 Palestinian refugees to their properties inside Israel ('Everyone has the right to own property alone as well as in association with others; and no one shall be arbitrarily deprived of his property', UDHR, Article 17).

The World Zionist Organization and its political goals

As pointed out above, political Zionism, as represented in the World Zionist Organization (WZO), is the dominant and hegemonic school of Zionism, namely, the school of thought and colonial practice to which all political Zionist parties subscribe.

All political parties of the Zionist movement, including Labour Zionism, Religious Zionism and Revisionist Zionism, share, above and beyond real historical differences of policy and political ideology (now much blurred), a common goal that has tied them all as members, albeit often conflicting members, of the World Zionist Organization: a fundamental commitment to the establishment and the continued existence in Palestine of a Jewish state as a state for all Jews throughout the world, aiming to guarantee in the law and in the practice of the state a demographic majority of members of the Jewish tribes (a demographic majority of ethnic Jews).

In other words, all political Zionist parties are committed to the normative statement that it is a good idea to establish and consolidate in the country of Palestine a sovereign state, a Jewish state, that attempts to guarantee in law (for example, the Absentees' Property Law of 1950) and in practice (for example the mass expulsion of the native indigenous Palestinian Arab people under the cover of the 1948–49 war) a demographic majority of the Jewish tribes in the territories under its control.

The establishment of the State of Israel on 15 May 1948 is correctly considered to be the crowning of the efforts of the World Zionist Organization (WZO), the Jewish Agency for the Land of Israel (JA), the Jewish National Fund (JNF) and affiliated organizations over the previous 50 years. During the preceding half a century or so, the administrative underpinnings for a Jewish state were laid in Palestine according to patterns that have been more or less standard in all Western colonial ventures. There was, however, one major difference that characterized the Zionist colonial effort in Palestine, and distinguished it from other western colonial efforts in Asia and Africa: the Zionist movement did not originally predicate its efforts in Palestine on the colonization of the native land through the dispossession and exploitation of the native people.

Rather, it has systematically followed a pattern of colonization that has emerged as much more cruel and disastrous for the native indigenous population: colonization through the dispossession and exclusion of the native people. Thus, among the key Zionist slogans were not only 'the conquest of the land' but, equally important, 'the conquest of labour'. As expressed in the programme of *Ha-Po'el ha-Tza'ir* ('The Young Worker') Party, 'The necessary condition for the realization of Zionism is the conquest of all branches of labour in *Eretz Israel* by Jews' (Goldstein 1976: 5).

As noted above, the political objectives of the World Zionist Organization were first defined in August 1897, at the First Congress of the WZO in Basle, Switzerland: 'The aim of Zionism is to create for the Jewish people a home in Palestine secured by public law.' The Zionist movement won its first crucial international political recognition in the 1917 Balfour Declaration submitted by the British foreign secretary, Lord Arthur James Balfour, to his compatriot, the banking magnate Lord Lionel Walter Rothschild, in which the British Empire committed itself to the Zionist objectives in the following terms:

Foreign Office
November 2nd 1917

Dear Lord Rothschild,

I have much pleasure in conveying to you on behalf of His Majesty's Government the following declaration of sympathy with the Jewish Zionist aspirations, which has been submitted to, and approved by the Cabinet.

His Majesty's Government view with favour the establishment in Palestine of a national home for the Jewish people and will use their best endeavours to facilitate the achievement of this object, it being clearly understood that nothing shall be done which may prejudice the civil and religious rights of existing non-Jewish communities in Palestine or the rights and political status enjoyed by Jews in any other country.

I should be grateful if you would bring this declaration to the knowledge of the Zionist Federation. (quoted in Davis 1977: 154)

Subsequent to the First World War, the Jewish Agency for the Land of Israel, or the Jewish Agency (JA), was recognized by the British Mandate Government, under the terms of the text of Article 4 of the

Mandate for Palestine as approved by the League of Nations in July 1922 (below), as the appropriate public body to advise the Mandate administration in such economic, social and other matters as may effect the establishment of the Jewish national home in Palestine:

> An appropriate Jewish Agency shall be recognized as a public body for the purpose of advising and cooperating with the Administration of Palestine in such economic, social and other matters as may effect the establishment of the Jewish national home and the interests of the Jewish population in Palestine, and subject always to the control of the Administration, to assist and take part in the development of the country.
>
> The Zionist organization, so long as its organization and constitution are in the opinion of the Mandatory appropriate, shall be recognized as such an agency. It shall take steps in consultation with His Britannic Majesty's Government to secure the cooperation of all Jews who are willing to assist in the establishment of the Jewish national home. (quoted in Mallison and Mallison 1986: 92)

Having been granted recognition by the British Mandate for Palestine and His Britannic Majesty's Government, the various departments of the World Zionist Organization became departments of the Jewish Agency and the chairman of the board of the WZO became the chairman of the JA. The JA thus became the executive arm of the WZO in the areas of Zionist immigration to Palestine, absorption of Jewish immigrants, settlement and economics, and was subsequently to provide the administrative, economic, military, political and other underpinnings for the Jewish state in the making. Until 1929, the World Zionist Organization was effectively identical to the Jewish Agency.[9]

Following the establishment of the State of Israel in 1948, the 23rd Zionist Congress, convened in 1951 (the first to convene in the State of Israel), replaced the said 'Basle Programme' with the 'Jerusalem Programme':

1. The task of Zionism is the consolidation of the State of Israel, the ingathering of exiles in *Eretz Israel* [the Land of Israel], and the fostering of the unity of the Jewish people.

The program of work of the Zionist Organization is:

1. Encouragement of immigration, absorption and integration of immigrants; support of youth *aliyah* [ascent, namely, Jewish immigration to Israel]; stimulation of agricultural settlement and economic development; acquisition of land as the property of the people.
2. Intensive work for *halutziut* [pioneering] and *hachsharah* [training for *halutziut*].

3. Concerted effort to harness funds in order to carry out the tasks of Zionism.
4. Encouragement of private capital investment.
5. Fostering of Jewish consciousness by propagating the Zionist idea and strengthening the Zionist movement; imparting the values of Judaism; Hebrew education and spreading the Hebrew language.
6. Mobilization of world public opinion for Israel and Zionism.
7. Participation in efforts to organize and intensify Jewish life on democratic foundations, maintenance and defence of Jewish rights. (http://www.thelikud.org/Archives/Structure%20of%20the%20World%20Zionist%20Organization.htm)

Following the 1967 war, the 27th Zionist Congress, held in Jerusalem in 1968, revised the 'Jerusalem Programme' above. The Revised Jerusalem Programme of 1968 reads as follows:

The aims of Zionism are:

1. The unity of the Jewish people and the centrality of Israel in Jewish life;
2. The ingathering of the Jewish people in its historic homeland, *Eretz Israel*, through *aliyah* from all countries;
3. The strengthening of the State of Israel which is based on the prophetic vision of justice and peace;
4. The preservation of the identity of the Jewish people through the fostering of Jewish, Hebrew and Zionist education and of Jewish spiritual and cultural values;
5. The protection of Jewish rights everywhere. (ibid.)

(The reference to 'Zionist education' was introduced into the text by the Zionist General Council XXXI/5 in 1991.)

With the termination of the British Mandate for Palestine and the establishment of the State of Israel in 1948 such departments of the Jewish Agency as paralleled the duties of government ministries (Foreign Affairs, Defence, Trade and Industry, Labour and more) were handed over to the government of the new state, and the status of the WZO, the JA and the JNF in the Jewish state was settled in the World Zionist Organization/Jewish Agency for the Land of Israel Status Law of 1952, the Jewish National Fund Law of 1953, the Covenant between the Government of the State of Israel and the WZO/JA of 1954 (which, following the reconstitution of the Jewish Agency, was replaced with a new Covenant between the Government of the State of Israel and the Reconstituted Jewish Agency for the Land of Israel of 1979) and the Covenant between the Government of the State of Israel and the JNF of 1961.

According to the World Zionist Organization/Jewish Agency (Status) Law of 1952, Article 4 (amended 1976) the 'State of Israel recognizes the World Zionist Organization and the Jewish Agency for Israel as the authorized agencies which will continue to operate in the State of Israel for the development and settlement of the country, the absorption of immigrants from the Diaspora and the coordination of the activities in Israel of Jewish institutions and organizations active in those fields'.

Except that the Constitution of the WZO commits the organization to 'the ingathering of the Jewish people in its historic homeland, *Eretz Israel*, through *aliyah* from all countries' (World Zionist Organization, *Constitution*, Article 2) and the functions of the reconstituted Jewish Agency for the Land of Israel (except with respect to activities and facilities which the Government of Israel is by law obliged to furnish) include 'Jewish immigration (*aliyah*) to and absorption of Jewish immigrants (*olim*) in Israel; social welfare Services in connection with Jewish immigration and absorption; health services in connection with Jewish immigration and absorption; fostering regional development and creation of centers of employment in peripheral areas for the absorption of Jewish immigrants (*olim*) and for their social and community integration in urban and rural sectors and absorption in agricultural settlement; Jewish immigrant housing' (*Agreement for the Reconstitution of the Jewish Agency for Israel*, Article 1C, 1994).

The quotes above do not represent the official World Zionist Organization English-language translation. They represent the translation by the author of the original Hebrew text, the reason being that, as we shall see below, the official WZO translation is rendered in such terms as are designed to veil from the world at large, and possibly from significant sections of the Jewish constituencies of the WZO and the JA, the apartheid objects of the WZO and the JA (for Jews only).

The duplicity of official Zionist narrative in English versus Hebrew is striking. It is useful to point out two highlights:

• The official name of the Jewish Agency in Hebrew is the 'Jewish Agency for the Land of Israel' (*Eretz Israel*, designating 'Greater Israel', namely the territory allegedly promised by God to the people of Israel in the biblical narrative), whereas the official name of the Jewish Agency in English is the 'Jewish Agency for Israel' (suggesting the State of Israel bounded by its 1949 armistice lines).

• The objects of the Jewish agency in Hebrew refer to *aliyah* (Jewish immigration) and *olim* (Jewish immigrants), whereas the official English-language translation refers to 'immigration' and 'immigrants', omitting the reference to Jews.

Needless to say, only people classified as 'Jews' are recognized under Israeli law as *olim*, namely Jewish immigrants.[10]

Achieving the goals of political Zionism

By the conclusion, in July 1949, of the Israel–Syria Armistice Agreements, which brought to an end the 1948–49 war, Israel had achieved a significant territorial expansion from 55.5 per cent of the territory of Mandatory Palestine, as allocated to the Jewish state by the 1947 UN General Assembly Resolution 181(II) recommending the partition of Palestine with economic union, to over 77 per cent (20,600 km²). Of the remaining area, the West Bank (6,400 km²) was annexed to the Hashemite Kingdom of Jordan in 1950, and the Gaza Strip (362 km²) came under Egyptian military administration. In the territories that have thus come under Israeli rule and occupation at the end of the 1948–49 war lived (prior to the war) some 900,000 Palestinian Arabs. They inhabited approximately 500 villages as well as all major and provincial cities: Bisan, Tiberias, Safad, Nazareth, Shafa'Amr, Acre, Haifa, Jaffa, Lydda, Ramle, Jerusalem, Majdal (Ashqelon), Isdud (Ashdod) and Beersheba. Of this population, only some 150,000 remained under Israeli rule inside Israeli armistice boundaries (the 'Green Line'). The majority of the native indigenous Palestinian Arab population who fled and/or were terrorized to flee during the hostilities, or were forcibly expelled by the Israeli army, have never been permitted by Israel to return; nor has Israel ever acknowledged the right of these people to the title of their properties inside Israel.

Having expelled the majority of the native indigenous Palestinian and/or Arab people from the territories that came under the control of the Israeli army in the course of the 1948–49 war, and being cognizant of UN General Assembly Resolution 194(III) of December 1948 'that the refugees wishing to return to their homes and live at peace with their neighbours should be permitted to do so at the earliest practicable date', the Israeli authorities then pursued the systematic destruction of their homes with the aim that there be no homes for the refugees to return to.

Of the 500 or so Palestinian Arab villages and cities, some 400 (385 according to the list compiled by the Israeli League for Human and Civil Rights; see Table 1.1) were destroyed and almost all razed to the ground by the Israeli army during the 1948–49 war and throughout the 1950s.[11]

As noted above, the State of Israel has consistently denied the right of return to the erstwhile Palestinian Arab inhabitants of the land,

and violated UN General Assembly resolutions recognizing their right of return and calling for their repatriation. In fact, all 1948 Palestinian Arab refugees and internally displaced persons are legislated in Israel as 'absentees' through the Absentees' Property Law of 1950. Thus some four million 1948 Palestine refugees today outside the 'Green Line' have been alienated from all rights to Israeli citizenship, to their lands, and to their properties in Israel. And of the 150,000 of the native indigenous Palestinian Arab people who found themselves in the wake of the 1948–49 armistice agreements inside the 'Green Line', the approximately one million Palestinian Arab citizens of Israel today, some 25 per cent, 250,000 persons, are internally displaced persons, 'present absentees', likewise denied all rights in their pre-1948 properties inside Israel.

The enormity of this nation-wide, systematic practice of war crimes is indicated in the Israeli League for Human and Civil Rights' list of destroyed Palestinian Arab villages. The list refers to Arab villages destroyed in pre-1967 Israel alone. The Arab population of the cities of Bisan, Tiberias, Safad, Majdal (Ashqelon), Isdud (Ashdod) Beersheba and West Jerusalem was expelled in its entirety. In Lydda, Ramle, Jaffa,

Table 1.1 Destruction of Palestinian Arab villages

Name of district	Number of villages (before 1948)	Number of villages today	Number of destroyed villages
1. Jerusalem	33	4	29
2. Bethlehem	7	0	7
3. Hebron	16	0	16
4. Jaffa	23	0	23
5. Ramle	31	0	31
6. Lydda	28	0	28
7. Jenin	8	4	4
8. Tul Karm	33	12	21
9. Haifa	43	8	35
10. Acre	52	32	20
11. Nazareth	26	20	6
12. Safad	75	7	68
13. Tiberias	26	3	23
14. Bisan	28	0	28
15. Gaza	46	0	46
Total	475	90	385

Source: Based on Israel Shahak, Israeli League for Human and Civil Rights, 'Arab Villages Destroyed in Israel', quoted in Davis and Mezvinsky 1975: 47.

Haifa and Acre, the surviving Arab population was largely confined to ghettoes.

It should be noted that the data in Table 1.1 are to some extent incomplete, partly because Shahak found it impossible to locate Arab tribes (many of them already settled and not migratory under the British Mandate). It should also be noted that in the months following the signing of the armistice agreements in 1949, thousands of Palestinian Arabs (such as the population of the Arab city of Majdal), many with Israeli ID cards, were forcibly deported.

The Israeli Central Bureau of Statistics lists 124 officially recognized Arab localities (see State of Israel 2001). According to the Association of Forty, there are as many unrecognized Arab localities inside Israel, many of which were there years before the State of Israel was established, as there are recognized localities.[12]

The vast number of properties classified under the Absentees' Property Law of 1950 as 'absentee property' can be further assessed if one recalls that, until 1947, individual or corporate Jewish land ownership in Palestine did not exceed 7 per cent of the territory of British Mandate Palestine, or 10 per cent of the territories that came under Israeli rule and occupation following the 1948–49 war. According to the Israeli Custodian of Absentee Property, almost 70 per cent of the territory of pre-1967 Israel consists of land classified as 'absentee property':

> The Custodian of Absentee Property does not choose to discuss politics. But when asked how much of the land of the State of Israel might potentially have two claimants – an Arab and a Jew holding respectively a British Mandate and an Israeli deed to the same property – Mr Manor [the Custodian in 1980] believes that 'about 70 per cent' might fall into that category. (Robert Fisk, 'The Land of Palestine, Part Eight: The Custodian of Absentee Property', *The Times*, 24 December 1980)

Jewish National Fund estimates, on the other hand, set the figure as high as 88 per cent:

> Of the entire area of the State of Israel only about 300,000–400,000 dunums [1 acre equals 4 dunums] … are state domain which the Israeli government took over from the mandatory regime [2 per cent]. The JNF and private Jewish owners possess under 2 million dunums [10 per cent]. Almost all the rest [i.e., 88 per cent of the 20,225,000 dunums within the 1949 armistice lines] belongs at law to Arab owners, many of whom have left the country. (Jewish National Fund, *Jewish Villages in Israel*, p. xxi, quoted in Lehn in association with Davis 1988: 132)

All these massive properties have been vested under the Absentees'

Property Law of 1950 with the Custodian of Absentee Property appointed by the Minister of Finance (Article 2[a]).

Under the said law, every right an 'absentee' had with regard to any property is vested with the Custodian, and the status of the Custodian was legislated to be the same as that of the owner of the property (4[a] [2]). The fact that the identity of an 'absentee' is unknown did not prevent the property from being classified as 'absentee property'.[13]

As Baruch Kimmerling notes:

> It is difficult to estimate the value of this property ... The UN Refugee Office estimated ... [in the late 1950s or the early 1960s] ... that all in all the value of Arab abandoned orchards, trees, movable and immovable property in the territory under Israeli jurisdiction was about 118–120 billion Pounds Sterling, an average of £130 ($364) per refugee. (Kimmerling 1983: 100)

Kimmerling qualifies these estimates ('this is probably high'), and quotes Gabbay (1959) as reference. However, in light of other assessments, his qualification seems misplaced. Consider, for instance, the following outline by Don Peretz:

> Much information concerning the use, amounts and distribution of abandoned Arab property and the government's policy toward it was secret. Records and most reports of the Custodian of Absentee Property were secret. Sessions of the Knesset's Finance Committee, when it discussed the problem, were closed. Even the United Nations, in spite of frequent requests, was unable to obtain adequate information about Israel's disposition of Arab property. In its Fifteenth Progress Report of October 4, 1956, the CCP [UN Conciliation Commission for Palestine] stated that its representatives had still received no reply to a request submitted to the Israel Government the previous February for information concerning the administration of Arab refugee property or the measures taken to protect it, safeguard its identity, and provide restitution to the refugee owners. Therefore much information in this Chapter and Chapter IX concerning absentee property necessarily came from indirect sources.
>
> The CCP Refugee Office estimated that although only a little more than a quarter was considered cultivable, more than 80 per cent of Israel's total area of 20,850 square kilometres represented land abandoned by the Arab refugees. Three-quarters of the former Arab land was sub-marginal land or semi-desert in the Negeb. Evaluation of the property varied from that of the United Nations – £P120 million – to the Arab League's estimate of more than ten times that amount.

Abandoned property was one of the greatest contributions toward making Israel a viable state. The extent of its area and the fact that most of the regions along the border consisted of absentee property made it strategically significant. Of the 370 new Jewish settlements established between 1948 and the beginning of 1953, 350 were on absentee property. In 1954, more than one third of Israel's Jewish population lived on absentee property and nearly a third of the new immigrants (250,000 people) settled in urban areas abandoned by Arabs. They left whole cities like Jaffa, Acre, Lydda, Ramle, Baysan [Beit Shean], Majdal [Ashqelon]; 388 towns and villages and large parts of 94 other cities and towns, containing nearly a quarter of all the buildings in Israel. Ten thousand shops, businesses and stores were left in Jewish hands. At the end of the Mandate, citrus holdings in the area of Israel totalled about 240,000 dunums of which half were Arab owned. Most of the Arab groves were taken over by the Israel Custodian of Absentee Property. But only 34,000 dunums were cultivated by the end of 1953. By 1956 73,000 dunums were either cultivated or fit for cultivation. In 1951–52, former Arab groves produced one-and-a-quarter million boxes of fruit, of which 400,000 were exported. Arab fruit sent abroad provided nearly 10 per cent of the country's foreign currency earnings from exports in 1951. In 1949 the olive produce from abandoned Arab groves was Israel's third largest export, ranking after citrus and diamonds. The relative economic importance of Arab property was largest from 1948 until 1953, during the period of greatest immigration and need. After that, as the immigrants became more productive, national dependence upon abandoned Arab property declined relatively.

The CCP estimated that the amount of Israel's cultivable abandoned Arab land was nearly two and a half times the total area of Jewish-owned property at the end of the Mandate. The Israel Custodian of Absentee Property estimated that only two and a half million of the four million dunums of Arab land held by him were cultivated. No account was given for the discrepancy between the amount of cultivable area cited by the CCP (4,574,000 dunums) and the cultivated area held by the Custodian. Neither was the difference between the total of four million dunums of absentee property held by the Custodian and the CCP's total of 16,324,000 dunums clearly explained ...

In 1951 abandoned cultivable land included nearly 95 per cent of all Israel's olive groves, 40 thousand dunums of vineyards, and at least 10 thousand dunums of other orchards excluding citrus.

Twenty thousand dunums of absentee property were leased by the Custodian in 1952 for industrial purposes. A third of Israel's stone production was supplied by 52 Arab quarries under his jurisdiction.

The amount and value of movable Arab property was never accurately determined. In the chaotic war conditions which prevailed after the Arab flight most of their property was destroyed, looted or lost. More than four million pounds' worth of movable property was in the warehouses of the Custodian in 1951. The CCP's Refugee Office estimated that the approximate value of all movable Arab refugee property was about 20 million Palestine pounds. (Peretz 1958: 142–6)[14]

By all accounts, the properties vested in the Custodian of Absentee Property following the 1948–49 war constituted the primary rural and urban resources for post-1948 Israeli, exclusively Jewish, settlement projects, cultivation and development. As Moshe Dayan noted in his famous speech before students at the Israel Institute of Technology (Techniyon) in 1969:

> We came here to a country that was populated by Arabs, and we are building here a Hebrew, Jewish state. In a considerable portion of localities we purchased the land from the Arabs. Instead of the Arab villages Jewish villages were established. You even do not know the names of these villages and I do not blame you, because these geography books no longer exist. Not only the books, but also the villages no longer exist. Nahalal was established in the place of Mahalul, Gevat in the place of Jibta, Sarid in the place of Hanifas and Kefar Yehoshu'a in the place of Tel Shamam. There is not a single settlement that was not established in the place of a former Arab village. (Dayan, 19 March 1969; as quoted in *Haaretz*, 4 April 1969)

Regularizing the irregular: the regulation of apartheid in Israel

With the establishment of the State of Israel in May 1948, the legal status of the landholdings, properties and operations of *inter alia* the World Zionist Organization, the Jewish Agency for the Land of Israel and the Jewish National Fund inside the State of Israel had to be regularized. Following the establishment of the state, a fundamental legal and political circle had to be squared. On the one hand, the new state was politically and legally committed to the values of the Universal Declaration of Human Rights, the Charter of the United Nations Organization, and the standards of international law, which, since the Second World War, have informed most, if not all, liberal western democracies and enlightened world public opinion. On the other hand, the driving force underpinning the efforts of political Zionism since its establishment at the First Zionist Congress was not liberal democratic, but ethnocratic, namely, the attempt to establish in Palestine a state that would be as 'Jewish' as England was 'English' – in other words, establish and consolidate in the country of Palestine a sovereign state, a Jewish state, that attempts to guarantee in law and in practice a demographic majority of the Jewish tribes in the territories under its control: an apartheid state.

Clearly, the political Zionist efforts to create in all or in a part of the country of Palestine a Jewish majority *ex nihilo* could not but further entail the dispossession and expulsion of the majority of the native indigenous population from the territories of the projected Jewish state, and the legislation of the remnants of the non-Jewish, largely Palestinian Arab, population remaining under Israeli rule into the status of second- and third-class citizens.

Racism is not apartheid and apartheid is not racism. Apartheid is a political system where racism is regulated in law through acts of parliament. Racism is prevalent in all states, including liberal democratic states such as the current western liberal democracies. But in liberal democratic states, those victimized by racism have legal recourse to seek the protection of the law under a democratic constitution, namely a constitution that embodies the values of the Universal Declaration of Human Rights. In an apartheid state, on the other hand, the state enforces racism through the legal system, criminalizes expressions of humanitarian concern and obligates the citizenry through acts of parliament to make racist choices and conform to racist behaviour.

But it was equally clear to the political Zionist leadership that successfully steered the establishment of the Jewish state from its modest beginning in the first Zionist Congress in 1897 through to its admission as a member state in the UN some 50 years later in 1949 that, for a state constituted by UN General Assembly Resolution 181(II) and admitted to the UN on the basis of its declaration that the State of Israel 'unreservedly accepts the obligations of the United Nations Charter and undertakes to honour them from the day when it becomes a member of the United Nations',[15] it was imperative to be able to project the Jewish state as 'the only democracy in the Middle East'. Israel's admission to the UN, and its continued membership in the UN, depended on it.

The liberal democratic world community, having defeated the Nazi Third Reich, emerged, scarred and smouldering, from the devastation and the horrific slaughter of the Second World War with the Universal Declaration of Human Rights, adopted by the UN General Assembly on 10 December 1948 (five months prior to the admission of Israel as a member state of the UN on 11 May 1949), declaring that:

Whereas recognition of the inherent dignity and of the equal and inalienable rights of all members of the human family is the foundation of freedom, justice and peace in the world;

Whereas disregard and contempt for human rights have resulted in barbarous acts which have outraged the conscience of mankind, and the advent of a world in which human beings shall enjoy freedom of speech and belief and freedom from fear and want has been proclaimed as the highest aspiration of the common people;

Whereas it is essential, if man is not to be compelled to have recourse, as a last resort, to rebellion against tyranny and oppression, that human rights should be protected by the rule of law ...

The State of Israel would not have been able to project itself in the West as successfully as it has done since its establishment in 1948 as the 'only democracy in the Middle East' without elaborately veiling its apartheid legislation. As Musa Mazzawi points out, the discussions at the UN Security Council suggest, the holocaust notwithstanding, that the UN would have been reluctant to allow the admission of the Jewish state as a member state had the UN not received formal and solemn assurances from the Government of the State of Israel that Israel would abide by Resolution 181(II) of November 1947 recommending the partition of Palestine with economic union, and Resolution 194(III) of December 1948 resolving that the 1948 Palestinian refugees wishing to return to their homes and live at peace with their neighbours should be permitted to do so at the earliest practicable date (see note 15). It goes without saying that, under the circumstances, had the new state failed to project itself as anything other than an international-law-abiding state, it would have seriously jeopardized the prospects of its admission as a member state in the UN.

And by the same token, all governments of the State of Israel and the pro-Israel and pro-Zionist lobbies in the West worked relentlessly since 1975 for a period of over fifteen years to nullify one of the most significant achievements of the PLO and the international Palestine solidarity movement, including the anti-Zionist Jewish opposition inside and outside Israel, namely, UN General Assembly Resolution 3379 of November 1975. All parties to the Israeli–Palestinian conflict were aware that the passage of this resolution could provide a platform for UN sanctions against Israel directed to assist rogue Israeli governments to comply with UN Security Council resolutions, and ultimately provide an instrument to effect the suspension of Israel's membership in the UN in the event that it fails to do so.

The nullification of the said resolution by the UN General Assembly in December 1991 represents a massive setback for the struggle of the Palestinian people to regain their rights under international law. It is for these and related legal and political considerations that the legal regulation of apartheid in Israel is structured in terms that are rather different from the structures of legal apartheid in the Republic of South Africa.

One, there is no UN resolution recommending the partition of South Africa into a 'White state' and a 'non-White' state; and second, given the specificity of the establishment of the State of Israel outlined above, blatant Israeli violations of UN General Assembly Resolution 181(II) and 194(III) under the cover of the 1948–49 war had to be covered from public view by a veil of legal ambiguity in a way apartheid in South Africa did not. (After all, the Republic of South Africa was not the creation of the United Nations organization.)

Thus the official Israeli claim that the record of the State of Israel on the question of racism is not better, but also not much worse relative to many other member states of the United Nations Organization is basically correct. But it also serves to veil the fact that Israel is probably the last remaining apartheid state member of the UN as well as the reality of Israeli apartheid, namely the regulation of racism in law through Acts of the Israeli Parliament (the Knesset), resulting in 93 per cent of all the territory of pre-1967 Israel being designated in law through Acts of the Knesset for cultivation, development and settlement by, of and for Jews only. It is in order to note in this connection that Israeli apartheid legislation in the area of land tenure (the core of the Israeli–Palestinian conflict) is more radical than apartheid legislation in the Republic of South Africa at the heyday of the apartheid governments there, when some 87 per cent of the land was designated in law for cultivation, development and settlements for 'Whites only'.

Apartheid in Israel is an overarching legal reality that determines the quality of everyday life and underpins the circumstances of living for all the inhabitants of the State of Israel. In the decades preceding 1994, when the official and hegemonic ideological value system of the Republic of South Africa was apartheid, the key legal distinction in South African apartheid legislation was between 'White', 'Coloured', 'Indian' and 'Black'. The official hegemonic ideological value system in the State of Israel is political Zionism, and the key legal distinction in Zionist apartheid legislation in Israel is between 'Jew' and 'non-Jew'.

The introduction of this key distinction of 'Jew' and 'non-Jew' into the foundation of Israeli law is, however, accomplished as part of a two-tier structure. It is this structure that has preserved the veil of ambiguity over Israeli apartheid legislation for over half a century.

The first tier, the level at which the key distinction between 'Jew' and 'non-Jew' is rendered openly and explicitly, is in the Constitutions and Articles of Association of all the institutions of the Zionist movement and, in the first instance, the WZO, the JA and the JNF. Thus the Constitution of the Jewish Agency stipulates:

> Land is to be acquired as Jewish property and ... the title of the lands acquired is to be taken in the name of the JNF to the end that the same shall be held the inalienable property of the Jewish people. The Agency shall promote agricultural colonization based on Jewish labour, and in all works or undertakings carried out or furthered by the Agency, it shall be deemed to be a matter of principle that Jewish labour shall be employed. (Article 3 [d] and [e])

Similarly, the Memorandum of Association of the Keren Kayemeth Leisrael (JNF) Ltd, as incorporated in the United Kingdom in 1907, defines the primary object of the company as follows:

> To purchase, take on lease or in exchange, or otherwise acquire any lands, forests, rights of possession and other rights, easements and other immovable property in the prescribed region (which expression shall in this Memorandum mean Palestine, Syria, and other parts of Turkey in Asia and the Peninsula of Sinai) or any other part thereof, for the purpose of settling Jews on such lands. (Article 3, subclause 1)

In parallel, the Memorandum of Association of the *Keren Kayemeth Leisrael* (JNF) as incorporated in Israel in 1954, defines the primary object of the Israel company as follows:

> To purchase, acquire on lease or in exchange, etc. ... in the prescribed region (which expression shall in this Memorandum mean the State of Israel in any area within the jurisdiction of the Government of Israel) or any part thereof, for the purpose of settling Jews on such lands and properties. (Article 3 [a])

The second tier is the level at which this key distinction between 'Jew' and 'non-Jew', as institutionalized in the Constitutions and Articles of Association of all the bodies affiliated to the World Zionist Organization, is incorporated into the body of the laws of the State of Israel, notably the body of strategic legislation governing land tenure.

Until 1948, it could have been argued with some justice that the WZO, the JA, the JNF and the various other bodies of the Zionist movement are institutional expressions of a technically voluntary organization of primarily parochial interests, and that they should, therefore, be properly judged by standards relevant to similar establishments, for instance the establishment of the Catholic Church and its various corporate organizational and business subsidiaries.

It could further be argued that Zionist institutions are constitutionally restricted to the promotion of Jewish interests in terms very similar to the constitutional limitations on Catholic institutions to promote Catholic interests. I am not sure, though, that the analogy applies, in that I am not sufficiently acquainted with Catholic dogma and the constitutional charters of the various relevant Catholic establishments. However, to the extent that this analogy does apply, it applies only to the period of activity of the WZO, JA and JNF and their affiliated bodies in Palestine until 1948 and before the establishment of the State of Israel.

The situation alters radically after the establishment of the State of Israel, in that now the exclusivist constitutional stipulations of the WZO, JA and the JNF (for Jews only) are incorporated into the body of the laws of the State of Israel through a detailed sequence of strategic Knesset legislation initiated within two years of the establishment of the State of Israel in 1948, and by and large completed a decade or so later.

Thus organizations and bodies that, prior to the establishment of the State of Israel in 1948, could credibly have claimed to be voluntary have been incorporated, following the introduction of the strategic legislation listed below, into the legal, compulsory, judicial machinery of the state:

- 1950: Absentees' Property Law; Law of Return; Development Authority Law;
- 1952: World Zionist Organization – Jewish Agency for the Land of Israel (Status) Law;
- 1953: *Keren Kayemeth Leisrael* (Jewish National Fund) Law; Land Acquisition (Validations of Acts and Compensation) Law;
- 1954: Covenant between the Government of Israel and the Zionist Executive, also known as the Executive of the Jewish Agency for the Land of Israel;
- 1958: Prescription Law;
- 1960: Basic Law: Israel Lands; Israel Lands Law; Israel Lands Administration Law;
- 1961: Covenant between the Government of Israel and the Jewish National Fund.

In subsequent years this body of strategic legislation governing, in the first instance, the terms of tenure of 93 per cent of Israel lands was further refined in such pieces of legislation as the Agricultural Settlement

(Restriction on Use of Agricultural Land and Water) of 1967 and the Lands (Allocation of Rights to Foreigners) Law of 1980. The list above, however, represents the mainstay of Israeli apartheid, namely the body of strategic legislation enacted by the Parliament of the State of Israel, the Knesset, which, until the Israeli Supreme Court ruling in the case of Adil and Iman Qaadan versus the cooperative communal settlement of Qatzir in 2000, constituted the primary instruments of the denial of access in law and through Acts of Knesset to some 93 per cent of the territory of the State of Israel to non-Jews, Palestinian Arab citizens of Israel and 1948 Palestinian refugees in the first instance.

It should be pointed out that the laws listed above were promulgated in addition to previously available legal instruments such as the Land (Acquisition for Public Purposes) Ordinance of 1943 and in addition to the unlimited powers with regard to the requisition of lands and property which are vested in the Israeli authorities under the various Defence (Emergency) Regulations of 1945 and Ordinances that have been in force from 1948–49 up to the present. These are, *inter alia*: Defence (Emergency) Regulations of 1945; Emergency (Security Zones) Regulations (1949); Requisitioning of Property in Times of Emergency Law (1949); Emergency Regulations (Cultivation of Waste Lands) Ordinance (1949).

The juridical problems arising from the introduction of this two-tier mechanism of legal duplicity were clearly and eloquently articulated by the late Mr Zerah Wahrhaftig, then minister of religious affairs and chairman of the Knesset Constitution, Law and Justice Committee, when presenting the Basic Law: Israel Lands, on behalf of the Government before the Knesset on 19 July 1960:

> The reasons for this proposed law, as I put it before you, are as follows: to give legal garb to a principle that is fundamentally religious, namely, 'the land shall not be sold forever, for the land is mine' (Leviticus 25: 23). Irrespective of whether this verse is explicitly mentioned in the law, as one proposal had it, or whether it is not mentioned, the law gives legal garb to this rule and principle in our Torah. This law expressed our original view concerning the holiness of the land of Israel. 'For the land is mine' – 'the holiness of the land belongs to me' says *Gemara* [*Talmud*] in 'Tractate Gittin', page 47a. And Ibn Ezra explains why the land should not be sold forever: 'For the land is mine' – 'this is a most important reason'. And Nachmanides says: 'And the intelligent will understand'. I also trust that the educated will understand; therefore, I will not further explain the reasons for this principle ... Concerning the name, we gave this law the name Basic Law: Israel Lands. There were

a number of proposals with regard to the name. MK Harari proposed to name it 'The People's Lands'. On the face of it, I do not see any great difference between the two names. I admit that neither name hits the target. What is it that we want? We want something that is difficult to define. We want to make it clear that the land of Israel belongs to the people of Israel. The 'people of Israel' is a concept that is broader than that of the 'people resident in Zion', because the people of Israel live throughout the world. On the other hand, every law that is passed is for the benefit of all the residents of the state, and all the residents of the state include also people who do not belong to the people of Israel, the worldwide people of Israel.

Menachem Begin (*Herut* Movement): This is not expressed [in the law].

Zerah Wahrhaftig: We cannot express this. Whatever we write, Israel lands or people's lands, from the strictly legal point of view, the reference is necessarily to the people resident in Zion only. Every law is valid only in the area under the jurisdiction of the state, and therefore it makes no difference what we write … We thought it might be better to write 'Israel' rather than 'people'. It is also a question of tradition, of habit … MK Meridor was wrong when he said that there is no legal innovation in the law. There is therein a very significant legal innovation: we are giving legal garb to the Memorandum of Association and the JNF … As for the JNF, the legal innovation is enormous; it gives legal garb to a matter that thus far was incorporated only in the JNF's Memorandum. (*Knesset Debates*, Vol. 29 [9 May–23 August, 1960], pp. 1,916–20)

As noted above, it is through this two-tier mechanism that an all-encompassing apartheid system could be legislated by the Israeli Knesset in all that pertains to access to land under Israeli sovereignty and control without resorting to explicit and frequent mention of 'Jew', as a legal category, versus 'non-Jew'. The legal mechanism operates as follows: with the notable exception of the Law of Return of 1950, none of the laws listed above resorts, in the text of the law, to the distinction between 'Jew' and 'non-Jew'.[16] Thus, for example, the World Zionist Organization–Jewish Agency for the Land of Israel (Status) Law of 1952 makes the WZO responsible for 'settlement projects in the state' (Clause 3), but makes no overt reference to Jewish settlement. It is necessary to know that the WZO/JA are constitutionally restricted to promoting 'agricultural colonization based on Jewish labour', and that for the WZO/JA, 'it shall be deemed to be a matter of principle that Jewish labour shall be employed', in order to begin to appreciate how the Israeli mechanism of legal duplicity has allowed the legislation of an all-encompassing apartheid system in all matters pertaining to access to land inside the State of Israel to be covered in seemingly non-discriminatory legal terms.

Thus the Knesset, through its WZO/JA Status Law of 1952, committed the State of Israel by law to secure a monopolistic concession in the area of 'settlement projects in Israel' for an organization that is constitutionally restricted to 'agricultural colonization based on Jewish labour' for which it 'be deemed to be a matter of principle that Jewish labour shall be employed'. The law further authorizes the WZO to coordinate 'the activities in Israel of Jewish institutions and organizations active in . . . development and settlement of the country' (Clause 4). Prominent among these Jewish institutions – 'various bodies' (Clause 8), 'funds and other institutions' (Clause 12) of the WZO – is, of course, the JNF, over which the WZO holds absolute control. The law also identifies the Jewish Agency with the WZO (Clauses 3 and 7).

In addition to the above, in 1954 the legal status of the WZO inside the State of Israel was further underpinned by the covenant signed between the Government of the State of Israel and the World Zionist Organization Executive. Subject to the WZO/JA (Status) Law of 1952, 14 Articles are provided, of which the following are illustrative and noteworthy:

Article 1 defines the duties of the WZO Executive as:

[O]rganization of *aliyah* [Jewish immigration] from abroad and transfer of the *olim* [Jewish immigrants] and their property to the country; participation in the absorption of *olim* in the country; youth *aliyah*; agricultural settlement in the country and the purchase of land and its development by the institutions of the Zionist Organization: the JNF and the Foundation Fund; participation in the establishment and expansion of development projects in the country; encouragement of private capital investments in the country; assistance to cultural projects and institutions of higher education in the country; mobilization of funds to finance these activities; coordination of the activities in Israel of Jewish institutions and organizations which are active in the domains outlined above and are financed by public funding. (quoted in Lehn in association with Davis 1988: 98–9)

On the signing of this covenant, the government and the WZO Executive exchanged formal letters, all dated 26 July 1954, confirming and acknowledging the agreement, and specifying the position of the Executive functionaries in official ceremonies. For example, the chairman of the Executive ranks 'immediately after the members of the Cabinet', and the rank of the members of the Executive is 'equal to that of the members of the Knesset'. The letters confirm the impression that the WZO and its several institutions constitute, legally and effectively, an equal of the government, hence virtually a state within the State of Israel.

Until 1971 the chairman of the WZO was also the chairman of the JA and the distinction between the two bodies was essentially a question of terminology. The activities of the Zionist movement in Jewish communities throughout the world, with the exception of Palestine, and, since 1948, the State of Israel, were classified under 'World Zionist Organization', and the activities on behalf of the Jewish community in Palestine, and, since 1948, the State of Israel, were classified under 'Jewish Agency'.

Following the 1967 war and in light of the consolidation of the international consensus with regard to the illegality of the 1967 Israeli occupation of and settlement activities in the West Bank, the Gaza Strip, the Golan Heights and the Sinai Peninsula (until the Israeli staged withdrawal from the Sinai in the framework of the Camp David Accords of 1978 and the Israel–Egypt Peace Treaty of 1979, the implementation of which was completed in 1982), the tax-exempt status of Zionist fundraising in the USA seemed to have been endangered.

Since 1948 the tax authorities in the USA and in Europe were amenable to classifying the activities of the WZO, the JA and the JNF inside the State of Israel, within the 1949 armistice line (the 'Green Line') as charitable philanthropy and thus exempt from tax. But it seems that against the backdrop of the international consensus with regard to the illegality of the post-1967 Israeli occupation, the Zionist organizations were not able or, perhaps, did not even attempt to get the relevant tax authorities in the West to classify the Zionist settlement activities in the post-1967 occupied territories also as tax-exempt.

In fact, over time, intensified Zionist settlement activities in the post-1967 occupied territories put the entire Zionist fundraising enterprise in the West in jeopardy. Being regarded not as a charitable philanthropic activity, but rather as a political activity, and an illegal political activity at that, the failure to segregate monies earmarked for Zionist settlement in the post-1967 occupied territories from monies earmarked for Zionist settlement inside the 'Green Line' could have put the entire Zionist fundraising at risk of losing its tax-exempt status.

The danger was averted by reintroducing in 1971 the organizational and accounting separation between the World Zionist Organization, a typically political organization whose governing board is elected through democratic procedures, and the now reconstituted Jewish Agency, which is an organization funded by the various Zionist funds (United Jewish

Appeal in the USA and the Foundation Fund outside the USA) whose governing board is one-half appointed by the said Zionist funds.

Indeed Article A4 of the Agreement for the Reconstitution of the Jewish Agency for Israel reads:

> The functions and tasks and programs administered by the Agency, or to which it may contribute funds, shall be only such as may be carried on by tax-exempt organizations. (http://www.thelikud.org/Archives/Structure%20of%20the%20World%20Zionist%20Organization.htm)

The two Zionist bodies, now separated, agreed a division of labour on a geo-political basis. The Jewish Agency is active inside Israel and/or in relation to Israel, whereas the World Zionist Organization is active in all member states of the UN and/or in relation to Jewish communities in these states, save Israel. The covenants agreed in 1971 between the Government of the State of Israel and the World Zionist Organization on the one part and the reconstituted Jewish Agency for Israel (note 9) on the second part regulate the activities of the JA and the WZO inside Israel and the post-1967 occupied territories respectively.

The definition of the areas of activity designated for the WZO on the one part and the JA on the second part in their respective prescribed regions overlap to a large extent (but not completely). Subject to this arrangement, the Settlement Division of the WZO, funded by the Government of the State of Israel and/or by non-tax-exempt donations, is active in the post-1967 occupied territories, whereas the Israel department of the JA, funded by the various tax-exempt Zionist appeals, is active inside the State of Israel.

Following the reconstitution of the Jewish Agency, the 1954 covenant was replaced in 1971 with a new covenant between the Government of Israel and the World Zionist Organization.

The Preamble to the new covenant read as follows:

> The Covenant entered into between the Government of Israel (hereinafter – the Government) and the World Zionist Organization (hereinafter – the WZO) according to the World Zionist Organization and Jewish Agency for Israel (Status) Law of 1952 is hereby published.
>
> Whereas the Government is desirous to enhance the activities of the WZO and the WZO desires to cooperate and to act in full coordination with the State of Israel and its Government, in accordance with the laws of the State;
>
> Now therefore this Covenant is hereby entered into:
>
> And the functions of the WZO under the said Covenant include:

1. The organization of immigration abroad and the transfer of immigrants and their property to Israel.

2. Participation in immigrants' housing and in their absorption.

3. Health services in connection with immigration and absorption.

4. Youth *aliya* and youth care and training.

5. Maintenance and support in Israel and outside of Israel of cultural, educational, scientific, religious, sports and social service institutions.

6. Agricultural settlement and acquisition of property and its preparation by the institutions of the WZO.

7. Participation in the establishment and enlargement of development enterprises in Israel.

8. Encouragement of private capital investment in Israel.

9. Maintenance and support of cultural enterprises, institutes of higher education and research institutes.

10. The care of aged, disabled, handicapped and other persons in need of assistance and social services.

And only upon declaration by the WZO that it will implement only those activities, within the realm of functions described above, which the Jewish Agency does not actually implement, within its realm of functions.

The Annex to the said Covenant defines the 'WZO' as including Funds and other Institutions. 'The Funds and other Institutions of the WZO' to mean 1. *Keren Hayesod* (Foundation Fund) – the United Israel Appeal; 2. The Jewish National Fund; 3. Companies for the benefit of the public under the Charitable Trusts Ordinance exclusively controlled by WZO; 4. Any corporation wholly owned and controlled by the WZO and/or by any of the Funds and other Institutions mentioned above, wholly or partly, which is non-profit-making or whose activities and/or properties are exclusively devoted to the achievement of the purposes of the WZO and/or of the said Funds and Institutions; provided that in the event of the winding up of any such corporation all its residual assets shall be transferred to the WZO or to any such Fund or Institutions as aforesaid.

The Annex then stipulates that:

1. Subject to the following limitations and conditions, the WZO shall be exempt from the taxes and compulsory government charges bear [*sic*] income wholly devoted to the achievement of its purposes; 2. Fees under the Land (Fees) Regulations of 1975; 3. Land appreciation tax and additional tax under the Land Appreciation Tax Law of 1963; 4. Loans imposed by law; 5. Income tax and capital gains tax under the Income Tax Ordinance and any other tax imposed on income; provided that the exemption shall not apply to dividend or interest on debentures paid to

the WZO by a company engaged in any commerce, trade or business, for the purpose of the settlement of Israel or the absorption of immigrants; 6. Fees under the Companies (Fees and Forms) Regulations of 1976, imposed according to Clauses 1, 2(a), 2(b), 2(d), 3, 5, 6, 8 and 9 of the First Schedule, provided that the exemption shall only apply.

2. Stamp duty under the Stamp Duty on Documents Law of 1961 1. Debentures issued by the WZO, the redemption of which is guaranteed by the State of Israel; 2. The transfer or assignment to the WZO of shares in a company controlled by not more than five persons, and mainly concerned with the acquisition and holding of land; 3. Guarantees of debts of the WZO and guarantees given by the WZO of debts of bodies in whose budgets the WZO participates.

3. Licence fees under the Traffic Ordinance for vehicles other than private motor vehicles, of the WZO and its Funds and other Institutions 1. The *Hemnuta* Co., Ltd. is exempt from taxes and from compulsory Government charges imposed by the enactments detailed in Clauses 2(a), 2(b), 2(c), 2(d), 2(e) – with regard to income accrued by its land transactions and 2(g)(1), accordingly, under the limitations and conditions detailed in said clauses; 2. The exemptions specified in this Annex are in addition to and not in derogation of exemptions under the law. (based on <http://www.thelikud.org/Archives/Structure%20of%20the %20World%20Zionist%20Organization.htm>)

In other words, in the critical areas of immigration, settlement and land development the Israeli sovereign, the Knesset, which is formally accountable to all its citizens, Jews and non-Jews alike, has formulated and passed legislation ceding state sovereignty (including taxation) and entered into Covenants vesting its responsibilities with organizations such as the WZO, the JA and the JNF, which are constitutionally committed to serving and promoting the interests of Jews and Jews only. It is through this procedure of legal duplicity, the ceding of state sovereignty and vesting its responsibilities in the critical areas of immigration, settlement and land development with Zionist organizations constitutionally committed to the exclusive principle of 'only for Jews', that legal apartheid is regulated in Israel. And it is through this mechanism of legal duplicity that the State of Israel has successfully veiled the reality of Zionist apartheid in the guise of legal democracy since the establishment of the State of Israel to date.

The same procedure has been applied by the Knesset in order to veil the reality of clerical legislation in Israel. Israel is a theocracy in that all domains pertaining to registration of marriage, divorce and death are regulated under Israeli law by *religious courts*. In order to effect the transformation of Israel from a state ruled by secular law to a state ruled by religious law and in order to veil the reality of clerical theocracy in the guise of legal democracy, the Knesset formulated and passed the Jurisdiction of Rabbinical Courts (Marriage and Divorce) Law of 1953, thereby ceding its sovereignty in the said areas of registration of marriage, divorce and death to the religious courts. Under the terms of this law, the religious courts (Rabbinical, Shari'a and Ecclesiastic) are declared state courts (religious court judiciary draw their salaries from the state). To date, all matters pertaining to the registration of marriage and divorce are thus removed from the civil courts and vested in the religious courts, whose verdict in these areas is not subject to civil appeal. Civil (state) registration of marriage and divorce is not available in Israel.[17] (See Aloni 1971; see also Rosen-Zvi 1990 and Shava 1991.)

This was, and for all practical purposes still remains, the state of affairs pertaining to the regulation of apartheid in Israel, notably apartheid in access to the material resources of the State of Israel, first and foremost land and water, until March 2000 when the Israeli Supreme Court sitting as the High Court of Justice issued its ruling in the case of Adil and Iman Qaadan versus the cooperative communal settlement of Qatzir notwithstanding. (For the story of Qatzir see Chapter 5.)

The veiling of Israeli apartheid

With the legislation by the Knesset of the World Zionist Organization/Jewish Agency for the Land of Israel (Status) Law of 1952 and subsequently the Jewish National Fund Law of 1953, the responsibility for strategic projects of land development and the settlement of the country were vested *in law* with organizations (the WZO, the JA and the JNF) that are committed, under the terms of their respective Constitutions, to advance immigration and settlement for Jews (and only Jews) inside the State of Israel as well as 'any area within the jurisdiction of the Government of Israel'. Furthermore, these organizations are recognized *in law* as *the* authorized agencies for the objects *inter alia* listed above.

But it is equally important to point out that nowhere in the text of the law as passed by the Knesset is there any reference to 'Jews only'. The term 'Jews only' does not appear in the text of the law. It is only when one recognizes that, instead of making an explicit reference to 'Jews' and/or 'Jews' versus 'non-Jews' and/or 'Jews only' in matters pertaining to the development and settlement of the country, the law vests the development and the settlement of the country with organizations such as the WZO, the JA and the JNF that are committed, under the terms of their respective Constitutions, to advance immigration and settlement for Jews only and are regarded by the state *in law* as *the* authorized agencies for the objects *inter alia* listed above, that one begins to appreciate the significance of this two-tier system.

It is this two-tier apartheid legislation that made it possible for the State of Israel to veil its political Zionist apartheid policies in all matters pertaining to land development and settlement of the country (by, of and for Jews only) and successfully project itself in the West as 'the only democracy in the Middle East' unchallenged in law until the watershed ruling in March 2000 of the Israeli Supreme Court sitting as the High Court of Justice in the case of Adil and Iman Qaadan, stipulating, *inter alia*, that

> If the State, through its own actions may not discriminate on the basis of religion or nationality, it may not facilitate such discrimination by a third party. It does not change matters that the third party is the Jewish Agency. Even if the Jewish Agency may distinguish between Jews and non-Jews, it may not do so in the allocation of State lands. (*Judgments of the Supreme Court of Israel* [PADI], Case No. 6698/95)

On the implications of the said Qaadan ruling on the future of Israeli apartheid see Chapter 5.

With the establishment of the State of Israel in 1948 the Israeli legislator, the Knesset could, in principle, consider two alternative strategies:

- regard the World Zionist Organization and its various affiliates to have been a necessary scaffold to build the Jewish state, whereupon, once the State of Israel was established, the scaffold was to be dismantled; or
- regard the World Zionist Organization and its various affiliates to be further required as useful instruments for the consolidation and the continuity of the State of Israel as a Jewish state in the political Zionist sense of the term, and particularly useful in enabling the State of Israel to project itself as 'the only democracy in the Middle East', its Zionist apartheid legislation notwithstanding.

The Israeli legislator wasted no time in deciding the issue.

As will be detailed below, the elections for Israel's Constituent Assembly, stipulated in UN General Assembly Resolution 181(II) of November 1947 (recommending the partition of Palestine with economic union) were held in July 1949. Yet, when the Constituent Assembly convened, it became clear that an agreement had been reached by the major political Zionist parties represented in the Assembly to betray the mandate on which they had been elected to the Assembly. In violation of the stipulations of UN General Assembly Resolution 181(II) above, the elected delegates failed to fulfil the purpose for which the Assembly had been elected, namely, to adopt a Constitution for the newly established state. Instead, the Constituent Assembly passed the Transition Law (1949) transforming itself by fiat into the First Knesset, namely, into Israel's legislative Parliament.

In the absence of a Constitution, let alone a Constitution that conforms to the stipulations of UN General Assembly Resolution 181(II), the Israeli legislator, the Knesset, regarded itself to be free to ground the laws of the new state in the political Zionist interpretation of the idea of a Jewish state (namely, a state that aims to guarantee in the law and in practice of the state a demographic majority of members of the Jewish tribes, a demographic majority of ethnic Jews). Presumably, being aware that the political Zionist interpretation of the idea of a Jewish state represents a blatant violation of the terms of the said UN General Assembly Resolution 181(II), the Israeli legislator refrained from taking the legal route followed by the apartheid Government of South Africa, legislating petty apartheid at the surface of the law for all to see. Rather, the Israeli legislator chose to legislate Zionist apartheid (discrimination *in law* on the basis of 'Jew' versus 'non-Jew') by constructing a two-tier legal system. In the body of Israel's strategic apartheid legislation (with the notable exception of the Law of Return of 1950) there is no explicit reference to 'Jews' versus 'non-Jews' or 'Jews only'. Instead, the said strategic laws vest with the WZO and its various affiliates, notably the Jewish Agency (JA) and the Jewish National Fund (JNF), the authority to carry out and facilitate Zionist apartheid discrimination on behalf of the state on the basis of 'Jews only', subject to their respective Constitutions.

As pointed out by David Ben-Gurion, first prime minister of the State of Israel when introducing the WZO/JA Status Law for its renewed first reading in the Knesset:

> The Law as proposed before you is not an ordinary law, rather it is one of the central basic laws, characterizing this State, as a state designated to serve as an instrument and an anvil in the redemption of Israel. The Law therefore incorporates stipulations of principle, that though devoid of the formal contents of a law that entails penalty in the event of transgression or violation, encapsulate the special historical meaning of the State of Israel and determine the linkage of the State of Israel to the people of Israel. These stipulations also endow the World Zionist Organization with sovereign rights [*sic* – In Hebrew *Zekhuyot Mamlakhtiyot*] inside the State of Israel: the right to act inside the State of Israel with

the aim to develop and settle the country, absorb Jewish immigrants (*olim*) from their dispersion, and coordinate the activities of institutions and organizations active in these areas inside the State of Israel. (*Knesset Debates*, Vol. 13 [3 November 1952–26 March 1953], p. 24)[18]

By granting the WZO/JA a status 'that takes away a part of the sovereignty of the State of Israel' (to borrow the phrase of the late MK Meir Vilner, then as for many subsequent decades, a leading member of the Communist Party, in the said debate, ibid., p. 33) it was possible for the State of Israel to exclude *in law* its non-Jewish citizens, first and foremost its Palestinian Arab citizens (not to mention its 1948 Palestine refugees) from the development and settlement of the country and yet project this apartheid colonial project in the West as 'the only democracy in the Middle East'.

The critical importance of these structures of veiling and obfuscation cannot be sufficiently emphasized. They represent one of the primary vehicles that made it possible for official representatives and various apologists of the Zionist movement and the Government of the State of Israel to deliver the claim that the State of Israel was a democracy akin to western liberal democracies, the Palestinian *nakba* notwithstanding. In this way, it was possible for the same bodies that often challenged their critics to point out a single instance in the text of the laws of the State of Israel, with, perhaps, the exception of the Israeli Law of Return, of explicit discrimination on the basis of 'Jews' versus 'non-Jews' or 'Jews only', to engage in the building up and consolidation in the country of Palestine of an apartheid system (for Jews only) akin to the now defunct South African *herrenfolk* 'democracy' (for Whites only).

I have chosen to state the case of Israeli apartheid rather parsimoniously. In fact, as will become evident below, there are quite a number of instances of exactly such discrimination of 'Jew' versus 'non-Jew' or 'Jews only' in the body of Israeli law. According to the latest count by Adalah: Legal Center for Arab Minority Rights in Israel, there are no fewer than 17 such laws (Adalah 1998: 11).

My primary concern in this work, however, will focus on the strategic legislation put in place by the Israeli legislator, the Knesset, pertaining to the question of settlement and land, the core area of the Israeli–Palestinian conflict, aiming to examine such structures of this body of strategic legislation as enabled the State of Israel, an apartheid state, a state that enforces its citizens *in law* to make racialist choices on the basis of 'Jew' versus 'non-Jew', to project itself in the West over many decades as the 'only democracy in the Middle East'.

The case of the South African Forest, Golani Junction

Having read Mahmoud Issa's *Lubya: A Palestinian Village in the Middle East*, and having become aware that the Lavi Forest and the South African Forest were planted on the site of the Palestinian Arab village of Lubya, destroyed in the course of the massive ethnic cleansing operations carried out by the Israeli army under the cover of the 1948 war, I was motivated to visit the location.

I visited the South African Forest, Golani Junction, on Saturday 2 March 2002. One part of the forest has been developed as a recreational area and another part has been fenced off as a grazing area for cattle.

The South African Forest was planted on the site by the Jewish National Fund (JNF), together with the Israeli Ministry of Education, the Sports Authority, Regional Council of Lower Galilee, and Local Council of Kefar Tavor. The recreational area in the forest, with the children's playground named after Barney Nestadt of Johannesburg, was put there by the JNF, the Friends of the Jewish National Fund and the Women's Zionist Organization of South Africa in 1996.

It appears that the JNF of South Africa (together with the Israeli government and municipal bodies listed above) chose to plant the South African Forest and (together with the Friends of the JNF and the Women's Zionist Organization of South Africa) situate the recreational area and the children's playground on the ruins of the Palestinian Arab village of Lubya, located in Lower Galilee, inside pre-1967 Israel, ethnically cleansed under the cover of the 1948 war and subsequently razed to the ground.

Under Israeli law, notably the Absentees' Property Law of 1950, the thousands of 1948 Palestine refugees of Lubya and their descendants remain stateless refugees outside the borders of the State of Israel, and the hundreds of the internally displaced persons of Lubya inside Israel remain 'present absentees'. Some 25 per cent of the total of one million Palestinian Arab citizens of Israel are internally displaced persons known as 'present absentees', namely people who are present in Israel as citizens, yet, like their stateless refugee brethren, are classified as 'absentees' under Israel's Absentees' Property Law of 1950 and are denied their basic human rights under UN Charter and international law, notably their right to return to their destroyed village and their properties. Instead, their homes have been destroyed and planted over, in the case of Lubya, by the South African Forest with its recreational area.

By classifying 80 per cent of the native indigenous Palestinian Arab people resident in the territories that came under the control of the Israeli army in the 1948–49 war (today's approximately 4 million 1948 Palestine refugees) as 'absentees' in the eyes of the law, the State of Israel has not only defined them as aliens inside and outside their own homeland, but cast them outside legal existence altogether as far as their rights to their 1948 properties are concerned. As a consequence, there are in the State of Israel today 250,000 persons whose status is that of 'present absentees'. They are 'present' in that, unlike the approximately 4 million 1948 Palestine refugees, they have not been made stateless and are tax-paying citizens of the State of Israel with the right to vote and be elected to office, including Parliament and government. They are, however, 'absent' in that very much like the 4 million 1948 Palestine refugees under the Absentees' Property Law of 1950, they have lost the title to all of their movable and immovable 1948 properties inside the State of Israel. They are internally displaced persons.

I am fairly confident that when challenged, the JNF, the Friends of the JNF and Women's Zionist Organization of South Africa will attempt to rebut charges of complicity with the cover-up of war crimes, racism and apartheid by pointing to the absence of segregation in the forests and park recreational facilities, emphasizing that JNF forests and recreational facilities are as popular, if not more popular, with the Arab citizens of Israel as with the Jewish citizens.

But surely only a criminal mind would maintain that the fact that the Arab citizens of Israel have non-segregated access to JNF forests and recreational facilities can be conceived as a justification of an apartheid enterprise of depriving in law and through Acts of Parliament the 1948 Palestine refugees and their descendants, specifically the thousands of the 1948 Lubya refugees, including the hundreds who are internally displaced persons inside Israel, of their right to return and their property rights.

The case of the internally displaced persons inside Israel ('present absentees') brings the case into sharp focus. The hundreds of internally displaced persons of Lubya who are citizens of the State of Israel are able to take their families to picnic in the South African park and recreational facilities, as well as visit the ruins of their homes and what remains of their olive groves and gardens, but are denied in law the right to live in the neighbouring cooperative settlements of Kibbutz Lavi, Moshav Sedeh Ilan and the communal settlement of Giv'at Avni, let alone rebuild their homes in Lubya.

As noted above, a part of the South African Forest is fenced off and serves as grazing grounds for cattle herds of the nearby cooperative agricultural settlements of Kibbutz Lavi and Moshav Sedeh Ilan. The lands of the village of Lubya (38,578 dunums/9,644 acres) have been distributed among the surrounding Zionist cooperative agricultural and other settlements including the communal settlement of Giv'at Avni.

As already noted, most of the Palestinian Arab inhabitants of Lubya are now stateless refugees outside the border of the State of Israel. A few hundred, however, are internally displaced persons inside the State of Israel. Their status in Israel is that of 'present absentees'.

The Universal Declaration of Human Rights recognizes the right to return (Article 13) and the right to property (Article 17) as fundamental rights:

> Article 13 (1) Everyone has the right to freedom of movement and residence within the borders of each state; (2) Everyone has the right to leave any country, including his own, and to return to his country.

> Article 17 (1) Everyone has the right to own property alone as well as in association with others; (2) No one shall be arbitrarily deprived of his property.

The refugees of Lubya are denied their right to return to their home village and properties. Instead, the cattle of the so-called socialist cooperative Zionist settlements of Lavi and Sedeh Ilan are given access.

The war crime perpetrated by the Israeli army against the people of Lubya in 1948 is paradigmatic. Some 400 rural and urban Palestinian Arab localities have been similarly ethnically cleansed and razed to the ground in whole or in part. In many localities, Lubya and elsewhere, the crime is covered up by JNF forests (in the case of Lubya, funded by the JNF, the Friends of the JNF and the Women's Zionist Organization of South Africa).

Generally speaking most attempts at a cover-up fail, and the attempt by the Government of Israel, the WZO, the JNF and their friends to cover up the massive war crimes perpetrated by the Israeli army under the cover of the 1948–49 war are no exception. It is possible to bulldoze a Palestinian village to the ground and cover the ruins with a JNF forest. It is not possible to eradicate the native Palestinian village cactus, the *sabr*, which has traditionally served also as a hedge to demarcate the boundaries of family compounds and agricultural plots. Tear the *sabr* down, and it will always re-emerge. And indeed, as one wanders through the South African Forest, as through many other JNF forests, one repeatedly comes across hedgerows of *sabr*, growing vigorously under the shadow of the pine forests planted by the JNF. I doubt that the current Government of South Africa would consider afforestation activity of this kind to be legal, let alone charitable or deserving the status of tax exemption.

In this connection, it may be in order to point out again that apartheid is not racism. Apartheid is racism regulated *in law*. Israel is an apartheid state because racism in Israel is determined in law by Acts of Parliament, first and foremost in all that pertains to legislation of land tenure.

Should the JNF attempt a rebuttal along the line suggested above, their officials ought to be reminded that the question at hand is not whether their recreational facilities are segregated or otherwise, nor whether cattle are allowed to graze in JNF forests or otherwise, but why cattle are allowed to defecate on the site of the destroyed village of Lubya while the 1948 Palestine Lubya refugees and internally displaced persons are not allowed to return there.

Destruction of entire localities, the dispossession of their people and ethnic cleansing are classified as war crimes under international law. Planting forests and constructing recreational grounds on sites of destroyed 1948 Palestinian villages can hardly be classified as charitable activity, even if the said facilities are open to Arab citizens of Israel.

To my mind, assuming that the JNF, the Friends of the JNF and the Women's Zionist Organization of South Africa have a recognized charitable status in South Africa and assuming that donations to these and other Zionist bodies are tax-exempt, should these bodies wish to retain their charitable status and tax exemption privileges in South Africa and elsewhere, they would be well advised to begin the process of reconciliation with the refugees and internally displaced persons of Lubya; recognize their right to their properties now planted over by the JNF, the Friends of the JNF and Women's Zionist Organization of South Africa, and recognize their right to choose to return to Lubya and rebuild their homes there. As far as I can judge, other than the problems of apartheid, racism and greed, the only problem that might require some additional attention is locating alternative grazing grounds for the cattle of Kibbutz Lavi and Moshav Sedeh Ilan – not an insurmountable problem by any standards.

I would have thought that the case of the South African Forest, Golani Junction, would constitute sufficient grounds for the Government of the Republic of South Africa to commence a process of systematic inquiry into the activities of the Zionist organizations of South Africa in order to question such tax-deductible status of Zionist fundraising as it may enjoy in South Africa and elsewhere, specifically such tax deductions as may be granted to contributions to the JNF, the Friends of the JNF and the Women's Zionist Organization of South

Africa. The inquiry could begin by putting the following questions to the JNF, the Friends of the JNF and the Women's Zionist Organization of South Africa:

- Is the dispossession of the native indigenous people of Lubya, the razing down of their homes; the planting of forests on the ruins of their homes; and the appropriation of their properties to build recreational facilities regulated through Acts of Knesset?
- Is the JNF an official partner and beneficiary to the Government of Israel in the application of such instruments of Israeli legislation as the Absentees' Property Law of 1950?
- Is the JNF still committed to purchase, take on lease or in exchange, or otherwise acquire any lands, forests, rights of possession and other rights, easements and other immovable property (including 1948 Palestine refugees' property) for the purpose of settling Jews *and only Jews* on these lands?

Considerable academic research has been carried out with reference to the case of Lubya. In addition to the work of Mahmoud Issa above, relevant information can be accessed at Bir Zeit University Research Centre. The text below is based on the Bir Zeit University web-sites <http://www.birzeit.edu/crdps/village@.html> and <http://www.birzeit.edu/crdps/lub@vil.html>

Lubya before 1948 The village of Lubya was located on the summit of a rectangular, rocky hill that extended in an east–west direction and overlooked the plain of Tur'an to the south. It was divided into eastern and western parts by a secondary road that linked it to the Tiberias–Nazareth highway. The Crusaders knew the village as Lubia. Lubya was said to be the hometown of Abu Bakr al-Lubyani, a prominent Muslim scholar of the fifteenth century who taught Islamic religious sciences in Damascus. In 1596, Lubya was a village in the *nahiya* of Tiberias (*liwa'* of Safad) with a population of 1,177. It paid taxes on goats, beehives, and on a press that was used for processing either olives or grapes. The governor of Damascus, Sulayman Pasha, died in Lubya in 1743 on his way to confront Dahir al-'Umar, who became the *de facto* ruler of northern Palestine for a short period in the second half of the eighteenth century.

In the early nineteenth century the British traveller Buckingham described Lubya as a very large village on top of a high hill. The Swiss traveller Burckhardt noted in 1822 that wild artichokes covered the plain where the village was located.

Later in the nineteenth century, Lubya's population was estimated variously at 400 to 700, and was employed in the cultivation of olive and fig trees. The older stone houses were clustered on the eastern side of the site (as were the newer buildings constructed during the British Mandate), possibly because the eastern side of the hill overlooked the cultivated lands of the village. The villagers were predominantly Muslim. An elementary school was established in the village in 1895, and remained in use during the British Mandate. During the Mandate period, Lubya was the second largest village in Tiberias District in terms of area.

Lubya also had importance archaeologically – 2 km to the east of the village were the ruins of a structure known as Khan Lubya that contained the remains of a pool, cisterns and large building stones. This site was probably a caravanserai during medieval times.

The village economy was based on agriculture – its lands were fertile, and it was known in the region for its high-quality wheat. In 1944/45 a total of 31,026 dunums were allotted to cereals, and 1,655 to orchards and olives.

Occupation and depopulation The Palestinian press reported an attack by Zionist forces on Lubya during the night of 20 January 1948, which left one villager dead. This early raid was coordinated with another on the nearby village of Tur'an, according to an account in the newspaper *Filastin*. A 24 February skirmish with a Jewish convoy on the outskirts of the town lasted four hours and, according to the account in *Filastin*, left one Arab dead and two wounded, in addition to many casualties in the convoy. A third attack took place during the first week of March 1948. Palestinian historian 'Arif al-'Arif states that *Haganah* soldiers attempted to force their way through the road between Tiberias and al-Shajara, attacking Lubya at dawn. They reached the western edge of the village but were repulsed by the villagers themselves, who lost six men while killing seven of the attackers. *Filastin* reported another infiltration attempt on 11 March that was preceded by mortar shelling.

With the occupation of Tiberias in mid-April 1948, the people of Lubya were isolated and turned to Nazareth for help and guidance. They told Palestinian historian Nafez Nazzal that there was another attack on Lubya on 10–11 June, as the first truce of the war was about to go into effect. At the same time, the Arab Liberation Army (ALA) attacked the Israeli settlement of Sejerah to the south-west. Villagers recalled that an Israeli infantry unit took up positions at the southern end of the village, but withdrew by nightfall on 11 June. The village militia participated briefly in the fighting at Sejerah with the ALA, but returned to protect the village during the truce.

After the truce ended, Israeli forces launched Operation *Deqel*. On

16 July, some villagers brought the news of the fall of Nazareth. In the words of former residents of Lubya interviewed 25 years later, the villagers were 'terrified', but their request for military aid from the ALA was turned down. During the night of 16 July, most of the population fled north-west towards Lebanon, leaving behind the village militia and some elderly people. When an Israeli armoured unit approached the following day, the poorly armed militia decided to retreat. Eyewitnesses said that the occupying force shelled the village before entering it, and then destroyed a number of houses and commandeered others. Some elderly people took refuge in a nearby cave and a few later escaped – the fate of the rest is unknown. 'Lubiya fell without fighting,' the *History of the War of Independence* states, 'and the road to Tiberias was open to us.'

The village today The Lavi pine forest has been planted by the Jewish National Fund – the body of the World Zionist Organization in charge of land acquisition and development – on the western side of the site. Another forest has been planted nearby in the name of the Republic of South Africa. The debris of the houses is buried under these forests. Cacti, scattered cisterns (formerly used by the villagers for collecting rainwater), and pomegranate and fig trees further mark the site. The lands around the site are cultivated by the nearby settlement. A forest and a military museum have been established near the site in honour of the Golani Brigade of the Israeli army. The secondary road that once led from the village to the Tiberias–Nazareth highway is still recognizable.

2 · Israel

The establishment of the State of Israel as a Jewish state

Is the State of Israel a sovereign, independent and democratic state, or is Israel a Jewish state? Is the State of Israel governed by and for all of its citizens, or is Israel governed by and for all Jews throughout the world? Is the Israeli government accountable to all its citizens, Arabs and Jews, or is the Israeli government accountable only to Jews both inside and outside the land of Palestine, whether they are Israeli citizens or not?

These are not new questions in Israeli political discourse, for they have accompanied the process of the establishment of the State of Israel since its earliest days. The State of Israel was established by unilateral declaration on 15 May 1948. The Declaration of the Establishment of the State of Israel – known as 'Israel's Declaration of Independence' – does not declare Israel an independent state, nor does it declare Israel a sovereign state; rather it declares Israel a Jewish state:

> We, the members of the National Council representing the Jewish people in Palestine and the Zionist Movement, are met together in solemn assembly today, the day of termination of the British Mandate for Palestine, and by virtue of the natural and historic right of the Jewish people and of the Resolution of the General Assembly of the United Nations, we hereby proclaim the establishment of the Jewish state in Palestine to be called *Medinat Yisrael* (the State of Israel). (*Declaration of the Establishment of the State of Israel*, 15 May 1948, translated by the author from the original Hebrew)

What may seem to an uninformed outside observer a minor technical quibble was in fact the subject of explicit discussion and controversy at the meeting of the People's Council on 14 May 1948, the eve of the announcement of the establishment of the State of Israel.

It is instructive to point out that just as the seemingly minor quibble some 20 years later about the definite article 'the' in UN Security Council Resolution 242 of November 1967 was not minor, nor a quibble – the seemingly minor quibble above over the terms 'Jewish state', 'independent Jewish state' or 'sovereign independent Jewish state' was not minor nor a quibble either. Rather, both the former and the latter reflected as well as veiled a profound and unstated project that was to have devastating consequences for the native indigenous people of the country, the Palestinian Arab people.

Declaring the State of Israel in 1948 a 'Jewish state', rather than an 'independent Jewish state' or a 'sovereign independent Jewish state' both reflected and veiled the core programme of political Zionism, namely, the establishment of a Jewish state in Palestine as a state for all Jews throughout the world aiming to guarantee in the law and practice of the state a demographic majority of members of the Jewish tribes (a demographic majority of ethnic Jews) – not as a state for all of its citizens, Arabs and Jews alike, let alone a state for all of its citizens and 1948 Palestine refugees.

And resolving unanimously at the UN Security Council 20 years later in the wake of the 1967 war (UN Security Council Resolution 242 of November 1967) that the fulfilment of the principles of the Charter of the UN requires the establishment of a just and lasting peace in the Middle East, which would include, *inter alia*, 'withdrawal of Israel armed forces from territories occupied in the recent conflict' (rather than from *the* territories occupied in the recent conflict) similarly reflects as well as veils the global and regional power relations at the time, allowing the State of Israel to maintain with impunity to date the longest occupation in modern times in violation of international law, perpetrating in the process incalculable war criminal cruelty against the Palestinian Arab people.

The global, regional and local power relations that are reflected in the formulation of UN Security Council Resolution 242 above have dramatically changed in the decades since the 1967 war, sufficiently to compel the State of Israel to withdraw from part of the 1967 occupied territories, namely, the whole of the Sinai peninsula, liberated by Egypt in the wake of the 1973 war, and a part of the Golan Heights – but not sufficiently to compel Israel to withdraw from *all* territories occupied in the 1967 war.[19]

As documented below, the borders of the State of Israel were deliberately left undefined in the Declaration of the Establishment of the State of Israel in 1948, and the inclusion of a commitment to the right of 'both peoples' to a state of their own was refused. The Jewish state in the political Zionist sense of the term was to be an apartheid state.

As noted above, the question whether to declare the State of Israel a 'Jewish state' or an 'independent Jewish state' or a 'sovereign independent Jewish state' was discussed explicitly at the meeting of the

People's Council on 14 May 1948, the eve of the announcement of the establishment of the State of Israel.

The late Meir Vilner, a leading member of the Communist Party and a signatory to the said Declaration, pointed out:

> Members of the Council: we are all united today in recognition of the significance of this great day for the *Yishuv* [pre-state Jewish community in Palestine] and the Jewish people, the day of the abolition of the Mandate and the declaration of the independent Jewish state ... The *Eretz Israel* Communist Party [*sic*] supports the proposed resolution of the declaration of the Jewish state, has reservations on a number of issues, and proposes a few amendments and additions ... We propose, in accordance with the resolutions of the United Nations [General] Assembly, to add the following paragraph: 'The Council declares that a fundamental principle of its policy is that of the right of both peoples to self-determination and to independent states of their own.' In Section 9, where it says, 'Calling for the establishment of a Jewish state in *Eretz Israel*', we propose to add the word 'independent' namely: 'Calling for the establishment of an independent Jewish state in *Eretz Israel*.' ... At the end of Section 11 it says: 'We ... hereby declare the establishment of a Jewish state in *Eretz Israel*.' We propose to add the words 'sovereign independent', thus 'the establishment of a sovereign, independent Jewish state'. (State of Israel, People's Council, *Protocols of Debates*, Fourth Session, 14 May 1948, Government Printer, Tel Aviv, 16 May 1948, pp. 13–14, translated from Hebrew)

Vilner's proposals were not accepted. The debate, however, highlights the fact that those who formulated the draft consciously avoided words that would have specified the sovereignty and independence of the proposed state and the right of both peoples to self-determination and to independent states of their own, emphasizing the 'Jewishness' of the newly established State of Israel.

Thus, in the *Declaration of the Establishment of the State of Israel* the State of Israel was declared above all a 'Jewish state': 'We hereby proclaim the establishment of the Jewish state in Palestine to be called *Medinat Yisrael* [the State of Israel, namely, the state of the Jewish people].'

Significantly, the borders of the new state were intentionally left undefined. The relevant discussion was summarized by David Ben-Gurion in the same debate as follows:

> There was a discussion of this matter in the People's Executive. There was a proposal to determine borders, and there was opposition to this

proposal. We decided *to evade* (and I choose this word intentionally) the matter for a simple reason: If the UN fulfils all its resolutions and undertakings and maintains the peace and prevents bombardments and uses its powers to execute its own resolutions, then we on our part (and I express the opinion of the people) will honour all the resolutions in their entirety. So far the UN has not done so ... therefore, we are not bound by anything, and we have left this matter open. We did not say no UN borders, but neither did we say the opposite. We have left this matter open for developments. (ibid.: 19; emphasis in the original)

The infrastructures for the Jewish state were laid out over the first five decades of the twentieth century through the Zionist colonial effort in Palestine as institutionalized in the various departments and offices of the WZO and its executive arm, the JA, as well as through WZO-affiliated companies such as the JNF, the Foundation Fund, *Hemnutah* and more. It is interesting to note that in their capacity as voluntary Jewish tribal associations, the success of the various Zionist agencies in Palestine was fairly limited. The JNF, for instance, since the year of its incorporation in London in 1907 and throughout the period of its activity under the Ottoman and the British regimes until 1948, had failed to purchase more than 936,000 dunums of land, at most (Orni 1974: 66; Lehn in association with Davis 1988: 70), namely, some 3.5 per cent of the 1922 Mandate Palestine or some 4.5 per cent of the territory of pre-1967 Israel.

Following the establishment of the State of Israel, however, and the introduction of the legislation detailed above into the body of Israeli law, the legal situation governing the activities of the WZO, the JA, the JNF and their various subsidiaries was radically altered. Their respective restrictive constitutions, which were legally binding on what were, until 1948, technically voluntary organizations, are now incorporated into the legal foundations and the body of law of the State of Israel, thereby establishing in all matters pertaining to access to material resources of the new state, notably land and water, a situation of radical legal apartheid between 'Jew' and 'non-Jew'.

Israel and the UN

The legal basis for the establishment of a Jewish state in Palestine lies in United Nations General Assembly Resolution No. 181(II) of November 1947, recommending a partition plan for Palestine and the establishment of a 'Jewish state' on some 57 per cent of Mandatory Palestine (14,500 km[2]), and an 'Arab state' on the remaining approximately 43 per cent (11,000 km^2) with the city of Jerusalem as a *corpus separatum* under a special international regime administered by the United Nations (176 km^2). The Resolution was passed on 29 November 1947 with 33 votes in favour, 13 against, and 10 abstentions. Both the native indigenous Palestinian Arab population and the League of Arab States failed to see the justice of allocating Jewish sovereignty to 57 per cent of the land when Jewish individual and corporate landholdings in Palestine in 1947 consisted of less than 7 per cent of the total area of the country. At the same time, even inside the United Nations' proposed boundaries for the Jewish state, the Arab population had a slight majority over the Jewish population, which, in 1947, numbered only 500,000 persons in the whole of Palestine (509,780 Muslims and Christians and 499,020 Jews according to Appendix I to the Report of Subcommittee 2 to the Ad Hoc Commission on the Palestine Question, Official Records of the 2nd Session of the General Assembly, Doc. A/AC 14/32, p. 304, quoted in Cattan 1988: 39 and 41 n21).

One of the standard claims put forward by official representatives of the State of Israel as well as its NGO apologists alleges that the rejection of UN General Assembly Resolution 181(II) by the representative bodies of the native indigenous Palestinian Arab population and by the League of Arab States somehow nullified the said Resolution and gave licence to the Government of the newly established State of Israel to extend the borders of the new state beyond the boundaries of the 'Jewish state' as determined in the said UN Resolution by 20 per cent (from 57 per cent of the territory of British Mandate Palestine to 77 per cent).

Such a claim is seriously misguided. Transgressions against UN General Assembly and UN Security Council resolutions by one or more member states of the UN do not give licence to other member states to do likewise. No omission or commission by any party to an armed conflict allows other parties to the conflict to perpetrate war crimes and crimes against humanity, such as ethnically cleansing the majority of the native indigenous Palestinian Arab people from the territories that came under the control of the Israeli army and razing some 400 Palestinian rural and urban localities to the ground in whole or in part under the cover of the 1948–49 war.

The rule of law and the standards of international law apply to every individual and every member state of the UN on an equal footing, to the extent that they are consistent with the values of the Universal Declaration of Human Rights. Even if the member state in question is a 'Jewish state', it cannot hold the stick at both ends, claiming, in the name of the victims of the Jewish holocaust under the Nazi occupation of Europe during the Second World War, that UN General Assembly

Resolution 181(II) represents Israel's international legal birthright, and in the same breath prostituting the said claim and the memory of the Jewish and other victims of the Nazi occupation of Europe by blatantly violating the terms of the said UN General Assembly Resolution as well as subsequent General Assembly and Security Council Resolutions and perpetrating the crime against humanity of ethnic cleansing.

UN General Assembly Resolution 181(II) could be reversed, but it is important to note that it is the constitutive document of both the State of Israel (the 'Jewish state') and the State of Palestine (the 'Arab state') and that the only internationally legally recognized boundaries for the 'Jewish state' are the boundaries as determined in the UN Partition Plan for Palestine in 1947.

The territory of pre-1967 Israel is classified by international law under two categories:

1. the territory allocated for the Jewish state by the UN Partition Plan for Palestine (UNGA Resolution 181[II] of 29 November 1947); and
2. the territory occupied illegally by the Israeli army in the 1948–49 war beyond the boundaries of the 1947 UN Partition Plan.[20]

Under the UN Charter and Resolutions, Israel has no legitimate rule in either category. Israeli rule over the territories allocated for the 'Jewish state' by the 1947 UN Partition Plan was subject to a number of important conditions, notably compliance with the terms of the steps preparatory to independence and future constitution and government (see below), none of which has been upheld by the incumbent state.

Likewise, the Israeli occupation, in 1948–49, of territories beyond the boundaries specified in the 1947 UN Partition Plan, their colonization by exclusive Jewish settlements, and their subsequent annexation to the State of Israel are in violation of both the UN Charter and of international law, like all colonial occupation. From an international legal point of view, Israeli claims to West Jerusalem, Safad or Jaffa, occupied in 1948–49, are as thoroughly invalid as Israeli claims to East Jerusalem, Hebron or Gaza, occupied in 1967.

As noted repeatedly above, the full title of the 1947 UN Partition Plan for Palestine is 'Plan of Partition with Economic Union'. Under the terms of the Plan, the governments of both the proposed 'Jewish' and the proposed 'Arab' states were committed, *inter alia*, to hold elections to the Constituent Assembly, 'which shall be conducted on democratic lines':

> Qualified voters for each state for this election shall be persons over eighteen years of age who are (a) Palestinian citizens in that state; and

(b) Arabs and Jews residing in that state, although not Palestinian citizens, who, before voting, have signed a notice of intention to become citizens of such state. (*Plan of Partition with Economic Union*, 1947, Part 1 [B] Steps Preparatory to Independence [9])

The State of Israel has chosen to violate the constitutional stipulation posited by the United Nations General Assembly as a condition for its legitimate establishment.

UN General Assembly Resolution 181(II) (*Plan of Partition with Economic Union*) of November 1947 further requires that:

> The Constituent Assembly of each [of the Arab and Jewish] State shall draft a democratic constitution for its state ... guaranteeing all persons equal and non-discriminatory rights in civil, political, economic and religious matters and the enjoyment of human rights and fundamental freedoms, including freedom of religion, language, speech and publication, education, assembly and association. (*Plan of Partition with Economic Union*, 1947, Part 1: Future Constitution and Government of Palestine, Article 10)

Once elected, the Constituent Assembly of each state was to draft a democratic constitution for its state. The constitutions of both the Jewish and the Arab states were to embody, under the terms of the said Plan, Chapters 1 and 2 of the declaration provided for in Section C of the Plan. This declaration contains fundamental constitutional guarantees regarding holy places, religious buildings and sites, religious and minority rights, citizenship, international conventions and financial obligations.

This requirement for the drafting of a democratic constitution with the various guarantees was never met.

As noted above, the elections for Israel's Constituent Assembly, stipulated in the 1947 UN Partition Plan, were held in July 1949. The Constituent Assembly was elected by universal suffrage on 23 July 1949 for the explicit purpose of endorsing Israel's constitution. Earlier that month (8 July), the Provisional Council of State nominated a Constitution Committee to prepare the draft constitution for the consideration of the prospective Constituent Assembly. Yet, when the Constituent Assembly convened, it became clear that an agreement had been reached by the major political parties represented in the Assembly to betray the mandate on which they had been elected to the Assembly. In violation of the stipulations of the 1947 UN Partition Plan, contravening the UN Charter and international law, the elected delegates failed to fulfil the purpose for which the Assembly had been elected, namely, to adopt a constitution for the newly established state.

As noted above, the Constituent Assembly passed instead the Transition Law (1949) transforming itself by fiat into the First Knesset, namely, into Israel's legislative Parliament. As former member of the Knesset and former minister, Advocate Shulamit Aloni, pointed out:

> The Minutes of the First Knesset contain long Sections dealing with the controversy over this question. But the Minutes do not tell all. There does not appear anywhere in the records, for instance, that Mr Hillel Cook, a delegate to the Constituent Assembly, cried out: 'This is a political putsch! The Constituent Assembly must either adopt a constitution or disband!' (Aloni n.d.)

The task of formulating a Constitution for the State of Israel has been delegated by the Israeli Knesset to its Constitution, Law and Justice Committee. To date, 55 years after the Declaration of the Establishment of the State of Israel, the Committee has failed to present a constitution to the Knesset. Instead, eleven Basic Laws have been promulgated so far, including Basic Law: Human Dignity and Liberty of 1992 declared by Justice Aharon Barak, president of the Israeli Supreme Court, as representing a constitutional revolution in Israel.

Having successfully aborted the requirement stipulated by UN Resolution 181(II) for a democratic constitution, the newly established State of Israel was then enabled in the subsequent formative four decades to act without constitutional legal restriction, in violation of the specific terms of the said UN Resolution.

Additional to the constitutional violations detailed above, holy places, religious buildings and sites are not preserved, and rights in respect of holy places and religious buildings and sites are systematically denied. To illustrate but a handful of many thousands of cases of violation in this regard: the mosque of the city of Safad in the Galilee has been transformed into an art gallery; the mosque of the village of Ayn Hud in the Haifa district has been transformed into a restaurant and bar; the mosque of the village of Caesaria similarly serves as a restaurant and bar; the central mosque of Beersheba serves as the city museum; the Tel Aviv Hilton Hotel and the adjacent park, named Independence Park, are built on the site of a Muslim cemetery; the Jerusalem Plaza Hotel and the adjacent park, also named Independence Park, are likewise built on the site of a Muslim cemetery. Religious and minority rights have similarly been subject to outright and radical violation. For example, freedom of conscience and of worship are not available in Israel. Unfortunately, a fuller treatment of the subject is outside the scope of this work.[21]

It is in order, however, to cite one area of violation of religious and minority rights to illustrate the case. The State of Israel, through the Ministry of Religious Affairs, recognizes only one of the three contemporary Jewish confessions, namely, the minority orthodox Jewish confession.

Not only is atheism not recognized (the secular registration of marriage or divorce is not available in Israel), but the majority conservative and reform Jewish confessions are likewise denied recognition in Israel. Thus conservative and reform Jewish Rabbis can legally officiate in marriage, divorce, conversion and burial throughout the world, with the exception of the territory of the Jewish state. In the State of Israel, conservative and reform Jewish Rabbis cannot officially carry out their public duties.

But most significantly, the State of Israel is guilty of flagrant violation of the constitutional principle regarding citizenship as stipulated by the UN General Assembly in the 1947 Partition Plan for Palestine. There is no question that under the stipulations of the said Plan all the 1948 Palestinian Arab refugees and their descendants, by now some four million people defined under Israeli law as 'absentees', *are constitutionally entitled without qualification to Israeli citizenship.*

Thus, regarding citizenship, the following is stipulated as the relevant constitutional principle for both the Jewish and the Arab states:

> Palestinian citizens residing in Palestine outside the City of Jerusalem, as well as Arabs and Jews who, not holding Palestinian citizenship, reside in Palestine outside the City of Jerusalem shall, upon the recognition of independence, become citizens of the state in which they are resident and enjoy full civil and political rights. (1947 UN Partition Plan, C Declaration Chapter [3] [1])

The persistent denial of Israeli citizenship to this Palestinian constituency is an act of mass nullification of citizenship (denationalization), and a blatant violation of the UN Charter and international law, let alone Article 15 of the Universal Declaration of Human Rights:

1) Everyone has a right to a nationality;
2) No one shall be arbitrarily deprived of his nationality nor denied the right to change his nationality.

The Israeli procedure of denationalization is far more radical and far-reaching than its apartheid South African equivalent. The Republic of South Africa, in the framework of its apartheid policy, devised a legal mechanism intended to deprive 75 per cent of its inhabitants – the majority of its black people – of their South African citizenship. Under the Bantu Homeland Citizenship Act (1970) (amended as the Bantu Laws Amendment Act [1974]) every black person with South African citizenship was to become a 'citizen' of one of ten ethnic homelands, that were originally constituted as part of the Republic of South Africa.[22] In the period between 1976 and 1994 four homelands (Transkei, Bophuthatswana, Venda and Ciskei) were granted independence, thereby nullifying the South African citizenship of their eight million inhabitants, leaving 12 million (out of the 20 million black population) with a precarious right to be citizens of the Republic of South Africa.

In the Republic of South Africa, the principle of apartheid was applied under the categories of 'White', 'Coloured', 'Indian', and 'Black'. The 1984 'Constitution' did not bestow equal rights on 'White', 'Coloured' and 'Indian' people, but gave a 'parliamentary voice' to 'Coloured' and 'Indian' people (segregated politically in three separate Houses of Parliament, 'White', 'Coloured' and 'Indian' respectively), while the laws regarding access to education, land, and so on remained in place.

It remained the case, however, that South African apartheid recognized the legal personality of its black inhabitants in a way that Zionist apartheid with regard to the Palestinian Arabs does not. While intending to deprive all of its black inhabitants of citizenship in the Republic of South Africa, South African apartheid still recognized them as legal persons (albeit inferior), and thus predicated the legal mechanism of their exclusion on the replacement of their citizenship in the Republic of South Africa with an alternative citizenship, namely, citizenship in one of the ten bogus ethnic 'new independent states'.

As noted above, only four of the ten apartheid 'homelands' were granted 'independence', and thus only eight of the 20 million inhabitants of South Africa classified as 'Black' had their South African citizenship nullified through the South African Bantustan system. It must be noted that the South African Constitutions of 1994 and 1996 reinstated the citizenship rights of all South Africans.

But even though the black inhabitants of the bogus 'new independent states' were rendered legal aliens in their own homeland – they were not defined out of legal existence. They were, however, transferred out of the system.[23]

In the case of Israel, Zionist apartheid is applied under the categories of 'Jew' versus 'non-Jew'. Of the some five million non-Jewish Palestinian Arabs who are today entitled, under the constitutional stipulations of the 1947 UN Partition Plan, to Israeli citizenship, only 20 per cent (approximately a million persons) are citizens of the State of Israel.[24] As repeatedly noted above, of these approximately 250,000 (25 per cent) are classified as 'absentees' under the Absentees' Property Law of 1950, and are thus denied their rights to the titles of their pre-1948 properties inside the state of which they are citizens.

Having classified the 1948 Palestine refugees as 'absentees' in the eyes of the law, the Israeli legislator has thereby not only defined them as aliens in their own homeland, but has cast them outside legal existence as far as their rights to their pre-1948 properties are concerned.

All students of the Palestinian–Israeli conflict, Zionist apologists or otherwise, acknowledge that the 1947 UN General Assembly Resolution recommending the partition of Palestine was highly controversial. The State of Israel and the legitimacy of its continued existence as a Jewish state were (correctly, I submit) challenged at the outset, both locally in Palestine and regionally in the Middle East, as well as in all international, diplomatic and political arenas. As also repeatedly pointed out above, it was, therefore, politically impossible for the newly established State of Israel immediately to contravene the terms of the UN Charter by passing open and explicit apartheid legislation. For the newly established Government of Israel it was both politically and materially imperative to present Israel to the West as an advanced form of democracy and social progress.

In order to do so, it was necessary to veil its apartheid legislation from the view of the UN.

It is my hope that this book will make a significant contribution to the lifting of this veil, leading to the classification by the UN General Assembly of the State of Israel as an apartheid state and the imposition of international sanctions against Israel's rogue government.

Who is a Jew and the question of Palestinian return

The State of Israel was established as a Jewish state, and as was elaborated above, it was not intended as a state for all of its citizens, Jews and non-Jews alike. Rather it was primarily envisaged by its founders as a state for Jews, that is, a state of which every Jewish individual throughout the world would be a potential citizen. Thus, when the state was unilaterally established on 15 May 1948, it became imperative for its legislative body, the Knesset, to define in law those who would qualify as actual or potential citizens, and those who should be excluded – that is, non-Jews in general, and the native indigenous people of the land, the Palestinian Arab people, in particular. This was done without undue delay. In 1950 the Israeli Knesset passed two defining laws in this regard. In March of the said year the Knesset legislated the Absentees' Property Law, defining the boundaries of exclusion ('absentee') and in July, the Law of Return, defining the boundaries of inclusion ('Jew').

Under these laws, every Jew throughout the world is legally entitled to become a citizen of the State of Israel upon immigration to the country, while four million people, the 1948 Palestinian Arab refugees and their descendants, who were forcibly exiled as a consequence of the 1948–49 war, are denied the rights to citizenship. Nevertheless, their right of return is universally recognized in international law and in repeated UN resolutions (beginning with UN General Assembly Resolution 194[III] of December 1948). They are clearly not 'absent'. They clearly exist. Yet they are defined in Israeli law as 'non-existent', as 'absentees', and they are excluded in law from actual or potential citizenship in the Jewish state.

The Law of Return of 1950 is the cornerstone of Israel's Nationality Law of 1952. The details of the Law of Return of 1950 and the Israel Nationality Law of 1952, as well as the legal mechanism of exclusion that are codified in this body of legislation will be discussed in Chapter 3. It is important to note here, however, that the Knesset, having elevated the attribute of 'being Jewish' to the status of a legally determining principle of exclusion from, or inclusion into, the constituency of actual or potential citizens of the State of Israel, has brought into sharp focus the crisis of modern secular Jewish identity, which the Zionist movement claimed to have solved.

Under this body of legislation, as amended over the past five decades, it is not only the Palestinian non-Jews – first and foremost the Palestinian Arab 'absentees' – who are excluded from their undisputed right to citizenship. Also significant categories of Jews are similarly excluded: Jewish bastards, Jewish persons born to non-Jewish mothers, Jewish persons born to Jewish mothers who converted to another religion, and non-Jews converted to Judaism by conservative or reform Rabbis (only the Jewish orthodox conversion procedure is effectively recognized in Israel).

The question of 'who is a Jew' has bedevilled Israeli political practice and legislation since the passage of the Law of Return in 1950. As Akiva Orr noted:

> No one foresaw the problems that would emerge from embedding the term 'Jew' in the legal system. The issue exploded for the first time in the mid-1950s with the case of Fr. Daniel Rufeisen …
>
> The secular court was asked to decide whether Rufeisen was a 'Jew' from a legal point of view, but the authority of the court was immediately challenged by the religious authorities. This raised a whole new set of questions: who is qualified to decide who is a Jew? by what authority? according to what criteria? Rufeisen himself? The court? A government committee? The religious authorities? (Orr 1994: 32; see also Shahak 1994 and Orr 1983)

The case of Mr Abdallah Azeldin Alexander Tsiorulin brings the question at hand into sharp focus.

Mr Abdallah Azeldin Alexander Tsiorulin was born in Russia in 1952 and immigrated to Israel in 1992 with his second wife. His second wife is classified under Israeli law as 'Jewish'. He was granted Israeli citizenship 'by return' on the strength of his marriage to a 'Jew', and settled in Hederah, Israel. In or about 1999 he converted to Islam in Israel and changed his name to an Arabic name. Consequently, the Israeli Ministry of Interior changed the designation of his nationality on his Identity Card to 'Arab'.

The Israeli Ministry of Interior seems to be unable to accept that Islam is a universal religion embracing numerous nationalities, including Arab nationalities. Needless to say that ordering that the designation of the nationality of citizens be changed on their Identity Cards on the ground of conversion to Islam or any other religion represents in and of itself a blatant abuse of fundamental rights.

It was the critical historian Amnon Raz-Korkatzkin of Ben-Gurion University in the Negev who made the perceptive comment at the time to the effect that the State of Israel has manufactured a new definition for 'being Jewish'. The paraphrase of his comment would read something like the following:

Question: Who is a 'Jew' in the State of Irael today?

Answer: Not an Arab.

Political practice and legislation have been similarly bedevilled by the question of 'who is an Israeli' in the State of Israel. Clearly, the terms 'Israeli' and 'Jew' are not coterminous. One million of the over six million citizens of the State of Israel (17 per cent) are non-Jewish. They are Palestinian Arabs, the descendants of the remnants of the Palestinian people who survived the onslaught of the Israeli army in the 1948–49 war and have remained in Palestine under Israeli rule (150,000 in 1948–49). Classifiying the Palestinian Arab citizens of Israel as 'Israeli' is plainly offensive, since their status as citizens is not equal to the status of those citizens of the State of Israel who are classified in law as 'Jews'. Much of this volume will be devoted to the analysis and explication of the political and legal mechanisms in terms of which the State of Israel confers *a priori* privileged access to national resources, notably land and water, and services, notably religious services, on to its Jewish citizens, to the exclusion of its non-Jewish, mainly Palestinian Arab, citizens.

It is always necessary to remember, however, that Israeli legislation is not directed only against those non-Jews (namely, Palestinian Arabs) who are legally incorporated, albeit in terms of extreme legal discrimination, into the Israeli body politic as citizens of the Jewish state. Rather, the most damaging manifestation of Israeli legislation is directed against those non-Jews (namely, Palestinian Arabs) who are legally excluded as 'absentees' from the body of Israeli polity, first and foremost, the approximately four million 1948 Palestine refugees. Israeli Jewish homes are built on the ruins of *their* homes. Israeli Jews cultivate, develop and trade with *their* land. Thus each Israeli Jew has a shadow: the Palestinian Arab refugee of 1948 turned into an intifada activist, or a soldier in the Palestine Liberation Army, a *fida'i*, or an operative in one of the security arms of the Palestinian Authority.

Human beings will rebel, must rebel, in such circumstances, to reconstitute their full human existence, to reclaim their rights, if necessary by armed struggle, inside every part of the homeland from which they have been excluded. And to the extent that this struggle is carried out in conformity with international law the Palestinian Arabs deserve our full moral and material support.

Israeli–Palestinian dialogue

For Israeli–Palestinian dialogue to succeed, it must be based on truth; on critical awareness; on a fundamental commitment to the values of the Universal Declaration of Human Rights; and on the application of the standards of international law without fear or favour. Hypocrisy and duplicity mislead and misdirect.

The first truth on which, in my view, Israeli–Palestinian dialogue must be predicated is that as long as the 1948 Palestine refugees, reduced to the misery of refugee camps and exile, are excluded from any part of their homeland Palestine, including Bisan, Tiberias, Safad, Nazareth, Shafa'Amr, Acre, Haifa, Jaffa, Lydda, Ramle, Jerusalem, Majdal (Ashqelon), Isdud (Ashdod) Beersheba and, of course, Jerusalem, they are right to reassert their presence in the homeland from which they are excluded, if necessary, also by military means and armed struggle, subject to the standards of international law, and we must support them morally and materially in this struggle.

It is in order to point out in this connection that it is false and misguided to equate in any way moral and material support to organizations resisting occupation, colonization and apartheid, subject to the values of the Universal Declaration of Human Rights and the standards of international law, with expressions of support for 'acts of terrorism'.

'Acts of terrorism' target civilian populations. Armed struggle resisting occupation, colonialism and apartheid, subject to the values of the Universal Declaration of Human Rights and the standards of international law, does not target the civilian population, but, rather, is aimed at legal and legitimate targets, such as uniformed members of the security arms of the occupation, colonial or apartheid government. In terms of the values of the Universal Declaration of Human Rights and under the stipulation of international law it is occupation, colonialism and apartheid that are illegal, while resistance, including armed resistance, is legal.

Targeting the civilian populations is criminal in every context and must be morally condemned and politically rejected, with the proviso that crime, like all human action, is a human construct and ought not to be reified. A fundamental asymmetry obtains between the 'haves' and the 'have-nots', between the colonizer and the colonized. No armed action targeting civilians can be condoned. All 'acts of terrorism' ought to be condemned. But 'suicide bombing' by Palestinians is not 'just like' the strafing of Palestinian civilian residential quarters by Israeli Apache and Cobra helicopters with missiles, just as stealing food to feed the hungry is not 'just like' stealing money to feed a drug habit.

Many of those at the forefront of the 'war against terror', notably the Government of the State of Israel, seem to be unwilling to embrace an inclusive view of the phenomenon of 'terrorism' they so forcefully condemn. The first party victimized by 'acts of terrorism' is the Palestinian party – not the Israeli party. The majority of the victims of 'acts of terrorism' are Palestinian civilians – not Israeli civilians. The primary perpetrators of 'acts of terrorism' are the governments of the State of Israel sending death squads on assassination missions in the post-1967 occupied territories; strafing civilian residential areas with helicopter gunships; destroying clinics and medical infrastructure; devastating centres of learning, education and cultural heritage; subjecting the civilian population to protracted curfews; and denying the civilian population access to medical care. The primary 'terrorist' in the Israeli–Palestinian conflict is the Government of the State of Israel – not the Palestinian suicide bomber.

For Israeli–Palestinian dialogue to succeed all parties to the dialogue must take as the point of departure the values of the Universal Declaration of Human Rights and apply these values consistently. In May 2002 the Knesset legislated an Amendment to the Penal Code of 1977. Under the new legislation (Amendment No. 66 of 2002), expression of support for acts of 'violence or terror' are liable for prosecution and sentencing for up to five years' imprisonment ('violence and terror' being defined as 'an offence causing injury to the body of a person, or that places a person in danger of death or danger of serious injury'). All those committed to the values of the Universal Declaration of Human Rights without hypocrisy or duplicity would recognize that the first party that ought to be charged under this new legislation is none other than the Government of the State of Israel.

The second truth relevant to Israeli–Palestinian dialogue is that an Israeli–Hebrew people has been created in the process of the Zionist colonization of Palestine. This people, like all other peoples, must be guaranteed their full rights under international law and in conformity with all UN resolutions relevant to the question of Palestine.

It is in order to point out again in this connection that it is not the case that the United Nations Organization legitimized through the UN General Assembly Resolution 181(II) of November 1947 the establishment of a 'Jewish State' in the political Zionist sense of the term. Legally speaking, the UN *did not* intend the adoption of the said Resolution 181(II) as a licence for the armed forces of the Zionist organizations and subsequently the armed forces of the new State of Israel to perpetrate war crimes and crimes against humanity including the mass expulsion of the native indigenous Palestinian Arab people from their homeland.

In other words, it was and remains impossible for the General Assembly, conducting its business under the stipulation of the UN Charter, to have legally endorsed the political Zionist idea of the 'Jewish State', namely, a state that attempts to guarantee in law and practice a demographic majority of the Jewish tribes in the territories under its control.

The constitutional notion underpinning the idea of the 'Jewish State' in the said UN Resolution 181(II), as well as its sister 'Arab State', envisioned the partition of British Mandate Palestine into two essentially democratic states, one with 'Jewish' trappings and one with 'Arab' trappings, joined together in the framework of an economic union, with Jerusalem as *corpus separatum* under a special international regime to be administered by the United Nations, neither the capital of the 'Arab State' nor the capital of the 'Jewish State'.

One can only speculate as to what representations of 'Jewish', 'Arab' or 'international' trappings would be consistent with essentially democratic constitutions. One could imagine, for instance, that in the 'Jewish State' the first line on official road signs would be Hebrew, the second Arabic and the third English; in the 'Arab State' the first line Arabic, the second, Hebrew and the third English; and in the international city of Jerusalem road signs would be only in English to skirt the stupid thorny issue of whether the second line on official road signs should be Hebrew or Arabic.

In terms of the said UN General Assembly Resolution 181(II) all Arab inhabitants who were ordinarily resident in the territories designated by the UN for the 'Jewish State' were and remain entitled to 'Jewish State' citizenship; all Jews ordinarily in the territories by the said Resolution for the 'Arab State' were and remain entitled to 'Arab State' citizenship;

and all Arabs and Jews ordinarily resident in Jerusalem were and remain entitled to an international Jerusalem citizenship.

It thus follows that for Israeli–Palestinian dialogue to succeed it must take as point of departure a critical examination of the right of self-determination for the Hebrew people constructed in the process of the Zionist colonization of Palestine. Such critical examination would aim to dismantle illegal institutional representations of this right as were put in place by the Parliament of the State of Israel in violation of the values of the Universal Declaration of Human Rights and the stand-ards of international law (for example, the Absentees' Property Law of 1950), and replace them with alternative legal and other institutional representations such as are consistent with the same, notably with UN General Assembly Resolution 194(III) of December 1948 stipulating the right of return of all Palestinian Arab refugees.

It is in terms of this critical examination that the limitation of the Zionist 'peace camp', notably the work of Uri Avnery, is subject to scrutiny in Chapter 5.

'The Female Snake' and 'The Taste of Mulberries', by Havah ha-Levi

The Female Snake

Someone said something about Tantura …

Soft hills rolled silently into each other's embrace [towards the beach] and right on the edge of the hills there was a dense plantation of low palm trees clustered on the beach. A scenery of soft and misty dream. Only the feeling of nausea returns to trouble me.

At a short distance from the cluster of palms there was a group of empty houses. Some of them were slightly damaged, but generally, the houses were intact and beautiful. Everything [about the houses] was very neglected, empty and filthy. A few ancient shoes exposed their seams along the footpath. There in the deserted Village of Tantura the kibbutz *set up the summer camp for its children.*

The houses were cleaned up. A large long tent was erected to serve as a dining hall. The place was a paradise for children.

I remember the heat of the scorching sun over my tanned skin. The salt taste of the sea water. The swimming competitions. The beautiful and quiet beach. And thirty or forty happy children. Really happy.

And yet I listen to my memories. I try to redraw the lines that chart my memory. There are things that already had their beginning in another place.

There were these half-scornful sentences, such as: if the Arabs come, they will steal you first. You are blonde and the Arabs like blonde girls; if the Arabs come, they will see your golden head in the dark and will steal you first. They will think perhaps that it is a ball of gold; here is an Arab shoe. Such sentences …

Towards the end, two days before the conclusion of the summer camp, they asked who wanted to go on a tour and listen to Motke telling stories about the conquest of Tantura. I went, too.

We went into the cluster of palms, and the leader of the summer camp, a nice jovial kibbutznik, *who evidently loved children, was already there telling something.*

I lagged behind as usual. I walked along daydreaming and slightly bored. When I eventually caught up with the group, they were all standing near a large house which had perhaps originally been situated at the edge of the village, and I remember the words: 'We attacked at both ends. Most of them had already run away. Suddenly a huge Arab came out behind this house and began to run. I shot him, and he jumped in the air like a rabbit, turned a somersault and fell.'

Even today I do not know whether this was a factual description of what had happened. But at our place, they used to say that if you kill a snake, you should throw it away or hide it, because if it is left exposed, all the snakes (the family? the tribe?) will come to the place to look for it and this could be very dangerous. And that if you kill a bee that has stung you, it is likewise necessary to throw it away or hide it, since otherwise all the bees will come there after its smell. And that if you kill a lion, the lioness will always come to search for it.

And then, suddenly, together with the Arab, shot in the air with his white kufiyya *and black* aqal, *all the Arabs who had lived there in these houses, who had worn those shoes now discarded on the footpaths, the children who had run about naked on the beach, the fat, erect women who had carried the jars on top of their heads – they all came out suddenly in my imagination to look for him. I recalled the warning not to leave the corpse of the snake in the place where it had been killed because the female snake will come to look for it and I turned to look behind me, terrified. There was nothing there. Only the beautiful houses and the sea. A bit angry and a bit curious, I thought about this bad Arab who had come to attack our soldiers. I thought he had deserved to die like that, yet he did not seem to have been dangerous when he was shot there in the air, like a rabbit. I wanted to know if he was from this village, or from another place.*

We returned to the beach and ate a watermelon. I wanted to have the 'heart' of the watermelon, but I never got it because I always arrived late. Everything lost its taste.

I told my friend: Mira, I am already fed up with this summer camp. I want to go back home.

She looked at me surprised, beautiful, suntanned: 'Why?'

The Taste of Mulberries

The name of the villages was Sarkas, which probably refers to the former origin of its inhabitants, Circassians, who came, I would not know how, to the Middle East and settled here.[25] *Anyway, when I came to know the village, all of its inhabitants were Palestinian Arabs. In fact, I never came to know the village properly; I was never there, though this is only half the truth, and I shall return to that later.*

In our eyes, the eyes of children four or five years old, the village was repre-sented by two women: Khadija and Hanifa. Maybe they were more courageous than the rest, or maybe they served as something like the 'Foreign Office' of the village. They often walked about in the kibbutz, and as far as I can remember they were mainly preoccupied with the picking of khubeiza *[mallow] leaves, which grew in wild abundance along the roadside.*

When we asked why they pick the khubeiza, *we were told that the Arabs cook the leaves and eat them. And so, the first thing I ever knew about Arabs was that they eat* khubeiza. *I also knew, of course, that they ride on camels, since the camels used to pass through the kibbutz and occasionally camp there; I knew that they ride on donkeys along the white road which probably stretches up to the very end of the world. But at that time there were also in the area British soldiers [the Mandate] and Australian soldiers [Second World War], and thus it was imbedded in my consciousness that Eretz Israel consists of us, as well as passers by: Arabs, British, Australians ...*

About that time they all disappeared, and I really did not notice their disappearance all that much. Of course, the departure of the British was ac-companied by much talk on the radio and in the yard of the kibbutz. But as to the fact that Khadija and Hanifa ceased to show up – well, there are many events that pass through the universe of any child, and he or she accepts their appearance as well as their disappearance as a matter of fact. Later, I came to know that the village had been destroyed by bulldozers, and I was a little scared. And then I forgot, and many years passed before Sarkas again emerged before my eyes as a place where people lived.

The destroyed village was made into the kibbutz garbage dump. I do not know who was the first to discover that in the midst of the ruins and the dust and the stench there remained a mulberry tree. A huge mulberry tree, which, in summer, produced huge mulberries: black and deliciously sweet. The mulberry trees in the kibbutz were grown on much water and their fruit was therefore somewhat watery, and anyway they were much too high to climb. But this mulberry tree was low, spreading wide, and heavily laden with fruit, to the deep delight of a little girl who was rather quiet and clumsy and who loved mulberries. And thus, every Saturday we would go on pilgrimage to the mulberry tree, stand around it for hours and eat of its fruit and return home with hands and faces blackened by the dark dye of mulberry sap. Never, not once, while standing there among the ruins and the dust under the scathing sun did we talk or think of the inhabitants of Sarkas who lived here: where are they? Where did they go? Why?

From the distance of fifteen years of difficult political development, I watch this group of children devouring mulberries in the midst of a destroyed village, and I just cannot comprehend: how? Wherefrom this utter blindness?

For many years I would walk on Saturdays to Sarkas. At times with company. At times alone. Now Sarkas was no longer embodied in Khadija and Hanifa. Now Sarkas was reduced to the stench of the kibbutz garbage dump and the mulberries in summer. On either side of the road to Sarkas there were sabr cacti hedgerows along all roads, but today they have all disappeared, except in books and in Arab villages, where they still remain. In summer the sabr would bring forth their fruit, and raise masses of tiny red and orange flags glued to their rounded green flagpoles in a summer festival. And when the sabr fruit was ripe, the Arab women would appear out of nowhere, fill their big tin containers with the red and orange fruit and walk away.

Today I remember these Arab women and I ask myself: where did they come from? Who were they? Were they exiled inhabitants of the village? And in the evening, when they eat the fruit that they had gathered or when they sell it at the roadside, do they feel the taste of their lost homes?

But at that time I did not think of them in the least. The Arabs were something whose temporary provisional existence was eternal. They pass along the white road on a donkey-cart, emerging out of somewhere and going on to somewhere else. Only once, for some reason ... There was a big scout night game, a sort of test of courage. I hid behind the sabr hedgerows and waited for my pursuers to pass by. I sat there in the dark for a long time, quietly. I was not afraid. And all of a sudden they were with me. The women of Sarkas.

The women who pick khubeiza along the roadside. The women with the long knives who steal wheat from the fields of the kibbutz. The women with the water cans and the bundles of dry wood on their heads. Slowly, slowly, they slipped by on their bare feet, black and silent. Their round outline, like the sabr cacti leaves, merged with the darkness around, silent.

Today there stands on the site a huge plant for the processing of agricultural products. An exemplary cooperative venture. And the hill? The hill of the village of Sarkas, where is it? The entire area was levelled down, and around the huge factory orange groves were planted, and there is not one single cut stone left as testimony. Yet, I remember. I testify.

In 1961, a very young woman from Kibbutz Giv'at ha-Sheloshah married an Arab youth who was employed in her kibbutz. The kibbutz refused to allow them to remain there, and they applied to join 'my' kibbutz. The debate on whether they are to be admitted or whether they are not to be admitted extended over one and a half years and shook the kibbutz in a way that no other subject ever did, either before or since. The debate cut across families, and brought sons to rebel against their parents, brothers against brothers and husbands against wives. The leadership of the Ha-Shomer ha-Tza'ir kibbutz federation was called to present its position (opposed), and threats of leaving the kibbutz on this matter were voiced in both camps.

In the end, the 'mixed couple' was not admitted to the kibbutz. Both camps were already tired of endless debates and rows. In a bitter discussion which I (who supported their admission) had with one of the leading opponents he told me: 'Do you know that Rashid is a son of the village of Sarkas? Do you think he can live here, raise his children here and always see across the street the hill which was his village, and not think anything?'

At that moment, together with the scorching sun and the dust, I felt in my mouth the taste of the mulberries, and I understood what homeland means, and also, for the first time, vaguely and at a distance and a little bit afraid, I understood that this homeland, the homeland of the songs and of school textbooks, is simply just the taste of mulberries, and the smell of dust, and the moist earth in winter, and the colour of the sky, and that it is a homeland not only for me, but also for Rashid Masarwa. At that very moment, in the midst of the heated discussion, the taste of mulberries and the shock, I remembered one fearful memory.

It was towards the end of the 1948 war, after we had won the war and defeated the Arab armies and had a state of our own. We were lying in bed. Eight children in the children's house. It was night. From the distance we heard the heavy and rumbling noise. It was not very far away, but one could clearly hear that the noise did not come from inside the kibbutz. And the noise went on and on and on. I asked what this protracted and continuous noise was, and one of the children told me that two kibbutz members had gone with bulldozers to Sarkas to destroy the houses of the Arabs. In real fear of Arab revenge I asked: 'But what will the Arabs do when they come back and see that we have destroyed their homes?' And he then answered: 'That is why we destroy their homes, so that they do not come back.'

I then knew that the matter was lost. The home of Rashid was destroyed then so that he would not return. So that he, his mother in the long black robe who walks erect with the bundle of wood magnificently balanced on her head, and all his brothers and sisters who run barefoot on the stones would not return. And also now they will not let him come back.

In December 1972, the entire country was shaken with what was dubbed in the press as the 'affair of the espionage and sabotage network'. Some thirty Arab youths and six Jewish youths, Israelis, were arrested on charges of forming a 'sabotage organization', operated by Syrian intelligence, whose object was 'to damage the security of the state'. One of the Jewish detainees, a youth aged 26, was a son of 'my' kibbutz. Another detainee from the Arab village of Jatt was a youth named Mahmud Masarwa. In his defence speech he stated as follows:

The Honourable Court,
Your Honourable Judges,
  My father was born in the village of Sarkas, near kibbutz ... in the vicinity of Haderah. My father was the son of a peasant. In 1948, he was removed from his land, expelled by force. Their lands were confiscated. Their homes were destroyed. On the site a factory for the kibbutz was built. My father was compelled to go out and seek work as a labourer in order to feed ... [his family]. We went to live in such a tiny house: twelve people in the space of 2 metres times 3 metres. In 1957, I remember this quite well, one year after the Sinai war, my father told me and my brother who sits here [in the court room]: 'Go out to work in order that you at least help me to finance your studies ...' (Quoted from the official Protocol of the court proceedings)

'My brother who sits here in the court room!'

His brother who sat there was Rashid Masarwa who, in 1961, applied to be admitted to the kibbutz together with his Jewish wife. It was Rashid Masarwa who told the members of the kibbutz: 'I want to live here as a loyal kibbutz member like everyone else, but I want my children to know that their father is an Arab, and I want my children to know the Quran, and I want them to celebrate all the Jewish holidays, but also know what Ramadan is, and that their grandfather and grandmother will come to visit them here in the kibbutz, and that my children will also go to the village to be with their grandfather and grandmother in the holidays.'

Now he is sitting here, Rashid Masarwa, and watches his brother being sentenced for wanting to take by the force of arms what he himself had hoped to gain by application and consent, and all the brotherhood among the nations in the world could not be of any avail to them.

In the Ramle central prison the son of the dispossessing kibbutz and the son of the dispossessed village met again. Only one youth, one Udi Adiv, from that kibbutz resolved in his mind to cross the road. But the world has no space to accommodate the naive.

And if prisoners in jail do dream – both prisoners, no doubt, see in their dreams the colour of the sky, and perhaps they also savour the taste of mulberries.

3 · Israeli Apartheid

Israel and South Africa: two forms of apartheid

It is not the case that all Zionist and Israeli apologists would dismiss the subtitle above as a misrepresentation. As the late C. L. Sulzberger pointed out:

Afrikaner South Africa and Jewish Israel both began in 1948 when the Nationalist party gained control of this country [South Africa] and Palestine was partitioned. South Africa was one of the first states to recognize Israel. Its Prime Minister D. F. Malan was the first foreign chief of government to visit it.

The Afrikaner sees Israel as another small nation, surrounded by enemies, where the Bible and a revived language are vital factors. As Jannie Kruger, former editor of *Die Transvaler* wrote: 'The Afrikaners ... are *par excellence* the nation of the Book.' The fundamentalist Boers trekked northward with gun in one hand and Bible in the other ...

Like Israel, South Africa feels the role of language and religion are important to national survival. Prime Minister Vorster even goes so far as to say Israel is now faced with an apartheid problem – how to handle its Arab inhabitants. Neither nation wants to place its future entirely in the hands of a surrounding majority and would prefer to fight.

Both South Africa and Israel are in a sense intruded states. They were built by pioneers organizing abroad and settling in partially inhabited areas. The only people here when the first Dutch arrived were Bush-men and Hottentots but the Zulus would be living in Johannesburg were it not for the Boers' northward trek. (C. L. Sulzberger, 'Strange Nonalliance', *New York Times*, 28 April 1971, quoted in Stevens and Elmessiri 1977: 143)

And 25 years later South Africa's Archbishop Desmond Tutu observed that Israelis were 'treating Palestinians in the same way the apartheid South African government treated blacks':

In a commentary published on Monday by the *Guardian*, Tutu said: 'I've been deeply distressed in my visit to the Holy Land; it reminded me so much of what happened to us black people in South Africa.' ('Tutu

Hits Out at "Apartheid in Holy Land"', *Guardian*, 29 April 2002, quoted in <http://www.iol.co.za/index.php?art_id=qw1020058740124B253&set _id=1&click_id=2749&sf=2749>)[26]

But mainstream apologists for political Zionism and the State of Israel have so far preferred to take a different route. Israel, it is claimed, is not an apartheid state and ought not be classified as an apartheid state.

Is it not the case that the Palestinian Arab minority citizens of the State of Israel have an equal vote in the political process as the Jewish majority? (They do.) Are there not Palestinian Arab Members of Parliament in the Israeli Knesset? (There are.) Is it not the case that Palestinian Arab citizens of the State of Israel have an equal standing before Israeli courts of law as Jewish citizens? (They do, in principle.)[27]

And, the argument would then continue, since the Palestinian Arab minority citizens of the State of Israel have an equal vote in the political process as the Jewish majority; there are Palestinian Arab Members of Parliament in the Israeli Knesset; and Palestinian Arab citizens of the State of Israel have an equal standing before Israeli courts of law as Jewish citizens, it is not only misguided to attempt to classify Israel as an apartheid state, but, it is slanderous to do so, the slander being as obscene as the anti-Semitic blood libels against Jews in previous centuries, and motivated by the same sentiment, namely, anti-Jewish racism.

The evidence, however, suggests otherwise.

It is not the case that there is any fault in principle in pointing to the facts of Palestinian Arab minority citizens of the State of Israel having an equal vote in the political process as the Jewish majority, or to the participation of Palestinian Arab Members of Parliament in the Israeli Knesset, and the equal standing, in principle, of Palestinian Arab citizens of the State of Israel before Israeli courts of law as Jewish citizens as significant features of the Israeli political system.

It is, however, the case that pointing to these facts alone is tantamount to an exercise in misrepresentation, manipulating these significant features in order to veil the fundamental apartheid structures of the Israeli polity in all that pertains to the right to inherit property; to access the material resources of the state (notably, land and water); and to access the welfare resources of the state (for example religious services and child benefits) such as fully justify the classification of the State of Israel as an apartheid state.

It is in order to underline here that I refer to the term 'apartheid' in the narrow and technical sense of the word, namely, as a term designating a political programme predicated on discrimination *in law* on a racial basis; and I refer here to the term 'racial discrimination' as defined in Article 1(1) of the UN Convention on the Elimination of All Forms of Racial Discrimination of 1966 (any distinction, exclusion, restriction or preference based on race, colour, descent, or national or ethnic origin which has the purpose or effect of nullifying or impairing the recognition, enjoyment or exercise, on an equal footing, of human rights and fundamental freedoms in the political, economic, social, cultural or any other field of public life).

Classifying Israel as an apartheid state does not mean equating Israel with South Africa. Israeli apartheid is significantly different from South African apartheid, just as the Israeli occupation of Palestine is significantly different from the Nazi occupation of Europe. But the relevant differences (for example, that one million Palestinian Arabs in Israel are citizens, though not equal citizens) in the first case do not imply that the one (South Africa) is apartheid and the other (Israel) is not, just as the relevant differences in the second case (for instance, there is no Auschwitz under Israeli occupation) do not imply that the one (the Nazi occupation) is a crime against humanity and the other (the Israeli occupation) is not.

As early as 1982 Amos Oz published an interview with a certain Mr Tz., a Jewish settler in a cooperative settlement (*moshav*), which accurately captures the *Zeitgeist* of Israeli apartheid:

Leibowitz[28] is right. We are Judeo-Nazis, and why not? ... Even today I am willing to do the dirty work for Israel, to kill as many Arabs as necessary, to deport them, to expel and burn them, to have everyone hate us, to pull the rug from underneath the feet of diaspora Jews, so that they will be forced to run to us crying. Even if it means blowing up one or two synagogues here and there, I don't care. And I don't mind if after the job is done you put me in front of a Nurnberg trial and jail me for life. Hang me if you want as a war criminal ... What you lot don't understand is that the dirty work of Zionism is not finished yet, far from it. True, it could have been finished in 1948 ... (Oz 1983: 70–82)

The likes of Mr Tz. can be found in all walks of life in Israel's Zionist society, including today's government coalition.

Israel today and South Africa until 1994 represent two forms of apartheid. Either form of apartheid, South African or Israeli version, represents a flagrant violation of international law, notably the Covenant on the Suppression and Punishment of the Crime of Apartheid of 1973, a crime that ought be corrected by the international community applying all legitimate means available to the UN Security Council, notably the imposition of sanctions.

In what follows I hope to elucidate further the Israeli form of apartheid.

It is not always widely recognized that both Israeli apartheid and South African apartheid anchor their respective settler colonial projects in a fundamentalist interpretation of the Old Testament.

Once political Zionism settled, in the 6th and 7th Zionist Congresses of 1903 and 1905 respectively, the debate between the 'territorialists', who were open to consider Jewish colonial settlements in territories other than Palestine, and the 'Zion Zionists', opposed to Jewish colonial settlement in any territory other than Palestine, and anchored the Zionist political programme firmly in the settler colonial project in Palestine, the fundamentalist interpretation of the Old Testament came to play a similarly retrograde formative role in the institutionalization of Zionist nationalism.

Thus the Preamble to the Articles of Association of the JNF registered in 1907 in England defines the area of operation of the JNF in Article 3(1) as the 'prescribed region Palestine, Syria, any other parts of Turkey in Asia and the Peninsula of Sinai' (almost the 'promised land' allegedly covenanted by God to Abraham in Genesis 15:18–21: 'To your descendants I give this land, from the River of Egypt [the Nile] to the Great River, the river Euphrates') and its objects as 'purchase, take on lease or in exchange, or otherwise acquire any lands, forests, rights of possession and other rights, easements and other immovable property in the prescribed region … or any part thereof, for the purpose of settling Jews on such lands'.

And 50 years later the Declaration of the Establishment of the State of Israel proclaims 'the Land of Israel' as the birthplace of the Jewish people, a reference sufficiently ambiguous to extend from the boundaries of the territory of the 'Jewish state' as defined in the UN General Assembly Resolution 181(II) of November 1947 recommending the partition of Palestine into a 'Jewish state' and 'Arab state' with economic union and Jerusalem as a *corpus separatum* under UN administration, through to the boundaries of the said Biblical 'promised land'.

> *Eretz Israel* was the birthplace of the Jewish people. Here their spiritual, religious and political identity was shaped. Here they first attained to statehood, created cultural values of national and universal significance and gave to the world the eternal Book of Books.
>
> After being forcibly exiled from their land, the people kept faith with it throughout their Dispersion and never ceased to pray and hope for their return to it and for the restoration in it of their political freedom …

Placing our trust in the Almighty, we affix our signatures to this proclamation at this session of the Provisional Council of the State, on the soil of the homeland, in the city of Tel Aviv, on this Sabbath eve, the 5th Day of Iyar, 5709 (14 May 1948).

The ideological affinity between Afrikaner nationalism and political Zionism was recognized not only by perceptive international observers such as the late C. L. Sulzberger, but equally by the leadership of both camps rather early, and was clearly articulated in the alliance forged by their respective leaders Jan Smuts and Chaim Weizmann.

'I need not remind you', pointed out Smuts, Prime Minister of the Union of South Africa, addressing a reception given in his honour by the Jewish Community of South Africa, under the auspices of the South African Zionist Federation and the South African Jewish Board of Deputies in the Town Hall, Johannesburg, on 3 November 1919,

> that the white people of South Africa, and especially the older Dutch population, has been brought up almost entirely on Jewish tradition. The Old Testament, the most wonderful literature ever thought out by the brain of man, the Old Testament has been the very marrow of Dutch culture here in South Africa ...
>
> That is the basis of our culture in South Africa, that is the basis of our white culture, and it is the basis of your Jewish culture; and therefore we are standing together on a common platform, the greatest spiritual platform the world has ever seen. On that platform I want us to build the future South Africa. (Smuts n.d.)

And when, in 1961, consequent to Israel's decision to expand its diplomatic offensive in Black Africa, the Israeli delegation in the UN General Assembly was directed to support the motion of censure moved by the Afro-Asian member states condemning South Africa's apartheid as being 'reprehensible and repugnant to human dignity' (UN General Assembly Resolution 1598 [xv]), the response of the Afrikaans press and the South African government was equally revealing. *Die Transvaler* asked:

> And is there any real difference between the way that the people of Israel are trying to maintain themselves amid non-Jewish peoples and the way the Afrikaner is trying to remain what he is? The people of Israel base themselves upon the Old Testament to explain why they do not wish to mix with other people: the Afrikaner does this too ... (quoted in Stevens and Elmessiri 1977: 66)

And Prime Minister Dr Verwoerd is reported to have written:

People are beginning to ask why, if Israel and its Rabbis feel impelled to attack the policy of separate development here, the policy of separate development in Israel is not wrong in their eyes as well ... (ibid.)

And to have further observed that the Zionists

... took Israel from the Arabs after the Arabs had lived there for a thousand years. In that, I agree with them, Israel, like South Africa, is an apartheid state. (*Rand Daily Mail*, 23 November 1961)

As noted in the Preface above, for many decades prior to the release of Nelson Mandela in 1990, after 27 years of political incarceration, and the transformation of the Republic of South Africa in 1994 from an apartheid state into a state governed by a democratic constitution, the hard core of South African apartheid, the Dutch Reform Church, criminally educated its constituents and beyond that being 'a good Christian' entailed being 'pro-apartheid' and that being anti-apartheid was tantamount to being 'anti-Christ'.

And for many decades, since the destruction of European Jewry under the Nazi occupation, the education and information organs of the Zionist organizations and the State of Israel falsely educated their constituents and beyond that in order to be a 'good Jew' it is somehow necessary to be 'pro-Zionist' and that to be anti-Zionist is somehow tantamount to being 'anti-Jewish', in other words, 'anti-Semitic'.

Also as noted above, with the establishment of the State of Israel in May 1948, a fundamental legal and political circle had to be squared. On the one hand, the new state was politically and legally committed to the Charter of the United Nations Organization, the standards of international law and the values of the Universal Declaration of Human Rights, which, since the Second World War, have informed most, if not all, liberal western democracies and enlightened world public opinion. On the other hand, the driving force underpinning the efforts of political Zionism since its establishment at the First Zionist Congress was not liberal democratic, but ethnocratic, to attempt to establish in Palestine a state that would be as 'Jewish' as England was 'English', to establish and consolidate in the country of Palestine a sovereign state, a Jewish state, that attempts to guarantee in law and in practice a demographic majority of the Jewish tribes in the territories under its control – an apartheid state.

The ethnic cleansing perpetrated by the Israel army under the cover of the 1948–49 war and the consequent destruction of some 400 Palestinian rural and urban localities in the territories that came under Israeli sovereignty and control are crimes against humanity under international law. Granting citizenship to the remnants of the Palestinian people that survived the war crimes perpetrated by the Israeli army in the course of the 1948–49 war and remained in the territories that came under Israeli sovereignty and control subsequent to the 1949 armistice agreements was one effective way of veiling the crime.

Citizenship is a certificate representing a legal relationship between the individual and the state. Democratic citizenship is a certificate representing the recognition by the state of the right of every citizen to equal access to the political process of the state (e.g., to elect and be elected to all of the offices of the state); to the civil process (e.g., to equal standing before the law and to property); to social and welfare services (e.g., religious services); and to the material resources of the state (e.g., land and water).

Like all rights, democratic citizenship as we know it today is a right won by the struggle of the people *vis-à-vis* the state.

Unlike the US legislature, which recognizes, under a democratic Constitution, one universal citizenship for all US citizens without distinction of nationality, religion, language, tribe, sex, or any other social status, the State of Israel does not have one single universal citizenship for all of its citizens. Rather, informed by the dominant ideology of political Zionism, the Knesset legislated a schedule of four classes of citizenship based on racial discrimination and representing blatant inequality in law – in other words, representing another form of apartheid.

In the State of Israel the right of a citizen classified in law as a 'non-Jew' (namely, an 'Arab') to partake in the political process is formally equal to the right of a citizen classified in law as a 'Jew'. Likewise the standing of a citizen classified in law as a 'non-Jew' before the courts of law is in principle equal to the standing of a citizen classified in law as a 'Jew' (see note 27).

On the other hand the rights of a citizen classified in law as a 'non-Jew' to property, to the social and welfare services and to the material resources of the state are *not* equal to those of a citizen classified in law as a 'Jew', and, the ruling by the Israeli Supreme Court sitting as the High Court of Justice on the case of Qaadan *vs.* Qatzir in March 2000 notwithstanding, such citizens of the State of Israel as are defined in law as 'non-Jews' (namely, 'Arabs') are denied access to 93 per cent of the territory of pre-1967 Israel administered by the Israel Lands Administration (ILA).

In other words, the Israeli legal system is based fundamentally on the determination of at least two classes of citizenship: Class 'A' citizenship for such citizens as are classified in law as 'Jews', and, as such, are allocated in law a privileged access to the material resources of the state and the social as well as the welfare services of the state only because they are classified in law as 'Jews', versus Class 'B' citizenship for such citizens as are classified in law as 'non-Jews', namely, as 'Arabs', and, as such, are discriminated against in law with regard to their rights to equal access to the material resources of the state as well as the social and welfare services of the state, first and foremost their right to equal access to land and water, only because they are classified in law as 'non-Jews'.

But subject to Class 'B' citizenship above, there also exists in the State of Israel by force of the Absentees' Property Law of 1950 Class 'C' citizenship for such Arab citizens of the State of Israel as are present inside the state, yet classified in law as 'absent'. These Arab citizens are indeed present inside Israel as taxpayers and voters who cast (or refrain from casting) their vote in the election ballot – but, being classified under the said obscene law as 'absentees', they have been denied all their rights to their properties (lands, houses, corporations, shares, bank accounts, bank safes, and so on) such as were valid until 1948. It is estimated that some 25 per cent of the constituency of the Palestinian Arab citizens of Israel, approximately 250,000 persons, are classified in Israeli law as Class 'C' citizens, namely, as 'present-absentees'.

Also, subject to the said Absentees' Property Law of 1950, the Knesset determined in law a Class 'D' citizenship, namely, the denied citizenship of 750,000 1948 Palestine refugees and their descendants currently numbering according to UNRWA figures over four million persons. As pointed out above, under the terms of UN Resolutions 181(II) (Plan for Partition with Economic Union) of November 1947, the constitutive document of the State of Israel and the State of Palestine, recommending the partition of the territory of British Mandate Palestine into a 'Jewish State' and an 'Arab State' with economic union, and Jerusalem as a *corpus separatum*, the currently approximately four million 1948 Palestine refugees are entitled to the citizenship of the 'Jewish State'. Yet the Knesset, by force of the said Absentees' Property Law of 1950, and in violation of the norms of the Universal Declaration of Human Rights and the standards of international law, denationalized the mass of the 1948 Palestine refugees, denying their right to Israeli citizenship, thereby rendering them stateless.

It is in this context that the form of Israeli apartheid has to be considered, and judgement has to be exercised. Does the fact that the State of Israel has illegally nullified the citizenship of the majority of the Palestinian Arab population ordinarily resident in the territories allocated by UN Resolution 181(II) to the 'Jewish State' and annulled their rights to the titles of their properties inside Israel, while granting second- and third-class citizenship to the remnants of the Palestinian people that survived the crime against humanity perpetrated by the Israeli army under the cover of the 1948–49 war, justify Israeli claims to being 'the only democracy in the Middle East', or, rather, does the above justify the claims of those who submit to the international community that the State of Israel is possibly the last surviving apartheid state among the member states of the UN?

Needless to say, it is the view of this writer that the latter claim obtains. Israeli apartheid is indeed another form of apartheid, as the case of the destroyed Palestinian Arab village of Lubya and the South African Forest discussed above illustrates.

The Israeli apartheid legislator, unlike the South African apartheid legislator, did not insist on petty apartheid. The South African Forest, like all public spaces in Israel, is not segregated. There are no benches designated in law for 'Jews only' and benches for 'non-Jews'; buses for 'Jews' and buses for 'non-Jews'; beaches for 'Jews' and beaches for 'non-Jews' – but the South African Forest is planted over the ruins of the Palestinian Arab village of Lubya, veiling the war crime of the mass expulsion of its native indigenous population under the cover of the 1948–49 war, made stateless refugees outside the State of Israel and internally displaced persons inside the State of Israel. And the case of Lubya is far from unique. There are hundreds of such cases across the State of Israel.

The cattle of the neighbouring settlements of the so-called socialist cooperative Zionist settlements of Lavi and Sedeh Ilan are given access to graze there, but the 1948 Palestine refugees of Lubya are denied their right to return to their home village and properties there.

In all matters pertaining to the core of the Israeli–Palestinian conflict, the conflict between a settler-colonial state and the native indigenous population, namely, in all matters pertaining to the question of rights to property, land tenure, settlement and development, Israeli apartheid legislation is more radical than was South African apartheid legislation. The ruling by the Israeli Supreme Court sitting as the High Court of Justice on the case of Qaadan *vs.* Qatzir in March 2000 notwithstanding, to date some 93 per cent of the territory of the State of Israel is designated in law for settlement, cultivation and development for 'Jews only', whereas at the height of South African apartheid approximately 87 per cent of the territory of the Republic of South Africa was designated in law for the settlement, cultivation and development of 'Whites only'.

Not insisting on petty apartheid has veiled Israeli apartheid from scrutiny by the international community, allowed political Zionists and Israeli apologists to project Israeli apartheid as 'the only democracy in the Middle East', and shielded Israel from international sanctions for its blatant violation of international law, notably the Covenant on the

Suppression and Punishment of the Crimes of Apartheid of 1973. Let us hope that this state of affairs does not obtain for much longer.

Jewish presence, Arab absence: registration of births, citizenship and residence

Registration of births The registration of births in the State of Israel was regulated until 1965 by the Registration of Inhabitants Ordinance (1949), and as of 1965 by the Population Registry Law. Registration is administered by the Population Registry Division at the Ministry of the Interior. However, at the time of publication of *Israel: An Apartheid State*, the birth certificates issued in the State of Israel for newly born Jewish and non-Jewish babies differed in a number of important ways.

Birth certificates for Jews list the following categories:

- Religion (*dat*);
- Nationality (*leom*); and
- Citizenship (*ezrahut*) of the infant at the date of birth.

Birth certificates for non-Jews (Palestinian Arabs in our case) seemingly list the same categories:

- religion and confession (*al-din wa-al-taifa*);
- nationality (*al-qawmiyya*); and
- citizenship (*al-jinsiyya*) of the infant at the date of birth.

Closer examination of the forms current at the time of publication of *Israel: An Apartheid State*, however, revealed an important variation between the registration of the births of Jewish versus non-Jewish infants in the State of Israel. In the case of the Jewish infants, the registration of religion alone is stipulated. The registration of confession (orthodox, conservative or reform) is not required, presumably in order not to undermine the effective state-supported monopoly of the orthodox Jewish confession in Israel. (As already noted, conservative and reform Jewish Rabbis, who may legally lead their congregations in all parts of the world outside the territory of the State of Israel, are denied official recognition in the Jewish state.)

In the case of non-Jewish Palestinian Arab infants, however, the registration of confession (for example, Sunni Muslim, Shi'a Muslim) is mandatory, in line with the supreme policy of all Israeli governments to consolidate confessional divisions within the non-Jewish population.[29]

The examination of Jewish versus non-Jewish – in our case, Jewish versus Arab – birth certificates current at the time of publication of *Israel: An Apartheid State*, however, reveals a much more shocking practice: the citizenship of the Jewish infant is registered as Israeli at the time of his or her birth, whereas the citizenship of the non-Jewish Arab infant is left indefinite at the time of his or her birth. The documents reproduced below are facsimiles of the birth certificates of Mirah Doberzinsky, of Jewish religion and nationality, born on 14 May 1956 in Kefar Sava, and Mahmud Fawzi Aghbariyya, of Sunni Muslim religion and Arab nationality, born on 23 March 1957 in Umm al-Fahm. The citizenship of Mirah Doberzinsky at birth is *Israeli*. The citizenship of Mahmud Fawsi Aghbariyya at birth is *indefinite* (blank).

Both babies were born in the State of Israel. Both birth certificates were issued by the State of Israel, Ministry of the Interior, Population Registry Division. For the clerk at the Population Registry Division at the Ministry of the Interior a Jewish infant in the State of Israel has *Israeli* citizenship at birth, but an Arab infant in the State of Israel is *devoid of citizenship and is, therefore, stateless* at birth.

State of Israel
Ministry of Interior
Population Registry Division
Birth Registration Certificate
No. 61283
Name of the newborn: Mirah
Sex: Female
Family name: Doberzinsky
Place of birth: Kefar Sava Maternity Hospital
Date of birth: 14.5.1956
Religion & Nationality: Jewish
Name of parents:
Mother: Hannah Nussbaum
Father: Shimsbon Doberzinsky
The citizenship of the newborn on the date of birth: Israeli
Name of informant: Hannah Doberzinsky
Address of informant: Kefar Shemaryahu

I hereby certify that the newborn as registered above was registered on 27.5.1956 following the announcement of a live birth in the Residents Registry under Article 3 of the Registration of Inhabitants Ordinance – 1949, and in the Book of Births under Section 111 Paragraph (6) (1) of the People's Health Ordinance – 1940 according to Identity Number 5410167

This certificate was issued in the Population Registry Office, Herzliyyah Branch on 28.5.1956

(—) Registry Clerk

State of Israel
Ministry of Interior
Population Registry Division
Birth Registration Certificate
No. 17627
Name of the newborn: Mahmud
Sex: Male
Name of father: Fawsi
Name of grandfather: Abd al-Wahhab
Family name or Hamula [Tribe]: Aghbariyya
Place of birth: Umm Al-Fahm
Date of birth: 23.3.1957
Religion & Nationality: Sunni Muslim Arab
Name of mother: Ifat Aghbariyya
The citizenship of the newborn on the date of birth: –
Name of informant & address: Fawsi Abd al-Wahhab Aghbariyya, Umm al-Fahm

I hereby certify that the newborn as registered above was registered on 26.3.1957 following the announcement of a live birth in the Residents Registry under Article 3 of the Registration of Inhabitants Ordinance – 1949, and in the Book of Births under Section III Paragraph (6) (1) of the People's Health Ordinance – 1940 according to Identity Number H 447786

This certificate was issued in the Population Registry Office, Nazareth on 26.3.1957

(—) Registry Clerk

It is instructive, however, to realize that the unresolved ideological and legal dilemmas related to the question of 'who is a Jew' became more compounded over time. Given the significant increase over the last three decades of the existence of the State of Israel of the 'non-Jewish' component (estimated at up to 50 per cent) of the immigration to Israel from the former Soviet Union (totalling today approximately one million), the term 'Jew' became progressively more problematic as a designation of national identity for the national constituency that originates in the Zionist colonial enterprise in Palestine. Rather than accept that the term 'Jew' will not do as a designation of nationality in the multinational and multi-tribal State of Israel (see the Rufeisen case, above) and adopt a new term as a standard reference (such as Hebrew)[30] to designate the people concerned, the Israeli legislator chose to leave the dilemma unresolved and change the forms instead.

Today, Israeli identity cards no longer register nationality and

Israeli birth certificates no longer register citizenship. The registration (or otherwise) of citizenship of newborn babies has been moved to a form provided by the Ministry of Interior Population Administration to the hospitals entitled 'Announcement of Live Birth'. These forms are supplied to the hospitals in two versions: one with an Identity Card Number designated for the newborn baby and the second without an Identity Card Number designation.

The Ministry of Interior Population Administration provides the hospitals with detailed guidelines to determine which version to use with regard to each birth. Only if the mother and the father are citizens of Israel or if the mother and the father are residents of Israel and both have an Israeli ID card does the hospital invariably use the version with a designated Identity Card Number to announce a live birth. In all other cases the version without a designated Identity Card Number is to be used, and the parents are to be referred by the hospital for processing at the Regional Offices of the Population Administration of their region of residence.

Clauses 3.4.4 and 3.4.5 of the official guidelines issued by the Director of Monitoring and Control of the Ministry of Interior Population Administration caution the Regional Offices of the Population Administration 'not to leave with the parents the original copy of the Announcement of Live Birth form, nor any copy thereof', and suggest that the parents be given 'an official birth certificate instead' (3.4.4). The guidelines also direct the Regional Offices to 'transfer routinely, once a month', the original documents and copies of the Announcement of Live Birth forms pertaining to newborn babies whose live birth is registered on the version without a designated Identity Card Number to the central archive. 'It is imperative that no copies/photocopies/birth certificates are kept in the Regional Office' (3.4.5).

As noted above, the official birth certificate no longer registers the citizenship of the newborn on the date of his or her birth. The designation of an Identity Card Number is a necessary condition for registration of citizenship with the Population Administration, and as the above guidelines, notably Clauses 3.4.4 and 3.4.5, suggest, the Population Administration is anxious to keep the procedures relevant to registration of citizenship pertaining to newborn babies whose live birth was registered in hospital on the version of the form without a designated Identity Card Number as far as possible from public view.

Citizenship As noted above, citizenship is a certificate representing a legal relationship between the individual and the state. Democratic citizenship is a certificate representing the recognition by the state of the right of every citizen to equal access to the political process of the state (e.g., to elect and be elected to all of the offices of the state); to the civil process (e.g., to equal standing before the law and to property); to social and welfare services (e.g., religious services); and to the material resources of the state (e.g., land and water). Article 15 of the Universal Declaration of Human Rights stipulates that: (1) Everyone has the right to a nationality, and (2) No one shall be arbitrarily deprived of his nationality nor denied the right to change his nationality.

As noted above, it is the core argument of this work that Israeli citizenship, citizenship of the State of Israel, cannot be classified as a democratic citizenship. Unlike the US legislature, for instance, which recognizes, under a democratic Constitution, one universal citizenship for all US citizens without distinction of nationality, religion, language, tribe, sex, or any other social status, the State of Israel does not have one single universal citizenship for all of its citizens. Rather, informed by the dominant ideology of political Zionism, the Knesset legislated a schedule of four classes of citizenship based on racial discrimination and representing blatant inequality in law, representing another form of apartheid.

Under Israel Nationality Law of 1952, Israeli nationality – more accurately, Israeli citizenship (*ezrahut*) – is granted or denied i) by 'return' (as per Article 2); ii) by 'residence in Israel' (as per Article 3); iii) by 'birth' (as per Article 4); iv) by 'birth and residence in Israel' (as per Article 4a); v) by 'adoption' (as per Article 4b); vi) by 'naturalization' (as per Articles 5–8); or vii) by 'grant' (as per Article 9). Citizenship by naturalization is a derivative of the entitlement to citizenship by residence in that the law stipulates as a condition for the acquisition of citizenship by naturalization that the applicant be 'entitled to reside in Israel permanently' (Israel Nationality Law of 1952, Article 5[a] [3]).

Of the seven categories above, the first three deserve particular attention for our purpose. In this connection it is useful to distinguish in this context three separate yet – given Israeli legislation – closely related concepts or categories:

1. citizenship;
2. nationality; and
3. religion.

As noted below, these three categories constitute the three basic divisions of population registration in Israel (Population Registry Law of 1965). Entitlement or lack of entitlement to citizenship in the State of Israel for Jews is determined in the first instance by the Law of Return of 1950 (Article 1: Every Jew has the right to come to this country as an *oleh*). Citizenship in Israel, for Jews who are not born to parents one of whom is an Israeli citizen, is granted by 'return', and can be granted only by 'return', and that only Jews can be granted citizenship by 'return'.[31] Birth within the territory of the State of Israel *per se* does not constitute grounds for entitlement to citizenship.

In other words, a Jewish immigrant to Israel (*oleh*) and a Jewish infant born in Israel to parents who are not citizens of Israel both acquire citizenship by 'return'. Under the Law of Return of 1950, the acquisition of citizenship for Jews is 'automatic'. Should the Jewish immigrant concerned, or the parents (or guardians) of the newly born Jewish infant not wish to acquire citizenship in the State of Israel, they are expected to make an explicit statement to that effect. In the absence of such statement, they will be registered as citizens by default upon immigration or registration of birth.

As indicated by David Ben-Gurion in his speech of presentation of the Law of Return before the Knesset (3 July 1950):

> The Law of Return is one of the fundamental laws of the State of Israel. It embodies a central purpose of our state, the purpose of the ingathering of exiles. This law states that it is not this state which grants Jews from abroad the right to settle in it, but that this right is inherent by virtue of being a Jew, if one wishes to settle in the country ... This right precedes the State of Israel, and it is this right which built the State of Israel. (quoted in Orr 1983: 29; see Appendix II)

The normative paradigmatical registration for a Jewish citizen in the State of Israel would be:

- Citizenship: Israeli
- Nationality: Jewish
- Religion: Jewish.

As detailed above, fifty-odd years after the establishment of the State of Israel in 1948, this paradigm no longer obtains. Given the contradictions underpinning the definition of who is a Jew in the Jewish state, and faced with the reality of a growing constituency of hundreds of thousands of citizens of the State of Israel who are not Arab and not classified as 'Jews' under the Population Registry Law of 1965, notably immigrants from the former Soviet Union, the paradigmatic registration of a Jewish citizen in the State of Israel is being progressively challenged. In 2002 the reference to nationality in Israeli identity cards was removed altogether.

Citizenship by return The inherent fractures of secular Jewish identity and, specifically, secular Jewish identity as institutionalized in the State of Israel as a Jewish state in the political Zionist sense of the term, are embodied in the normative paradigm above. This paradigm would today be opposed by many among the new, Israeli-born, secular atheist 'Jewish' generation who regard themselves to be Israeli by citizenship, Israeli (or Hebrew) by nationality, with no religious affiliation, as well as by many new immigrants born to a non-Jewish mother, and many converts from Judaism to other religions who would regard themselves as Israeli by citizenship, Jewish by nationality and, for example, Catholic by religion.

Two critical cases are regarded in the literature as legal landmarks in this context. The first case was that of Oswald Rufeisen (Brother Daniel), a Polish Jew who converted to Catholicism during the Second World War. He joined the Carmelite Order, and immigrated to Israel in 1958. Rufeisen demanded the right of immigration and citizenship under the Law of Return as granted to every Jew. He insisted that he was a Jew by nationality and a Catholic by religion. The Israeli Ministry of Interior refused to recognize him as a Jew for the purpose of 'return', although under orthodox religious Jewish law (*Halakhah*) Oswald Rufeisen is defined as a Jew, his conversion to Catholicism notwithstanding.

The Israeli Supreme Court of Justice upheld the government refusal (*Judgments of the Supreme Court of Israel* [PADI], Case No. 72162, Vol. 16 [IV], 1962, pp. 2,428–52). Oswald Rufeisen was granted residence in Israel under the Entry into Israel Law of 1952, and subsequently, citizenship (by 'residence', not by 'return'). He was eventually registered under the Population Registration Law of 1965 as Israeli by citizenship, indefinite (blank) by nationality, and Catholic by religion.

The second case was that of Major Benjamin Shalit who, together with his wife, Ann Shalit (*née* Geddes) demanded that their children be registered as Israeli by citizenship, Jewish by nationality and indefinite (blank) by religion. The Shalit parents were conscientious atheists: Benjamin Shalit was an atheist of Jewish descent, and Ann Shalit an atheist of Christian descent. The Israeli Ministry of Interior rejected the Shalit request. In this case, the position of the government coincided with the ruling of orthodox religious Jewish law (*Halakhah*), which determines that children born to a non-Jewish mother are non-Jews.

The Israeli Supreme Court of Justice, however, upheld the Shalit appeal (*Judgments of the Supreme Court of Israel* [PADI], Case No. 58/ 68, Vol. 23 [II], 1969, pp. 477–608). The two Shalit children were thus registered under the Population Registration Law (1965) as Israeli by citizenship, Jewish by nationality and indefinite (blank) by religion. The verdict of the Israeli Supreme Court of Justice on the Shalit appeal was published in January 1970. Less than two months later, in March 1970, the Knesset passed an amendment to the Law of Return of 1950 and to the Population Registry Law of 1965 in order to prevent the ruling from becoming a legal precedent. The amendments read as follows:

Law of Return (Amendment No. 2), 1970
Addition of Sections 4A and 4B
1. In the Law of Return, 1950, the following sections shall be inserted after section 4:
Rights of members of family
4A. (a) The rights of a Jew under this Law and the rights of an *oleh* under the Nationality Law, 1952, as well as the rights of an *oleh* under any other enactment, are also vested in a child and a grandchild of a Jew, the spouse of a Jew, the spouse of a child of a Jew and the spouse of a grandchild of a Jew except for a person who has been a Jew and has voluntarily changed his religion.
(b) It shall be immaterial whether or not a Jew by whose right a right under subsection (a) is claimed is still alive and whether or not he has immigrated to Israel.
(c) The restrictions and conditions prescribed in respect of a Jew or an *oleh* by or under this Law or by the enactments referred to in subsection (a) shall also apply to a person who claims a right under subsection (a).
Definition
4B. *For the purpose of this Law, 'Jew' means a person who was born of a Jewish mother or who has become converted to Judaism and who is not a member of another religion* [emphasis added].

And the Population Registry Law of 1965 was amended accordingly to the effect that a new Clause 3A was inserted after Clause 3 as follows:

Power of registration and definition
3A. (a) A person shall not be registered by ethnic affiliation registration or religion if a notification under this Law or another entry in the Registry or a public document indicates that he is not a Jew, so long as the said notification, entry or document has not been controverted to the satisfaction of the Chief Registration Officer or so long as declaratory judgment of a competent court or tribunal has not otherwise determined.
(b) *For the purpose of this Law and of any registration or document thereunder, 'Jew' has the same meaning as in section 4B of the Law of Return, 1950* [emphasis added].

(c) This section shall not derogate from a registration effected before its coming into force.

(*Laws of the State of Israel* [authorized translation from the Hebrew prepared by the Ministry of Justice], Vol. 24, Jerusalem, 1969/70, pp. 28, 29)

Thus, when the third Shalit child was born in Israel after the passage of the above amendments, the child's nationality could no longer be registered as Jewish under the law (*Judgments of the Supreme Court of Israel* [PADI], Case No. 18/72, Vol. 26[I], 1972, p. 334).

Following the passage of the amendment, the question of 'who is a Jew' for the purpose of 'return' to the Jewish state was given a legally binding, quasi-religious definition: '"Jew" means a person who was born of a Jewish mother or who has become converted to Judaism and who is not a member of another religion' (Amendment No. 2 [4B]). In parallel, the State of Israel extended Israeli citizenship not only to any Jew throughout the world upon immigration into Israel, but, in addition, following the 1971 Amendment to the Israel Nationality Law, also to some Jews throughout the world *prior to* immigration into Israel:

> Where a person has expressed his desire to settle in Israel, being a person who has received, or is entitled to receive an *oleh* [Jewish immigrant] visa under the Law of Return, 1950, the Minister of Interior may, at his discretion, grant him, upon his application, nationality by virtue of return even before his *aliyah* [arrival of the Jewish immigrant at one of Israel's official ports of entry]. (Nationality [Amendment No. 3] Law, 1971)

Citizenship by residence in Israel The laws governing access to residence for non-Jews in Israel are as follows: Absentees' Property Law of 1950; Entry into Israel Law of 1952; and Israel Nationality Law of 1952.[32]

This exposition will focus on the Absentees' Property Law of 1950, it being the principal law passed by the Israeli legislator to regulate the residence of, or more precisely the denial of residence to, the majority of the Palestinian Arab inhabitants and their descendants of the territories that came under Israeli rule and occupation following the 1948–49 war.

For non-Jews both of whose parents are not citizens of the State of Israel, citizenship of the State of Israel is determined by 'residence', and the granting of resident status – temporary or permanent – is at the administrative discretion of the minister of the interior, whose effective policy is to discourage non-Jews from immigrating to or remaining in the

Jewish state. According to the stipulations of Israeli law, non-Jews cannot acquire citizenship by 'return'. Thus, under Israeli law, any Jew throughout the world has the right of immediate immigration to, settlement in and citizenship of the State of Israel after an alleged forced absence of 2,000 years, but the displaced Palestinian Arab refugees of 1948 and their descendants – some four million people today – are denied the same right, in violation of international law and United Nations resolutions, although their forced absence is less than 60 years.

The Israeli legislator does not recognize the term 'refugee' as far as the Palestinian Arab is concerned. In the view of the Israeli legislator, the Palestinian Arab population both inside and outside the territory of the State of Israel is divided into the two classes, as outlined above: those who, in the view of the law, exist and are 'present'; and, those who, in the view of the law, do not exist and as a consequence are classified as officially 'absent'. The division is not, however, as clear-cut as it may seem. The law manufactures the oxymoron of 'present absentees'.

'Present absentees' in the State of Israel are Palestinian Arab persons who, in some significant respects of the law, are 'present' as citizens of the State of Israel. For instance, as citizens who are 'present' they are eligible to vote and be elected to all state and other offices. On the other hand, in other significant respects of the law they are 'absent' – they do not exist in the view of the law. Since they are classified as 'absentees' under the Absentees' Property Law of 1950, their rights to the title of their movable and immovable properties acquired until 1948 inside Israel have been nullified, their 'presence' in Israel as citizens notwithstanding. The titles to their movable and immovable properties, like those of the some four million 1948 Palestine refugees outside the State of Israel, are vested in the Custodian of Absentees' Property. They are 'present absentees', namely, internally displaced persons.

Some 25 per cent of the total of one million Palestinian Arab citizens of Israel, approximately 250,000, are 'present absentees'. Once classified as 'present absentee' under Israeli law, one is destined to remain a 'present absentee'. It is important to note that the status of 'absentee' is inherited. Children of 'absentees', whether born inside or outside the State of Israel, are similarly classified as 'absentees'.

The Absentees' Property Law of 1950 defines 'absentee' as follows:

Interpretation
1. In this Law –
   (a) 'property' includes immovable and movable property, monies, a vested or contingent right in property, goodwill and any right in a body of persons or in its management;

(b) 'absentee' means –

(1) A person who, at any time during the period between 29 November 1947 and the day on which a declaration is published under Section 9(d) of the Law and Administration Ordinance (1948), that the state of emergency declared by the Provisional Council of State on 19 May 1948 has ceased to exist, was a legal owner of any property situated in the area of Israel or enjoyed or held it, whether by himself or through another, and who at any time during the said period – [33]

(i) was a national or citizen of the Lebanon, Egypt, Syria, Saudi Arabia, Trans-Jordan, Iraq or the Yemen, or

(ii) was in one of these countries or in any part of Palestine outside the area of Israel, or

(iii) was a Palestinian citizen and left his ordinary place of residence in Palestine

(a) for a place outside Palestine before 1 September 1948; or

(b) for a place in Palestine held at the time by forces which sought to prevent the establishment of the State of Israel or which fought against it after its establishment;

(2) A body of persons which, at any time during the period specified in paragraph (1), was a legal owner of any property situated in the area of Israel or enjoyed or held such property, whether by itself or through another, and all the members, partners, shareholders, directors or managers of which are absentees within the meaning of paragraph (1), or the management of the business of which is otherwise decisively controlled by such absentees, or all the capital of which is in the hands of such absentees.

The Absentees' Property Law of 1950, having defined the mass of the Palestinian Arab refugees from the territories that came under Israeli rule and occupation in 1948–49 out of existence as 'absentees', not only denies them their right of residence (and citizenship) in the Jewish state as stipulated by the 1947 UN Resolution, but at the same time denies them their right to their vast properties inside Israel.

It is difficult to see why leaving one's ordinary place of residence in Palestine for a place outside Palestine, or a place in Palestine held at the time by forces that sought to prevent the establishment of the State of Israel, or fought against it after its establishment, should entail losing the right to one's properties. The overwhelming majority of the Palestinian Arabs who were forcibly moved were non-combatants. The men, women and children who involuntarily left their ordinary place of residence in Palestine for a place outside Palestine (in the Middle East, Europe or elsewhere), or for a place in Palestine held at the time by forces that sought to prevent the establishment of the State of Israel, did so in an attempt to secure the welfare of their families when their country was ripped apart by war.

And anyway, individual rights to property are protected under the Universal Declaration of Human Rights and the standards of international law, regardless of whether the holders of the title to the said rights have left their ordinary place of residence voluntarily or otherwise.

Needless to say, the procedures of nullification of citizenship and alienation of property applied by Israeli legislation against non-Jewish Palestinian Arab persons under the Absentees' Property Law of 1950 are not applied against Jewish Palestinians. Their citizenship is guaranteed in any circumstance under the Law of Return of 1950, and their property is presumably secure in perpetuity through an alleged biblical title.

In the course of the escalation culminating in the Gulf War of 1991, Israel braced itself against possible Iraqi attacks against its civilian population by Scud missiles equipped with chemical and biological warheads. The population, almost without exception, carried their gas-masks on their persons at all times, and most households followed the spurious directives of the civilian defence and set aside 'gas-proof' rooms in their flats and houses.

With the outbreak of the war, however, a significant proportion of Jewish families inside Israel, notably in the metropolitan areas at the centre of the country, fearing for the safety of their children, decided that these protective measures were not good enough, and packed up to move to locations of relative safety. Some went abroad; others booked themselves into hotels in Jerusalem, assuming the Iraqi government would refrain from targeting the Holy City; still others took their families to the Dead Sea holiday resorts and health spas or to the southernmost town in Israel, the Red Sea resort town of Eilat; some were reported to have sought shelter with Arab friends in Arab cities and villages in Israel.

It is estimated that in January 1991 up to 50 per cent of the Jewish population of Tel Aviv evacuated the city in this way.

The mayor of Tel Aviv at the time, Reserve General Shlomo Lahat, was mortified; he accused the mass of his constituency who left their homes in Tel Aviv to seek better safety for their families of 'desertion', condemning the families who 'deserted' the city as having 'deserted the homeland'.

Needless to say, he was not heeded. For responsible families securing the safety of their children in times of war is a paramount consideration.

The war came and went. The fear of Iraqi missile attack proved to be much exaggerated. In total 39 fell inside the territory of the State of Israel in the Tel Aviv and Haifa areas. None carried chemical or biological warheads.

The mass of the Jewish families who left their homes to seek more secure shelter elsewhere packed their belongings and returned home. They parked their cars next to their apartment blocks or their suburban homes; took their door keys out of their pockets and opened their homes; went to the nearby ATM and drew money out of their bank accounts; called their employers and resumed their jobs (assuming their jobs were still there); contacted their brokers to review their investment portfolios and suchlike. In short, most of the Jewish families who left their homes to seek more secure shelter elsewhere correctly assumed that they would be able to pick up after the war where they had left off, and in the majority of cases this was indeed the case.

Their mayor, Shlomo Lahat (Linder), was an officer in the Giv'ati battalion in the 1948–49 war who took part in nearly all the major battles on the Jerusalem and southern fronts, may or may not have acted in, for example, Abu Shusha in conformity with such criminal 'orders of the day' as were issued in the daily battle-sheets of the political commissar of the Giv'ati battalion, Abba Kobner, a survivor of the Nazi occupation of Europe and the Kobna Ghetto rebellion, who turned to Nazi rhetoric himself (see below). Shlomo Lahat saw fit to vilify his constituency for their failure to demonstrate fortitude in crisis; for their lack of patriotism; for their alleged 'desertion of the homeland' – but he did not proclaim that the titles to the flats, houses, lands and other immovable shares, deposit boxes, bank accounts, jewellery and other movables owned by the families who left Tel Aviv in fear of war would be vested with the families who remained in Tel Aviv.

After all, the Tel Aviv constituents at the receiving end of his abuse were Jews – not Arabs, and clearly not the 1948 Palestine refugees forcibly expelled from their homes, *inter alia*, by his Giv'ati battalion.

Following the establishment of the State of Israel, the Palestinian Arab population remaining within the boundaries of the new state was immediately subject to a separate administration of the military government under the Defence (Emergency) Regulations of 1945, introduced by the British Mandate, and incorporated lock, stock and barrel by the Knesset into the legal corpus of the new state, previous condemnation of these Regulations by leading political Zionist lawyers as worse than 'Nazi laws' notwithstanding (see below). The country was divided into three regional Commands: the Northern, the Central and the Southern. This separate military government was administered by the commanders of the said three commands in their capacity as military governors, appointed by, and accountable to, the chief-of-staff. Every aspect of the life of the Palestinian Arab population inside Israel was regulated and determined by the military government until 1966.[34] In Israel, the military government was dismantled in 1966, only to be set up one year later in the post-1967 Israeli-occupied territories: the West Bank, the Gaza Strip, the Sinai (returned to Egyptian sovereignty in 1982), and the Golan Heights (annexed to Israel in 1981).

It is important to note that it was the separate administration of the military government inside pre-1967 Israel that was dismantled, not the Defence (Emergency) Regulations of 1945. These have remained in force in all the territories under Israeli rule and occupation since the declaration of the state of emergency by the Provisional Council of State on 19 May 1948, four days after the declaration of the establishment of the State of Israel on 15 May of that year.

In due course, all Palestinian Arabs who remained under Israeli jurisdiction following the 1948–49 war were granted permanent residence in Israel and regular identity cards (see below). They were not, however, necessarily granted citizenship. A belated insight into the legal reality of the citizenship of the Palestinian Arab population inside pre-1967 Israel was provided in 1980 by the Israeli minister of the interior, Joseph Burg, following passage by the Knesset in July of that year of the Fourth Amendment (1980) to the Israel Nationality Law of 1952:

> An announcement concerning the granting of Israeli citizenship to more than 30 thousand Arab residents in the state … was made yesterday by Minister of Interior Joseph Burg in the course of his visit to Arab villages in the western Galilee … This applies to residents who left the country in the War of Independence, and were not here in 1952 when Israel Nationality Law was passed in Parliament. ('Burg Announces the Granting of Israeli Citizenship to 30 Thousand Arabs', *Haaretz*, 21 November 1980)

And *Maariv* of the same date explains in somewhat greater detail:

> The new citizenship law, which enables the Arabs who live in Israel to apply for Israeli citizenship, will now enable more than 30 thousand Arab residents who are defined as present-absentees to obtain Israeli citizenship. This applies to people who fled from Israel in the War of Independence, and who returned to their villages and their families in various ways, mainly after 1952. ('Arabs Who Fled and Returned Can Get Citizenship', *Maariv*, 21 November 1980)

In other words, we now know that by 1980, thirty-two years after the establishment of the State of Israel, at least 5 per cent of the Palestinian Arab population, residents of the State of Israel inside its pre-1967 borders, were stateless. The Fourth Amendment (1980) to the Israel Nationality Law of 1952, ratified by the Knesset on 29 July 1980, modifies Article 3 of the law as follows:

Extension of nationality by residence to additional categories of persons

3A(a) A person born before the establishment of the State shall be an Israel national by residence in Israel from the date of the coming into force of the Nationality (Amendment No. 4) Law, 1980 (hereinafter referred to as 'the date of the 1980 amendment') if he meets the following requirements:

(1) He is not a resident of Israel by virtue of any other provision of this Law;

(2) he was a Palestinian citizen immediately before the establishment of the State;

(3) on 14 July 1952 he was a resident of Israel and was registered in the Register of Inhabitants under the Registration of Inhabitants Ordinance, 1949;

(4) on the date of the 1980 Amendment, he was a resident of Israel and registered in the Population Register;

(5) he is not a national of one of the states mentioned in section 2A of the Prevention of Infiltration (Offences and Jurisdiction) Law, 1954.

(b) A person born after the establishment of the State shall be an Israel national by residence in Israel from the date of the 1980 amendment if he meets the following requirements:

(1) He is not an Israel national by virtue of any other provision of this Law;

(2) on the date of the 1980 amendment, he was a resident of Israel and was registered in the Population Register;

(3) he is a descendant of a person who meets the requirements of paragraphs (1) to (3) of subsection (a).

The full implications of Article 3 prior to its amendment in 1980 were outlined by Member of the Knesset Eliezer Peri (United Workers' Party [MAPAM]) in the Knesset debate on the proposed law at the time:

Section 3, which essentially applies to the 170,000 Arabs in the country, may deny citizenship to over 90 per cent of the Arabs. For an Arab inhabitant to get automatic citizenship, he must pass through four sieves … I doubt that even the five Arab members of Parliament, affiliated with MAPAI and supporters of the coalition, have a Palestinian passport or

Palestinian certificate of citizenship by which they could prove that they were Palestinian citizens ... In order to obtain citizenship, the person in question had to be registered by 1 March, 1952. There are considerable numbers of Arabs who have failed, not by their own default, to register at the Registration of Inhabitants Offices; others, because of negligence were denied, under the law, automatic Israeli citizenship ... The third sieve through which the Arab has to go is the determination of his being entitled to permanent residence in Israel. The law fails to specify who is entitled to become an Israeli resident. These three requirements are necessary but not sufficient. In addition a fourth requirement is demanded: that the person in question lived in the country from the date of the establishment of the State of Israel to the day of coming into force of this law. 1 doubt if as many as ten per cent of the Israeli Arab population could prove that they answer positively to all the four requirements demanded by the law ... This law gives the administration innumerable possibilities. If the administration so wills, it will grant citizenship to Arabs, and if it so wills, it will deny citizenship to over 90 per cent. (quoted in Davis and Mezvinsky 1975: 95, 96)

It must also be emphasized, however, that under this Amendment only a portion, not necessarily the majority, of the stateless Palestinian Arab residents of Israel who were born after the establishment of the state are entitled to citizenship, and that is because Subsection (b) Paragraph (3) makes the granting of Israeli citizenship conditional on being an offspring of at least one parent who, on the eve of the establishment of the state, was a Palestinian subject (see Subsection [a] Paragraph [2] above).

Thus the legal situation has not, in fact, altered at all for an undis-closed number of Palestinian Arabs born in Israel after the establish-ment of the state, who did not become Israeli citizens under any other stipulation of this law, and who, on the date of the 1980 Amendment were registered in the Israel Population Registry, but who are the offspring of parents who could not prove that they were Palestinian subjects on the eve of the establishment of the state. Their status remains that of people who are stateless in their own homeland.

For the approximately four million expelled 1948 Palestine refu-gees and exiles outside the boundaries of pre-1967 Israel, the status of 'absentee' entails both denationalization, namely, denial of Israeli citizenship, and the alienation of their properties, denial of all of their rights of ownership inside the State of Israel.

Following the passage of the Fourth Amendment (1980) to the Israel Nationality Law of 1952, for the approximately one million Palestinian

Arabs resident inside the boundaries of the pre-1967 State of Israel, the status of 'absentee' no longer entails denationalization. It is estimated that all 'present absentees' are now citizens of the State of Israel.[35] But the entitlement to Israeli citizenship does not in any way alter their status of 'absentees' as far as their right to property is concerned. The alienation of their properties – acquired or inherited prior to the establishment of the State of Israel in 1948 – under the Absentees' Property Law of 1950 remains in force irrespective of whether the persons concerned are Israeli citizens, or otherwise. As noted above, the status of 'absentee' is inherited, and only non-Jews in the Jewish state, first and foremost Palestinian Arabs, can be so classified.

Also as noted above, unlike the US legislature, which recognizes, under a democratic Constitution, one universal citizenship for all US citizens without distinction of nationality, religion, language, tribe, sex, or any other social status, the State of Israel does not have one single universal citizenship for all of its citizens. Rather, informed by the dominant ideology of political Zionism, the Knesset legislated four schedules of citizenship based on racial discrimination and representing blatant inequality in law, in other words, representing another form of apartheid.

In the State of Israel the right of a citizen classified in law as a 'non-Jew' (namely, an 'Arab') to partake in the political process is formally equal to the right of a citizen classified in law as a 'Jew'. Likewise the standing of a citizen classified in law as a 'non-Jew' before the courts of law is in principle equal to the standing of citizen classified in law as a 'Jew' (see note 27). On the other hand the right of a citizen classified in law as a 'non-Jew' to the social and welfare services and the material resources of the state and to property are *not* equal to those of a citizen classified in law as a 'Jew'. The ruling by the Israeli Supreme Court sitting as the High Court of Justice on the case of Qaadan *vs*. Qatzir in March 2000 notwithstanding (see Chapter 5), the State of Israel was established, and so far remains, an apartheid state.

Citizenship by birth Under the Israel Nationality Law of 1952 (Amendment No. 4):

4(a) The following shall, from the date of their birth, be Israel nationals by birth:

(1) a person born in Israel while his father or mother was an Israel national;

(2) a person born outside Israel while his father or mother was an Israel national –

    (a) by return;

    (b) by residence in Israel;

    (c) by naturalization;

    (d) under paragraph (1).

(b) For the purpose of this section, where a person is born after the death of one of his parents, it shall be sufficient if that parent was an Israel national at the time of his or her death.

Needless to say, the option of citizenship by birth is denied to the constituencies that under UN Resolution 181(II) of November 1947 are entitled to claim it – the 1948 Palestine refugees.

Histadrut: *continuity and change*

The *Histadrut* ('The Federation') was established in 1920 as the General Federation of Hebrew Workers in the Land of Israel in an effort by the two rival major labour Zionist parties, *Ahdut ha-Avodah* and *Hapo'el ha-Tza'ir*, to coordinate Jewish labour matters. Until 1948 the *Histadrut* incorporated the primary economic infrastructure of the Jewish *yishuv* (Zionist community) in Palestine, controlling the mainstream of Zionist instruments of colonization, economic production and marketing, labour employment and defence (the *Haganah*), with trade union activity as only one division of its activities.

In the period of the British Mandate government of Palestine (1922–48) a *modus vivendi* based on a *de facto* division of labour was established between the colonial British government (in charge of enforcing 'law and order', security and taxation), the WZO/JA (representing the *yishuv* before the British government and controlling Zionist foreign relations and fundraising) and the *Histadrut* (managing and developing the economic infrastructure of the *Yishuv*, directing the political mobilization of the Jewish workers and controlling the organized Zionist labour force).

The *Histadrut* established the network of agricultural cooperative (*kibbutz*, *moshav* and other) settlements; General Sick Fund (*Kupat Holim Kelalit*); educational network of kindergartens and schools (Workers' Section); daily newspaper (*Davar*); publishing house ('*Am Oved*); construction companies (*Solel Boneh*); industrial and manufacturing concerns and holding companies (Kur); housing associations (*Shikun 'Ovdim*); banks (*Bank ha-Po'alim*); insurance companies (*Ha-Seneh*); tourism (*Histour*); agricultural marketing companies (*Tenuvah*); supplies company (*Ha-Mashbir*); labour exchange offices for unemployed workers; and more.

In other words the *Histadrut*, rather than being a trade union federation in the social democratic European sense of the term, was founded (together with the WZO/JA) as a primary forerunner institution of the State of Israel in the making. After the establishment of the State of Israel in 1948, the *Histadrut* developed to become the second largest employer in Israel, which also had a Department for Trade Unions. Half a century after its establishment the *Histadrut*-owned enterprises incorporated in the framework of the Workers' Company contributed just under 20 per cent of Israel's GNP. Needless to say, in these circumstances it was difficult for the *Histadrut* to maintain a balance between its interests as the second largest employer in Israel (second to the state) and the trade union interests of the workers, including its own employees organized in the framework of the *Histadrut* Department for Trade Unions.

Since the establishment of the State of Israel in 1948, however, the *Histadrut* has undergone progressive change, reflecting and responding to economic, social and political changes inside Israel, as well as the Middle East region and the world as a whole.

The changes began immediately in the wake of the establishment of the State of Israel when in 1948 certain functions hitherto under the control of the *Histadrut*, such as education and labour exchanges, were transferred to the state whereas other functions, mainly in the area of agricultural settlements, were intensified. These changes culminated in 1994, when MK Haim Ramon's New *Histadrut* list (RAM) won plurality in the May 1994 elections for the 17th *Histadrut* General Congress (46.42 per cent of the vote) and Haim Ramon became chairman. Under his leadership the bureaucratic and corporate structure of the *Histadrut* was reformed. The reforms were officially launched in the 17th *Histadrut* General Congress convened in two Sessions, Session One in July 1994 and Session Two (the 'Session of Reforms') in January 1995; and the *Histadrut* was renamed the New *Histadrut* (New General Federation of Workers).

The reforms included the overall sale of the *Histadrut* lucrative industrial and manufacturing assets as well as other holdings (such as Kur, *Bank ha-Po'alim*) in the private market. The sale made it possible for the *Histadrut* to plug its mounting financial deficits and also reduced the degree of conflict of interests between the interests of the *Histadrut* as employer and the duties of the *Histadrut* Department for Trade Unions.

Below I propose to consider some milestones in this process of change.

Change of name of the Histadrut *and Arab membership* True to its name and commitment to Zionist ideology and practice, until 1960 the *Histadrut* did not allow Arab citizens of Israel into its ranks. It was only in 1960 (at the ninth *Histadrut* convention) that legal provisions were made extending membership in the *Histadrut* to Arab workers who were citizens of Israel. In 1966, the tenth *Histadrut* convention introduced the official change of the name of the *Histadrut* federation from the 'General Federation of Hebrew Workers in the Land of Israel' to the 'General Federation of Workers in the Land of Israel' and corresponding adjustments were made in the Constitution of the *Histadrut*. The reference to 'Hebrew' workers was removed from the name of this *Histadrut* and from Chapter 1, Article (1) of the Constitution ('The Foundations of the *Histadrut*'), otherwise leaving the original pre-1966 text intact.

The change of the official name of the *Histadrut* was strongly debated, and through the debate, the underlying motives for the introduction of the change were revealed. Prominent among the opponents of the change was future prime minister, Member of Knesset (MK) Shimon Peres, then representing the Israel Workers' List (RAFI).[36] This is what he had to say:

> The question of the change of name will become more serious if we recall that though the name of the Histadrut Federation implies no limitation, it does imply a commitment. Are we not a Federation aiming – and not just chanting in its anthems – for *aliyah* (Jewish immigration)? A Federation dealing with the absorption of *aliyah*? A Federation dealing with the teaching of the Hebrew language? This is clearly a General Federation. This is clearly a Hebrew Federation in Israel. Let us not make it nameless. Let us not make it devoid of identity. Let us not deny its anthems. Let us not manipulate its challenges. This is not a Federation that ends with a question mark. I heard that one of the additional arguments for change of name is: What will they say in the world? I do not consider the proposed apologetics as necessary. (Joseph Olitzki [ed.], *The Tenth Histadrut Convention, 3–7 January 1966, Tel Aviv-Jaffa: Complete Protocols of the Debates*, p. 541)

The late MK Israel Yeshaayahu, Chairman of the *Histadrut* Standing Committee, responded to the comments made by Shimon Peres above, assuring him that although a new reality had been created with the opening of the gates of the *Histadrut* to Arab workers, and although it was necessary to effect a change in the name of the *Histadrut* to make it compatible with the changes effected by this new reality, 'the content and the mission of the *Histadrut*' were not thereby altered (ibid.: 547).

It should be pointed out that the change of name entailed the removal of the term 'Hebrew', but not the removal of the reference to the 'Land of Israel'. The Amendment proposed by the Israeli Communist Party (MAKI) to alter the name of the *Histadrut* to the 'General Federation of Workers in Israel' was turned down. After all, in 1966 the *Histadrut* saw no reason to replace its commitment to the Zionist mission in the Land of Israel for the more modest territorial Zionist commitment inside the boundaries of the State of Israel.

It is also important to point out that Israel is an apartheid state and that all Zionist parties and institutions – political and other differences notwithstanding – are committed to the aim of guaranteeing in law and in practice an ethnic majority of 'Jewish' citizens in the State of Israel. The watershed debate inside Israeli political, economic and military establishments, including the *Histadrut*, is how 'Jewish' ethnocracy can be best guaranteed in law and practice.

One year later, the Israeli victory in the 1967 war indeed gave ample scope for the *Histadrut* to demonstrate that the said change of name did not in any way entail alteration of the Zionist mission of the *Histadrut*, and that the General Federation of Labour in the Land of Israel could effectively accommodate itself to the reality of post-1967 Israeli occupation, and abandon the Palestinian-Arab workers of the occupied West Bank and Gaza Strip to the most extreme and degrading forms of economic exploitation and social and political repression.[37]

The late MK Israel Yeshaayahu, however, was both right and wrong. The change of name did not in any way affect the content and the colonial mission of the *Histadrut*, especially not in the area of Zionist agricultural settlements. But, in parallel, the opening of the gates of membership in the *Histadrut* (first the *Histadrut* trade union structures, and subsequently the Workers' Company) to Arab workers who were citizens of Israel did contribute significantly to the progressive empowerment of the Palestinian Arab community in Israel inside the governing institutions of the *Histadrut* as well as outside.

It seems that the last bastion of *Histadrut* Zionist exclusion of non-Jewish members, first and foremost the Arab citizens of Israel, remains the land. In the area of corporate Zionist agricultural settlement, notably the *kibbutz* and *moshav* cooperative agricultural settlements, the *Histadrut* remained very much and officially exclusively Hebrew. To the best of my knowledge there has not been to date a single admission of an Arab citizen of Israel as a *kibbutz* and/or *moshav* and/or community settlement member, the ruling by the Israeli Supreme Court sitting as the High Court of Justice on the case of Qaadan *vs.* Qatzir in March 2000 notwithstanding. While the name of the *Histadrut* was changed to remove the reference to 'Hebrew' workers from its title, as was the name of the Workers' Company (see below), the name of the holding company of all cooperative *kibbutz* and *moshav* settlements, *Nir Shitufi*, remained unaltered (*Nir Shitufi*: An All Country Cooperative Association for the Settlement of Hebrew Workers in Israel Ltd), highlighting the apartheid nature of this particular so-called experiment in socialism (see below).

As noted above, the name of the *Histadrut* was officially changed again at the 17th *Histadrut* General Congress from the 'The General Federation of the Workers in the Land of Israel' ('the *Histadrut*') to the 'The New General Federation of Workers' ('the New *Histadrut*') as was the *Histadrut* logo.

It is important to underline in this context that such changes as did take place over the years need to be understood in the context of the progressive process of empowerment of the Palestinian Arab citizens of Israel pursuing together with Hebrew democratic citizens of Israel, decade after decade, since 1948 all avenues of struggle against the official policies of discrimination by all Israeli governments as well as all Zionist institutions, including the *Histadrut*.

Over the decades the sustained struggles of the Palestinian Arab community in Israel, highlighted by the Day of the Land in 1976, can boast considerable achievements, outside and inside the *Histadrut*, including the appointment of Arab members to the Management of the Workers' Company (see below).

One would like to hope that, led by a democratic leadership, this process of empowerment together with the progressive integration of Israeli economy into the globalized economic market (privatization, including the *Histadrut*-controlled corporations) may lead to the breakdown of the last bastion of Zionist apartheid settler institutions, leading, notably, to the admission of Arab citizens of Israel to *kibbutz* and *moshav* and other cooperative settlements.

Increasing attention is being applied by human rights organizations in Israel to this subject, pioneered by AL-BEIT: Association for the Defence of Human Rights in Israel (see Appendix IV).

Change of name of the Workers' Company The Workers' Company was established in 1923 as the 'General Cooperative Company of the Hebrew Workers in the Land of Israel'. The first aim of the company was 'to unite on a cooperative foundation the Hebrew workers of the Land of Israel in all professions of labour, both manual and spiritual' (Article 1). To advance this aim the Articles of Association of the Workers' Company empower the company to engage in every conceivable settlement, financial, manufacturing and other economic activity.

As noted above, the Workers' Company represented considerable economic muscle, manufacturing some 20 per cent of Israel's GNP. In its heyday, the Workers' Company had serious interests in almost all branches of Israeli economy including agricultural production, fishing, shipping, food processing, water works, mining, metal industries, construction, transport, retail, banking, insurance, arms manufacture, electronics, tourism, publishing and more.

The process of selling *Histadrut* manufacturing and other concerns to the private market in order to plug progressive *Histadrut* financial deficits began before Haim Ramon won the leadership of the *Histadrut*, but became official overall policy at the 17th *Histadrut* General Congress, from which point it was pursued by the New *Histadrut* in an accelerated manner.

In parallel, as part and parcel of the New *Histadrut* reforms, the aims of the Workers' Company were also altered radically in 1994 and 1995. To its pre-1994 aims to 'unite on a cooperative foundation the Hebrew workers of the Land of Israel in all professions of labour, both manual and spiritual' (1923 Constitution) and 'initiate, maintain and carry out the economic and market activities of the General Federation of Workers in the Land of Israel' (1967 Amendment) was now added the aim of 'mak[ing] available the properties of the Workers' Company ... to the *Histadrut* for the purpose of realizing its [the *Histadrut*'s] objectives, provided that making such properties available to the *Histadrut* as aforementioned not prejudice the ability of the [Workers'] Company to uphold all its [financial] obligations on such dates as they may be due' (1994 and 1995 Amendment).

Under this last Amendment the vast proceeds of the sale of the Workers' Company assets were made available to the *Histadrut* to plug its huge financial deficits (see below).

The change of name of the Workers' Company, however, was effected in 1979, at the 98th Council of the Workers' Company. Thirteen years after the change of the name of the *Histadrut*, the Workers' Company caught up with the *Histadrut* and resolved to change the name of the Workers' Company from 'General Cooperative Company of Hebrew Workers in the Land of Israel Ltd' to 'General Cooperative Company of the Workers in the Land of Israel Ltd'. *But only the name was changed* and, one can only presume, changed for the same reasons that motivated the change of name of the *Histadrut* 13 years earlier. The constitutional aims of the Workers' Company remained unaltered.

For the Council of the Workers' Company, as for all Zionist bodies and institutions, the legal exclusion of the non-Jew and the apartheid discrimination against the Arab was not a problem; these were fundamental elements in the formulation of the aims. The problem, rather, was how to maintain effectively the lie that had made it possible for the State of Israel to project itself in the West as allegedly the only 'democracy in the Middle East' and the *Histadrut* as allegedly a socialist trade union federation, while at the same time maintaining intact their colonial apartheid legal structures and policies.

For this, it seems, the removal of the reference to 'Hebrew Workers' (but not the 'Land of Israel') from the name of the *Histadrut* and the Workers' Company was sufficient.

But adherence to racism in this context could not be expected to be consistent. In 1960 the gates of the *Histadrut* were opened to Arab membership, and since each member of the *Histadrut* was by constitutional definition also a member of the Workers' Company, a constitutional contradiction was introduced into the legal structure of the Workers' Company. As the Palestinian Arab community in Israel became progressively more empowered and as Zionist ideological dogmatism weakened alongside the progressive integration of Israeli economy into the globalized economic market, Arab members of the *Histadrut* slowly won their way to senior positions in the Workers' Company including the management. In the current management of the Workers' Company there are two Arab citizens of Israel (Dr Hamra Majid and Nimr Ghanem).

But in the area constituting the core of the Israeli–Palestinian conflict – Zionist colonization of the land – the *Histadrut* continues to maintain the exclusion of its Arab members, denying them access to membership in *kibbutz* and *moshav* and other cooperative settlements. Here apartheid still rules undented.

Change of name of Nir Shitufi Until 1977 all *kibbutz* and *moshav* cooperative agricultural settlements in Israel were incorporated as daughter companies of the *Histadrut*-owned holding company, *Nir Shitufi*: An All Country Cooperative Association for the Settlement of Hebrew Workers in Israel Ltd (previously 'NIR: A Cooperative Company for the Settlement of Hebrew Workers Ltd', established 1924). Until 1977 *Nir Shitufi* was fully owned and controlled by the Workers' Company, the holding company of *Histadrut* agricultural, marketing, service and manufacturing corporations and associations. In 1977 the Workers' Company surrendered its controlling share in *Nir Shitufi* and control reverted to the Zionist cooperative federations for the settlement of Hebrew workers.

It should be pointed out that in 1977 the labour Zionist parties (the first Rabin government) lost the elections to their historical Zionist opponent, the Likud, headed by Menachem Begin.

One speculation has it that, fearing Likud takeover of the *Histadrut*, the *Histadrut* labour leadership sought to protect its settlement and land assets by severing the legal linkage between the Workers' Company on the one part and *Nir Shitufi* on the second part, vesting control of *Nir Shitufi* directly with the *kibbutz* and *moshav* and other cooperative settlement federations rather than with the Workers' Company and the *Histadrut*.

Nir Shitufi, however, was sufficiently unknown in the West to allow the reference to 'Hebrew workers' to remain in the name of the company, although in 1973, with the restructuring of the company, the name was changed from '*Nir*: A Cooperative Company for the Settlement of Hebrew Workers Ltd' to '*Nir Shitufi*: An All Country Cooperative Association for the Settlement of Hebrew Workers in Israel Ltd'.

The principle of the legal exclusion of non-Jews is clearly the constitutional unifying norm in all *kibbutz* and *moshav* and other cooperative agricultural settlements. These remain incorporated as daughter companies of *Nir Shitufi*. Membership in the *kibbutz* or the *moshav* constitutionally requires the endorsement of *Nir Shitufi*. Since *Nir Shitufi* is an 'All Country Cooperative Association for the Settlement of Hebrew Workers in Israel Ltd', the company is constitutionally obligated to veto the possible applications for membership of non-Jewish *kibbutz* and *moshav* and other cooperative settlement candidates.

The claim of the *kibbutz* and *moshav* and other cooperative agricultural and non-agricultural settlements to socialism is misguided, since they are, in the first instance, incorporated as apartheid settler organizations, constitutionally obligated to exclude and discriminate against non-Jews only because they are non-Jews. The attempts by socialist Zionist parties to reconcile Zionism, socialism and brotherhood among peoples have always been predicated upon a calculated lie.

Where the *kibbutz*, the *moshav* or other cooperative settlements as well as *Nir Shitufi* have turned a blind eye (such as the admission of European non-Jewish spouses – mostly women – of *kibbutz* and *moshav* members), they have done so in violation of the law, *not* in conformity to the law.

When the same principle is directed against Jews, the practice is rightly condemned as anti-Jewish racism (anti-Semitism). For whatever reason, when such racist principles and practices are applied against Arabs, the international cooperative and trade union movement, rather than expel the *Histadrut* as well as the *kibbutz* and *moshav* federations out of their ranks as racist organizations, allows itself to be misguided into embracing the *Histadrut* and the Israeli agricultural cooperative settlements federations as a legitimate affiliate organization.

The Haim Ramon new Histadrut *reforms* The lever for the reform of the *Histadrut* was forged by MK Haim Ramon as minister of health before he decided to run in the 1994 *Histadrut* elections. As minister of health in the second Rabin government he pioneered the National Health Law, 1995, which denied the *Histadrut* one of its major sources of income.

Until the passage of the said law, it was legal for the *Histadrut* to obligate all subscribers to the *Histadrut* health insurance programme (*Kupat Holim Kelalit*) to become members of the *Histadrut* and pay the compulsory dues of what was known as the 'Uniform Tax' (*Mas Ahid*). This tax was quantified progressively, relative to income, at something like 4–5 per cent of the gross salary of the individual member or member's family. Since *Kupat Holim Kelalit* was the largest health service in the country and since in many localities it was the only health service available, membership in the *Histadrut* was in many areas of the country less than voluntary.

The new law de-coupled this linkage, allowing citizens of the State of Israel to subscribe to the services of the *Histadrut*-owned *Kupat Holim Kelalit* without having to become members of the *Histadrut* itself. As a consequence the *Histadrut* suffered an immediate and massive drop in income, which was a primary consideration in its decision to accelerate the sale of its Workers' Company assets to the private market.

The subsequent election of MK Haim Ramon as *Histadrut* secretary-general completed the process.

Following the 1994 elections, the 17th *Histadrut* General Congress also endorsed the reform of the *Histadrut* election law to allow a direct ballot for the chairman of the *Histadrut*. Whereas previously the *Histadrut* was headed by the secretary-general, following the reforms the system of governance in the *Histadrut* is now patterned in analogy to the system of governance of the state, with the chairman of the *Histadrut* exercising 'presidential' powers. The electoral reforms took effect with the 1998 *Histadrut* elections to the 18th General Congress.

The first chairman of the *Histadrut* (and the last to be elected under the old system) was MK Haim Ramon, a senior member of the Labour Party and former minister of health, who on the eve of the *Histadrut* elections broke away from the Labour Party to launch the New *Histadrut* list (RAM), which carried him to victory.

The first chairman of the *Histadrut* to be elected under the rules of the reformed system was Amir Peretz, current chairman of the *Histadrut*, who took office following the 1998 elections. (In the 1998 elections *Histadrut* members placed three separate ballots in the ballot box: one to elect the chairman; one to elect their representatives to the Region; one to elect their representative to the General Congress (with women members of the *Histadrut* having a fourth ballot to the NA'AMAT Working and Volunteer Women's Movement).

There is no doubt that in the two years of his chairmanship MK Haim Ramon steered far-reaching reforms throughout the *Histadrut*. The reforms were thorough and, in addition to yet another change of name, included change of structure and change of substance. Having completed the reforms, Haim Ramon returned to the Labour Party, his political home, where he resumed a senior position. These reforms will now be considered in further detail.

Name At the 17th *Histadrut* General Congress the name of the *Histadrut* was officially changed again from the 'The General Federation of the Workers in the Land of Israel' ('the *Histadrut*') to the 'The New General Federation of Workers' ('the New *Histadrut*') and the logo changed from a logo depicting a combination of a hammer and an ear of wheat to a logo designed around the Star of David.

Structure The *Histadrut* General Congress (*Ve'idah*) remained in place. Elected every four years in general *Histadrut* elections on a party-political basis, the General Congress currently consists of 2001 delegates. But the *Histadrut* Council (*Mo'etzet ha-Histadrut*), previously elected by the General Congress, was nullified. Instead, the General Congress now elects a new body named *Histadrut* Parliament (*Beit Nivharei ha-Histadrut*), equivalent to what was until 1994 the *Histadrut* Executive Committee (*Ha-Vaad ha-Po'el*). The *Histadrut* Parliament, currently consisting of 171 delegates, is the highest authority of the *Histadrut* between one General Congress and the next.

The executive body of the New *Histadrut* is the Steering Committee (*Hanhagat ha-Histadrut*), equivalent to what was until 1994 the *Histadrut* Coordinating Committee (*Vaadah Merakezet*). The Steering Committee, consisting of at least 13 and no more than 27 members, is appointed by the *Histadrut* chairman on a party-political coalition basis, in a process very much like the forming of a government coalition by the prime minister.

Substance The most dramatic strategic change was the reform of the Workers' Company. Most of the major financial, industrial and manufacturing holdings of the Workers' Company were sold off to the private market by the New *Histadrut* leadership. By 1996:

• Workers' Company shares in Kur Industries (22.51 per cent of the shares and the voting rights) were sold to the US multinational Shamrock for approximately US$252 million;

- Workers' Company shares in *Bank ha-Po'alim* (Bank Hapoalim) (3.5 per cent of the shares) were sold to the private sector for approximately US$62.5 million;
- *Shikun u-Binui* Holdings incorporating *Solel Boneh* and *Shikun Ovdim* were sold for approximately US$94 million;
- the *Histadrut* daily *Davar* was shut down;

and more.

As a consequence the paradigmatical contradiction characterizing the *Histadrut* since its establishment in 1920, forever trying to balance between its interests as the second largest employer in Israel (second only to the state) on the one part and the trade union interests of the workers, including its own employees, organized in the framework of the *Histadrut* Department for Trade Unions on the second part, was now much reduced.

It would be true to say that today, following the Haim Ramon reforms, the *Histadrut* is much 'leaner' and closer to a trade union in the social democratic European sense of the term than to the organization underpinning the economic infrastructure of the State of Israel as the Jewish state in the making and becoming, after 1948, the second largest employer with a Department for Trade Unions.

However, it is necessary to bear in mind that the *Histadrut* remains very much committed to the values underpinning all Zionist parties, first and foremost to the aim of guaranteeing in law and in practice an ethnic majority of 'Jewish' citizens in the State of Israel.

There is no question that globalization and privatization weaken the hold of the Zionist ethnocratic institutions inside Israel and abroad, and in this regard work to the benefit of democratization of the Israeli political establishment as a whole, and the *Histadrut* establishment in particular, and therefore to the benefit of the Palestinian people as a whole, and the Palestinian citizens of Israel in particular.

There is a limit, though, to incremental reforms in institutions operating in the legal framework of apartheid states. It seems that in order to bring the incremental changes outlined above to full fruition Israel has yet to undergo the kind of structural legal transition that led to the release of Nelson Mandela in 1990 and transformed the Republic of South Africa from an apartheid state into a democratic state.

The case of Dr Sa'ad Murtada, First Egyptian Ambassador to Israel

The story of Dr Sa'ad Murtada, First Ambassador of the Arab Republic of Egypt to Israel, and his residence at Kefar Shemaryahu is perhaps an appropriate illustration, highlighting the workings of Israeli apartheid.

The Jewish settlement of Kefar Shemaryahu was established in 1937, technically as a *moshavah* (colony), and settled by a group of middle-class, German Jewish immigrants to Palestine. The lands for Kefar Shemaryahu settlement were purchased in 1935 from some of the large feudal landowners of the neighbouring Palestinian Arab village of Haram Sayyiduna 'Ali, by the Jewish Agency-owned Rural and Suburban Settlement Company Ltd (RASSCO). These lands consisted of 826 dunums (Bloc 6,665). An additional area of 365 dunums (Bloc 6,671) was purchased by RASSCO for Kefar Shemaryahu in 1939. The land was parcelled out into plots of 11 and 13 dunums each, which were subsequently sold to the settlers under individual titles of ownership.

As noted above, less than 7 per cent of the entire territory of pre-1967 Israel is similarly privately owned. In the course of the 1948 war, the inhabitants of the village of Haram Sayyiduna 'Ali were displaced, together with the mass of the Palestinian Arab population. Their extensive properties in lands and houses were classified under Israel's Absentees' Property Law (1950) as 'absentee property' and were immediately given over to the expansion of the existing neighbouring Jewish settlements of Rishpon (established 1936), Kefar Shemaryahu (established 1937) and Nof Yam (established 1946). As 'absentee property', the lands and the homes of the inhabitants of Haram Sayyiduna 'Ali were initially placed under the administration of the Custodian of Absentee Property, and were subsequently transferred to the Development Authority following the passage in the Knesset of the Development Authority Law of 1950.

The case of Haram Sayyiduna 'Ali is further underlined by the fact that some of the erstwhile Palestinian Arab inhabitants of the village are presently citizens of the State of Israel. They are among some currently 250,000 Palestinian Arab citizens of the State of Israel who are legally classified as 'present absentees', that is, they are present as citizens of the State of Israel, yet they are 'absent' as far as their rights to their pre-1948 properties in Israel are concerned. Like the mass of the Palestinian Arab people made refugees and exiled during and after the 1948 war, the inhabitants of Haram Sayyiduna 'Ali have been denied all rights to their pre-1948 properties under Israel's Absentees' Property Law of 1950.

Like the majority of the Palestinian Arab communities who were expelled in the course of the 1948 war under the impact of premeditated massacres and terror campaigns, the inhabitants of Haram Sayyiduna 'Ali left their village to seek temporary shelter and safe refuge for their dependants outside the heartland of Jewish settlement along the seaboard of Palestine. Some of the Palestinian Arab refugees of Haram Sayyiduna 'Ali sought shelter in the Arab village of Muqaybila (six kilometres north of Jenin), where they had property. When the 1949 Israel–Jordan Armistice Agreements were signed, those villagers of Haram Sayyiduna 'Ali who sought refuge in Muqaybila came under Israeli sovereignty. In this way they became inhabitants, and eventually citizens, of the new State of Israel.

This did not, however, alter the status as 'absentees' under Israel's Absentees' Property Law of 1950. Thus Kefar Shemaryahu, originally established on an area of 1,191 dunums (826 dunums purchased in 1935 and 365 dunums purchased in 1939) had, by 1956, doubled its lands. This was accomplished over a period of a few years. In 1950, the RASSCO colony of Kefar Shemaryahu was recognized by the state as an independent local municipal council. In 1954, an area of 409 dunums (Bloc 6,674) was annexed to the municipal area of Kefar Shemaryahu, which was further expanded in 1956 through the annexation of 90 dunums (Bloc 6,664), 529 dunums (Bloc 6,672) and 293 dunums (Bloc 6,673), increasing the municipal area of Kefar Shemaryahu to a total of 2,512 dunums. Almost all the additional territory annexed to the Kefar Shemaryahu Local Municipal Council is the property of the 1948 Refugees of Haram Sayyiduna 'Ali, both 'absentees' and 'present absentees'.

Over the years, Kefar Shemaryahu developed into an exclusive, fashionable and very expensive northern suburb of Tel Aviv, possibly the hottest real estate in Israel. The very rich purchase or lease the former agricultural farms, pulling down the original modest middle-class homes, and building expensive mansions and villas in their stead. Today, only multi-millionaires can afford to have homes in the locality, with the exception of a small minority of 'survivals': individuals and families, either themselves or whose parents happened to build their homes there well before the 1960s. Any sufficiently wealthy Jew from anywhere in the world can purchase or lease a plot of land in the locality and build his home there, but of the native indigenous Palaestinian Arab inhabitants of Haram Sayyiduna 'Ali, now citizens of the State of Israel, even those who today could materially afford to purchase or lease land there are prohibited under Israeli law from re-establishing residence in what remained of their native village or any of their properties in the vicinity.

The only physical evidence of Palestine in this heartland of apartheid prosperity are the Haram Sayyiduna Ali al-'Alaym mosque and a small cluster of the original Palestinian Arab homes. These are now occupied by the remnants of the population of the oriental Jewish slum established in the early 1950s on the site of the village of Haram Sayyiduna 'Ali, and subsequently evacuated when the area became attractive and property values in the area (Kefar Shemaryahu, Herzliyyah-Pituah and Nof Yam) soared. Kefar Shemaryahu and Herzliyya-Pituah became a favourite residential area for families of the diplomatic corps and foreign missions in Israel. In 1958, the Walworth Barbour American International School was inaugurated in Kefar Shemaryahu, with the assistance of the American Embassy, as a private co-educational institution offering an American educational programme to English-speaking students of all nationalities. The school services the entire diplomatic community in Israel, as well as Israeli citizens, and its existence further consolidated the prime residential status of the area.

Following the 1979 Israel–Egypt peace treaty and the subsequent exchange of ambassadors between the two states, Kefar Shemaryahu presented itself quite obviously as an appropriate address for the newly incumbent First Egyptian Ambassador to Israel, Dr Sa'ad Murtada. To this end, the Egyptian Embassy negotiated the lease of one of the most luxurious homes in the village, the mansion of Mr Boris Senior. The story of Dr Sa'ad Murtada's residence in Kefar Shemaryahu is linked to the legal history of Bloc 6,674. Until 1948 the land was owned by inhabitants of Haram Sayyiduna 'Ali; following the 1948 war, it was classed as 'absentees' property'.

As 'absentees' property', it was transferred by the Custodian of Absentees' Property to the Development Authority, and shortly thereafter was incorporated in the second lot of one million dunums transferred by the Development Authority to the Jewish National Fund. While the 1,191 dunums of the original body of Kefar Shemaryahu lands are under private ownership, the plots of Bloc 6,674 are under JNF ownership. Until 1960, they were available to individual lessees under JNF contracts of leasehold. Since the establishment of the Israel Lands Administration in 1961, they have been available to individual lessees under Israel Lands Administration contracts of leasehold. Mr Boris Senior was a suitable enough choice as business partner and landlord for Dr Sa'ad Murtada. Born in Johannesburg in 1924, and educated at Hilton College, Natal, and London University, he came to Israel prior to the 1948 war in the framework of the Foreign Volunteers Corps (MAHAL: *Mitnadvei Hutz la-Aretz*). A colonel in the air force, he joined the senior command of the nascent Israeli Air Force, which, in the 1948 war, was organized, commanded and to a large degree staffed by foreign volunteers and foreign air force veterans on special contracts.[38] Between 1947 and 1952 he served as chief of operations and deputy commander of the Israeli Air Force. He retired from professional military service in 1952, and became one of Israel's private industrial magnates (Orbi Ltd and Ingram & Glass Ltd), and an important member of Israel's social and industrial elite. One of his daughters is married to Yuval Rabin, son of the late Prime Minister Yitzhak Rabin.

Unfortunately for all parties concerned, however, the prospective tenant, Dr Sa'ad Murtada, happened to be an Egyptian Arab Muslim, and Mr Boris Senior's mansion happened to be located not in the original privately owned RASSCO-developed core municipal area of Kefar Shemaryahu, but on a 30-dunum plot in Bloc 6,674, which, as 'absentees' property', was transferred to the Development Authority, subsequently registered under JNF ownership, and annexed to the municipal area of Kefar Shemaryahu in 1950. Had the mansion been located on privately owned, originally RASSCO lands, the relevant legalities may have proved to be quite complex, since it seems that these lands are also restricted by the 'Jewish' clause. Yet it is doubtful whether the Israel Lands Administration could have intervened or would have wished to intervene, since privately owned lands do not fall under its administration.

The mansion in question, however, is built on land registered in the name of the JNF, and the case thus became a major legal and diplomatic headache for the Israel Lands Administration, and, obviously, for the Israel Ministry of Foreign Affairs. The matter was prominently reported in the Israeli Hebrew-language press, although the relevant legalities were consistently referred to in less than honest, and rather oblique, terms:

> The Israel Lands Administration Council will discuss next Sunday the leasing of a villa in Kefar Shemaryahu to the Egyptian Ambassador Sa'ad Murtada.
>
> The Egyptian Ambassador is interested in obtaining the lease of this villa, but under the existing law the owner of the villa is not permitted to lease it because it is built on JNF land. Minister of Defence Ezer Weizman made a personal appeal by telephone to the director of the Israel Lands Administration Jacob Aqnin, and asked him to arrange the matter. But Aqnin himself is not permitted under the law to do so, and the matter will, therefore, be brought for adjudication before the Israel Lands Administration Council.
>
> It seems that difficulties are envisioned in this case since there is considerable resistance in the Administration itself to the leasing of the villa. The opponents argue that if the law prohibiting the sublease

of property which is built on national land is violated this time, the case will constitute a precedent which will open the way for many to follow. The villa concerned is owned by the businessman Boris Senior, Yitzhak Rabin's in-law. Its owner is presently staying abroad. The villa is built on grounds encompassing 30 dunums. ('Israel Lands Administration to Debate the Lease of a House to Murtada', *Yediot Aharonot*, 21 March 1980)

This report is probably deliberately false. Under the terms of the Israel Lands Administration Law, Regulations and Stipulations of Leasehold, the sub-lease of property in part or in whole is possible and perfectly legal, provided the prior consent of the lessor is duly requested and obtained. Similarly, under the terms of the Memorandum and Articles of Association of the JNF, the sub-leasehold of JNF property in part or in whole is equally possible and perfectly legal, also provided that the prior 'express written authority of the Association' is obtained. The difficulty, therefore, resides elsewhere, and not in any insurmountable legal restrictions on possibilities of sub-lease, but in the explicit legal prohibition of the lease or the sub-lease of JNF lands, or any properties built on JNF lands, to non-Jews. The case must have been hotly contended inside the JNF and the Israel Lands Administration, and the intervention of Ezer Weizman, then minister of defence and an old air force friend and comrade of Mr Boris Senior, was called for.

We now know by which legal loophole the issue was finally resolved. The lease of the said property to the Egyptian Ambassador Sa'ad Murtada was eventually ratified, probably under the strong pressure of the Israeli foreign minister, as a two-year lease with an option for a third year. The daily *Yediot Aharonot* reported the decision:

Now that the lease is permitted because of the recommendation of the Foreign Ministry, the [Israel Land] Administration has decided to increase the leasehold fees for the Patrimony ... ('The Lease of Boris Senior's Villa to the Egyptian Ambassador Is Permitted', *Yediot Aharonot*, 28 March 1980)[39]

Under Israeli land tenure legislation, a three-year leasehold does not endow the lessee any occupancy or other rights whatsoever. Strictly speaking, under the Constitutions and Articles of Association of all Zionist bodies (WZO, JA, JNF and others) it 'shall be deemed to be a matter of principle that Jewish labour shall be employed', let alone allowed access as lessees or sub-lessees. But the above loophole, plus the increase of leasehold fees, helped the bodies concerned turn a blind eye in this case and evade a major diplomatic embarrassment, just as the bodies concerned turn a blind eye to the violation of their Constitutions and Articles of Association in cases where European women who are non-Jewish access *kibbutzim* and *moshavim* as spouses of Jewish *kibbutz* and *moshav* members. It is easier, however, for the said bodies to turn a blind eye in the latter case where the non-Jewish persons concerned are non-Arabs than in the former case, where the non-Jewish person concerned was an Arab.

The legal underpinnings of Israel's apartheid land policies are widely known inside Israel. Note, for instance, the following presentation by former MK and minister Shulamit Aloni:

> There are in Israel many laws and by-laws which allow for the taking of land from its occupiers and cultivators, beginning with the Emergency Regulations State, Citizenship, Land (Cultivation of Waste Lands) Ordinance (1949), the Absentees' Property Law (1950), the confiscations for public interest, and the declaration of areas as firing zones and army manoeuvre areas.
>
> On the other hand, the Arab citizen in Israel, or his representatives, has no voice concerning the right of the lease of lands for cultivation or agricultural settlement. In all the government or public committees on this subject, there is not one single non-Jewish representative. *Furthermore, all options for agricultural settlement are carried out through the Jewish Agency, and any person who is non-Jewish, even if he (or she) is the spouse of a Jew, cannot be a farmer here in this country, even if he (or she) is a citizen.* (Aloni, 'Law and Order or Law and Justice', *Yediot Aharonot*, 16 April 1979; emphasis added)

Shulamit Aloni is well acquainted with the details of Israel land legislation, both as a former MK and minister and as the wife of the late Mr Reuben Aloni, former Director of the Israel Lands Administration, as well as a private citizen whose home in Kefar Shemaryahu is built on 'absentee' land owned by Palestinian Arab refugees of the now destroyed village of Haram Sayyiduna 'Ali, subsequently registered in the name of the Development Authority. MK Shulamit Aloni happens to be a neighbour at Kefar Shemaryahu of Dr Sa'ad Murtada, the Arab Republic of Egypt's First Ambassador to Israel, but then she also happens to be Jewish. To her credit she was the one who made public the legal loophole that enabled Ambassador Sa'ad Murtada to sub-lease Boris Senior's villa.

4 · Political Repression in Israel

Given what goes on in the West Bank and the Gaza Strip, writing about political repression in Israel is like a guest taking residence in a Third World seaside resort hotel and complaining that his steak is not properly grilled, while the people in whose midst the hotel is located are starving.

As I write this book in the Arab city of Sakhnin, Central Galilee, there are no tanks outside the windows of my flat; no imposition of severe restrictions on movement, prolonged curfews and besiegement of towns and villages; no roadblocks denying kidney patients dialysis treatment, cancer patients oncological treatment and women in labour access to the maternity wards of the nearby hospitals; no malnutrition; no Apache helicopters strafing civilian homes or targeting civilian vehicles; no bulldozers digging up roads to make them unusable; no cars smashed under the tracks of vandalizing tanks; no women raped by invading soldiers.

Yet it would be unwise to disregard the instruments of political repression inside Israel, if only because the political structures of the State of Israel are currently undergoing dangerous transformations.

The mainstream of the constituency of Jewish citizens of the State of Israel recognizes the still significant limitation that the democratic resistance inside Israel to Israeli apartheid, the democratic struggle within, places on the capacity of the government to perpetrate still further atrocities, war criminal abominations against the native indigenous Palestinian Arab people, notably the crime against humanity of the mass expulsion of the remainder of the Palestinian Arab people from their localities inside the occupied West Bank, Gaza Strip and Israel.

At the time of writing, Israel is led by a Likud government headed by General (Reserves) Ariel Sharon (inveterate war criminal of *inter alia* Sabra and Shatila and former minister of defence) as prime minister, General (Reserves) Shaul Mofaz (confirmed war criminal of *inter alia* Jenin and former chief of staff) and minister of foreign affairs and former prime minister Benjamin Netanyahu (who regards his senior colleagues Sharon and Mofaz as 'soft' on what he terms 'the war on

Palestinian terrorism'). There is little doubt that in this context the margins of democratic resistance available to democratic formations inside the State of Israel, notably the margins of democratic resistance available to the constituency of the Palestinian Arab citizens of the State of Israel, are being whittled down.

Defence (Emergency) Regulations of 1945

It is important to emphasize at the outset that the primary legal instrument of political repression inside Israel within its pre-1949 armistice boundaries is identical to the instrument applied in the post-1967 occupied territories, namely, the Defence (Emergency) Regulations of 1945.

The establishment of the State of Israel was declared on 15 May 1948. Four days later, on 19 May, the Provisional Council of State declared a state of emergency under the Defence (Emergency) Regulations of 1945.[40] The state of emergency has been consistently extended by all Israeli Knessets since that date, a decision motivated not only by Israeli government perceptions of Israel's national security, as understood in political Zionist terms, but also by very weighty correlative material considerations. The vast properties of the Palestinian Arab people inside the State of Israel remain vested with the Custodian of Absentee Property under the Absentees' Property Law of 1950 so long as 'the state of emergency declared by the Provisional Council of State in 1948' has not been declared to have ceased to exist. Presumably, when the said 'state of emergency' is declared to have ceased to exist, all 1948 Palestinian refugees' property vested with the Israeli Custodian of Absentees' Property could be claimed back by its 'absentee' owners.

The characterization of the State of Israel as being permanently, since its establishment in 1948, in a state of emergency is not only a settler colonial political statement but, perhaps more significantly, a settler colonial legal statement in that so long as 'the state of emergency declared by the Provisional Council of State in 1948' has not been declared to have ceased to exist, the State of Israel is administered under a dual system of law: civilian law (itself structured as a two-tier apartheid system) versus military law.

This legal dualism obtains in all the territories under Israeli rule and occupation. Military law, namely, the Defence (Emergency) Regulations of 1945, obtains throughout the country of Palestine (1922 British Mandate territory) by virtue of the continuous extension of these regulations by all Israeli Knessets since 1948. Military law is, therefore, in force throughout the territories apportioned for the Jewish state by the 1947 UN Partition Plan for Palestine; in the territories occupied by

Israel during the 1948–49 war beyond the 1947 UN boundaries, all of which were subsequently annexed to Israel; and the territories occupied in 1967, some of which (East Jerusalem and its hinterland in the West Bank and the Golan Heights) were also subsequently annexed.

At present, Israeli civilian legislation applies *alongside* the Defence (Emergency) Regulations of 1945 in the territories allocated to the Jewish state by the 1947 UN Partition Plan for Palestine; in the territories occupied by Israel in the 1948–49 war; in East Jerusalem and its annexed hinterland in the West Bank; in the Golan Heights; and in the municipal territories of all Jewish settlements in the post-1967 occupied territories.

The 1967 war was launched by Israel on 5 June. Hostilities ended within six days in a notable Israeli blitzkrieg victory. Less than three weeks later, on 27 June 1967, the Knesset passed the necessary legislation to make possible the application of Israeli civilian law in all post-1967 occupied territories at such time as the government may deem fit.[41] In other words, the formal annexation of what remains of the occupied West Bank and the Gaza Strip to Israel requires no additional Knesset deliberation, and can be made effective by government decree at such time as the government may find appropriate.

In parallel to the dual (military versus civilian) legal system that obtains in Israel, a dual hierarchy of courts (military versus civilian) operates throughout the country as adjudicators of military and civilian justice respectively.

Every resident of the State of Israel may be prosecuted under either the civilian code or the military code. The decision as to which legislation (civilian or military) to invoke regarding any given offence is entirely at the discretion of the authorities. Jewish residents of the territories allocated to the Jewish state by the 1947 UN Partition Plan, the territories occupied in 1948–49, and the territories occupied in 1967 are, almost without exception, prosecuted in civilian courts under civilian legislation. Palestinian Arabs who are resident in pre-1967 Israel, Palestinian Arab residents of East Jerusalem, and Syrian residents of the annexed Golan Heights are conventionally prosecuted in civilian courts under civilian legislation.[42] Palestinian Arab residents of the portions of the West Bank and the Gaza Strip which are under Israeli occupation but have not yet been formally annexed are conventionally prosecuted in military courts under the Defence (Emergency) Regulations of 1945.[43]

The Defence (Emergency) Regulations of 1945, introduced into Palestine by the British Mandate authorities, were rightly condemned by leading Jewish lawyers at the time of their enactment. Jacob Shimshon Shapiro, subsequently legal adviser to the government of the newly established state of Israel and later minister of justice, condemned the Regulations in the following terms:

> The established order in Palestine since the Defence Regulations is unparalleled in any civilized country. Even in Nazi Germany there were no such laws ... Only in an occupied country do you find a system resembling ours. They try to reassure us by saying that these laws apply only to offenders and not to the whole of the population, but the Nazi governor of occupied Oslo said that no harm would come to those who minded their own business ... It is our duty to tell the whole world that the Defence Regulations passed by the government in Palestine destroy the very foundation of justice in this land. It is mere euphemism to call the military courts 'courts'. To use the Nazi title, they are no better than 'Military Judicial Committees Advising the Generals'. No government has the right to draw up such laws. (*Ha-Praklit*, February 1946, pp. 58–64, as quoted in Jiryis 1976: 12–13)

In similar vein, Dr Dov Yosef (Bernard Joseph) of the Jewish Agency, also subsequently minister of justice, commented:

> As for these Defence Regulations, the question is: Are we all to become victims of officially licensed terrorism or will the freedom of the individual prevail? Is the administration to be allowed to interfere in the lives of the people with no protection for the individual? As it is, there is no guarantee to prevent a citizen from being imprisoned for life without trial. There is no protection for the freedom of the individual; there is no appeal against the decision of the military commander; no means of resorting to the Supreme Court ... while the administration has unrestricted freedom to banish any citizen at any moment. What is more, a man does not actually have to commit an offence; it is enough for a decision to be made in some office for his fate to be sealed ... The principle of collective responsibility has become a mockery. All of the six hundred thousand [Jewish] settlers could be hanged for a crime committed by one person in this country. A citizen should not have to rely on the good will of an official; our lives and our property should not be placed in the hands of such an official ... In a country where the administration itself inspires anger, resentment, and contempt for the laws, one cannot expect respect for the law. It is too much to ask of a citizen to respect a law that outlaws him. (Jiryis 1976: 11–12)

The above is a rather accurate description of the legal underpinnings of the post-1967 Israeli occupation.

It is instructive to quote some of the more pernicious Articles of the Defence (Emergency) Regulations of 1945 in detail:

Detention: 111 – (1) A Military Commander may by order direct that any person shall be detained for any period not exceeding one year in such place of detention as may be specified by the Military Commander in the order.

Deportation: 112 – (1) The High Commissioner shall have power to make an order under his hand (hereinafter in these Regulations referred to as 'a Deportation Order') requiring any person to leave and remain out of Palestine.

Taking possession of land: 114 – (1) A District Commissioner may – if it appears to him to be necessary or expedient so to do in the interests of the public safety, the defence of Palestine, the maintenance of public order or the maintenance of supplies and services essential to the life of the community – take possession of any land, or retain possession of any land of which possession was previously taken under regulation 48 of the Defence Regulations, 1939, and may, at the same time or from time to time thereafter, give such directions as appear to him to be necessary or expedient in connection with, or for the purpose of, the taking, retention or recovery of possession of the land.

Forfeiture and demolition of property, etc.: 119 – (1) A Military Commander may by order direct the forfeiture to the Government of Palestine of any house, structure, or land from which he has reason to suspect that any firearm has been illegally discharged or any bomb, grenade or explosive or incendiary article illegally thrown or of any house, structure or land situated in any area, town, village, quarter or street the inhabitants or some of the inhabitants of which he is satisfied have committed or attempted to commit, or abetted the commission of, or been accessories after the fact to the commission of any offence against these Regulations involving violence or intimidation or any Military Court offence, and when any house, structure or land is forfeited as foresaid, the Military Commander may destroy the house or the structure of anything growing on the land.

Closed areas: 125 – A Military Commander may by order declare any area or place to be a closed area for the purpose of these Regulations. Any person who, during any period in which any such order is in force in relation to any area or place, enters or leaves that area or place without a permit in writing issued by or on behalf of the Military Commander shall be guilty of an offence against these Regulations. (Supplement No. 2, *Palestine Gazette*, No. 1442, 27 September 1945)

Under these Articles incalculable suffering has been inflicted on the Palestinian Arab people by the State of Israel over the past five odd decades. Some of the suffering is presented in this book. Other areas, given the priorities of this work, have not been documented here. Basic data regarding torture and the conditions of imprisonment and detention in Israeli jails, curfews, imprisonment and besiegement of towns and villages, deportation, expropriation and destruction of land, demolition of property, collective punishment, including economic strangulation, deliberate impoverishment, and denial of the right to food and water are essential to a comprehensive presentation of the Defence (Emergency) Regulations of 1945 and, indeed, the measures of occupation and colonization that they regulate. The reader will, however, have to consult other sources for further documentation of the measures employed and the effects of their application.[44]

The June 1967 war in many ways marked both the zenith and the beginning of the decline of Zionist and Israeli achievements. Unlike the 1948 war, which successfully engineered the evacuation of the majority of the Palestinian Arab population from the territories which subsequently became the State of Israel, after June 1967 the majority of the Palestinian Arab population in the occupied West Bank and the Gaza Strip remained. From a Zionist point of view, given that the aim of political Zionism was and remains predicated on the attempt to guarantee in law and in practice a demographic majority of the Jewish tribes in the territories under its control, this represents a major setback.

Furthermore, Israel's options are by now increasingly restricted, and thus the option of effecting a major evacuation of the Palestinian Arab population under the cover of the battle is no longer as readily available. In the 1948 war, as in the 1956 and 1967 wars, the war initiative was firmly in Israeli hands. This is no longer the case. The October 1973 Egyptian and Syrian limited war initiative, the altering directions of international political constellations, and the shifts in the international balance of power forced Israel into the frame of reference of the Egyptian president's peace initiative (Sadat's visit to Jerusalem, 19 November 1977), the Camp David agreement (17 September 1978), and the Israel–Egypt peace treaty (26 March 1979). As a consequence, Israel committed itself to complete withdrawal from the Sinai Peninsula occupied in the June 1967 war and the dismantlement of all Israeli settlements established on occupied Egyptian territory beyond the British Mandate international border between the two states. For the first time in Zionist history, a legal commitment was made to dismantle Jewish settlements in the framework of political negotiations and under diplomatic (as distinct from military) pressures.

The 1982 Israeli invasion of Lebanon has further underlined the decline of Israel's power position regionally and internationally. All these are indications of weakness, not of strength. However, the weakness of the State of Israel at this stage is not yet such that the national and political rights of the Palestinian Arab people, namely, the right of return of the 1948 Palestine refugees and the right of the Palestinian Arab people to self-determination and national independence may be secured.

Nevertheless, there is little doubt that the Zionist impetus and the capacity of the State of Israel to implement its Zionist objectives of establishing Jewish sovereignty and a Jewish numerical majority in all parts of British Mandate Palestine are very much impaired. The current leadership of the State of Israel shows every sign that it aims to utilize the first opportunity it believes is afforded by the international constellation to correct the decline of political Zionism, and to do so by resorting to still more war crimes.

At the time of writing, the government of the State of Israel is a *de facto* transitional government, a government not accountable to Parliament and immune to votes of no confidence. With a government headed by Ariel Sharon as prime minister, Shaul Mofaz as minister of defence and Benjamin Netanyahu as foreign minister, we can only expect the worst.

This war criminal leadership is hoping that it will be given an opportunity to complete today the crime against humanity of the mass expulsion of the Palestinian people, begun and not completed in 1948 – and is mad enough to seriously attempt to carry this criminal project out. As Tanya Reinhart perceptively notes:

> Sharon, now Israel's prime minister, describes its present war against the Palestinians as 'the second half of 1948.' Israeli military echelons had already used the same description in October 2000, at the outset of the second *Intifada* – the present Palestinian uprising. By now, there can be little doubt that what they mean by that analogy is that the work of ethnic cleansing was only half completed in 1948, leaving too much land to Palestinians. Although the majority of Israelis are tired of wars and of the occupation, Israel's political and military leadership is still driven by the greed for land, water resources, and power. From that perspective, the war of 1948 was just the first step in a more ambitious and far-reaching strategy. (Reinhart 2002: 10–11)

The 1980 Knesset legislation

In July 1980, the Knesset passed a series of laws that, under the guise of legality and due democratic process, radically altered the framework of public and political life under Israeli law. The new legislation was rushed through in the four weeks of July 1980 and completed before the Knesset withdrew for its long summer recess (August through October). In this section, considerable attention will be given to the legislation of repression passed by the Knesset at that time in an attempt further to suppress, in the framework of the civilian criminal code, independent political expression and organization, specifically, independent national Palestinian Arab political expression and organization. The legal tools of repression forged by the Knesset in the summer of 1980 are civilian additions to the draconian measures available to the authorities under the Defence (Emergency) Regulations of 1945.

First, on 23 July, the Knesset passed the Foundation of Law of 1980. This law replaces Section 46 of the Palestine Order in Council (1922–47), and introduces into Israeli legislature a new legal foundation, namely:

1: Where the court, faced with a legal question requiring decision, finds no answer to it in statute law or case-law or by analogy, it shall decide it in the light of the principles of freedom, justice, equity and peace of Israel's heritage. (*Laws of the State of Israel* [authorized translation from the Hebrew prepared by the Ministry of Justice], Vol. 34, Jerusalem, 1979/80, p. 181)

Needless to say, the amendment proposed by MK Meir Vilner to Article 1, namely:

Where the court, faced with a legal question requiring decision, finds no answer to it in statute law or case-law or by analogy, it shall decide it in the light of the principles of freedom, justice, equity and peace of the universal heritage of humanity as a whole (*Knesset Debates*, Vol. 27, 26–28 May 1980, p. 4,027)

was turned down.

MK Shulamit Aloni's comments on the subject are, indeed, instructive:

One can count a string of such distortions which are contrary to the principles of honesty, justice and equality which have established themselves in Israel in the name of *Halachic* law and coalition agreements. Now there are those who wish to make these distortions the foundation of legislation ... This is the reason for the objection to add to this proposed law the principles of the Declaration of Independence. This is the reason why the text of the law does not include the phrase ... 'principles of freedom, justice, honesty and peace without discrimination on the grounds of origin, race, nationality, religion or sex'. Such non-discrimination stands contrary to 'the heritage of Israel' as it is interpreted today in the State of Israel. (Aloni, 'Foundation Laws, Justice and Heritage of Israel', *Haaretz*, 17 June 1980)

Next the Knesset passed, on 28 July, the Law of Associations, *Amutot* [Charities; Friendly Societies] Law of 1980, which stipulates as follows:

> 2: An application for registration of an *amuta* [charity] shall be submitted by the founders to the Registrar of *Amutot* (hereinafter referred to as 'the Registrar'), including the name, objects and address in Israel of the *amuta* and the names, address and identity numbers of the founders.

> 3: An *amuta* shall not be registered if any of its objects negates the existence or democratic character of the State of Israel or if there are reasonable grounds for concluding that the *amuta* will be used as a cover for illegal activities. (*Laws of the State of Israel* [authorized translation from the Hebrew prepared by the Ministry of Justice], Vol. 34, Jerusalem, 1979/80, p. 239)

Until the coming into force of this new *Amutot* Law on 1 April 1981, the bulk of civil society life in Israel had been carried out within the legal framework of the Ottoman Associations Law, 1909, which was incorporated into the body of British Mandatory law in Palestine and, in 1948, into the body of law of the State of Israel.

Under the said Ottoman Associations Law, any association of two or more adults (resident in the State of Israel) established to promote stated non-profit objectives was rendered legal upon the submission of a formal announcement to that effect to the Registrar of Associations at the Ministry of the Interior. Any violation of Israeli law by the recognized legal persons of Ottoman Associations was dealt with under the existing body of Israeli legislation.

Until the coming into force of the new legislation, the Ottoman Associations under Israeli law were relatively autonomous. This is precisely why the major body of independent, civil society, non-profit, and charitable activity in Palestine before and after 1948 has taken place in the framework of the Ottoman Associations Law. Israeli universities, multi-million-dollar health insurance funds and friendly societies, on the one hand, and civil rights organizations such as the Israeli League for Human and Civil Rights and the Committee for the Defence of Political Prisoners in Israeli Jails, on the other, regulated their activities as Ottoman Associations until the passage of the said *Amutot* Law of 1980. Similarly, much of the independent charitable initiative, secular as well as religious, in the Jewish sector and the Arab sector in Israel was regulated within the framework of Ottoman Associations.

The import of the new law is, however, clear. Any association concerning which 'there are reasonable grounds for concluding that ... [it] will be used as a cover for illegal activities' will not be registered. Because what constitutes 'reasonable grounds' is undefined, as are 'illegal activities', the law is open to serious abuse. The 1980 law can thus serve, and indeed does serve, as the basis for new measures of repression. For instance, it took the Association for the Rights of the Internally Displaced in Israel some two years before the Registrar of *Amutot* finally registered the Association, and not before the founders of the Association served an injunction against the Registrar at the District Court in Jerusalem in 1999.

All Ottoman Associations existing prior to the coming into force of the new legislation were required to re-register with the Registrar of *Amutot* within one year of the coming into force of the new law, or else be declared disbanded. The new law also empowers the Registrar to launch, on his own initiative, an enquiry into the finances and any other dealings of any association; to postpone a general meeting of any association to a date determined by the Registrar (Article 37 and Article 40); and to initiate litigation to disband an association (Article 49). Finally and significantly, the new law does not apply to Ottoman Associations that are existing political parties, or employees' or employers' organizations (Article 67). After all, political parties and, in the first instance, the major Zionist political parties, the *Histadrut* and its various workers' organizations and Workers' Company-owned business concerns, as well as the employers' organizations, must be protected from the exigencies of a law that is clearly aimed at curbing the legal expression of opposition and autonomous activity of civil society associations.

This law was rightly condemned by MK Uri Avnery (SHELI) as an added measure in 'the campaign of the Minister of Justice to limit and eliminate democracy in Israel'. He proposed the complete elimination of Article 3:

What does it mean, 'the democratic character' [of the State of Israel]? I submit that the tendencies as expressed by the statements and actions of MK Geulah Cohen [Revival Party leader and initiator of the Basic Law: Jerusalem, the Capital of Israel] deny the democratic character of the State of Israel. I think, as a matter of course, that Gush Emunim denies the democratic character of the State of Israel. One could submit that [the religious orthodox] *Agudat Israel* Party denies the democratic character of the State of Israel since it aspires to transform the state of Israel into a *Halachic* theocracy where legislation is determined by the laws of God dated three thousand years ago, and not by the laws of the Knesset. Others could submit that the Communist Party denies the democratic character of the State of Israel since communist doctrine advocates the dictatorship of the proletariat. Anyone can claim against any other that he denies the democratic character of the State of Israel according to his convictions. The law does not determine what is the democratic character of the State of Israel. (Uri Avnery, *Knesset Debates*, Vol. 89, 28 July 1980, p. 4,118)

And Meir Vilner (RAKAH-affiliated Democratic Front for Peace and Equality) correctly pointed out that:

The Likud government, on the eve of the termination of its office, introduces and passes the Knesset laws whose meaning is the fascisiza-tion of life in the State of Israel. It is greatly regrettable that these laws are introduced in Israeli garb when they are more anti-democratic than the laws that applied under the foreign regime of the British Mandate in the same domains. Even the Associations Law under Ottoman rule in the country was more democratic. I think that in this law there are elements that give the government, the authorities, the possibility to liquidate any organization they wish to liquidate ... What is the 'democratic character' [of the State of Israel]? In my view, even today this democratic character is very limited; I wish to expand greatly this democratic character. There is discrimination against the Arab popula-tion in Israel, in this law as in all domains of everyday life. Lands are stolen on racialist nationalist grounds. Is this democracy? Arab students are expelled from universities. Is this democracy? (Meir Vilner, ibid., pp. 4,119–20)

Clearly, however, Israel's sovereign body, the Knesset, determined that the measures so far outlined were not sufficient, and that the Jewish state required further legal protection.

The Fourth Amendment (1980) to Article 3 (nationality by residence in Israel) of Israel Nationality Law of 1952 passed on 29 July 1980, and the granting of Israeli citizenship to the body of 'present absentees' resi-dent inside the boundaries of pre-1967 Israel has already been discussed. But the Fourth Amendment also introduced and passed a modification to Article 11 (Annulment of Nationality) of the law. This modification, known as the 'Shilonsky Amendment', reads as follows:

11(b) The Minister of Interior may terminate the Israel nationality of a person who has done an act constituting a breach of allegiance to the State of Israel. (*Laws of the State of Israel* [authorized translation from the Hebrew prepared by the Ministry of Justice], Vol. 34, Jerusalem, 1979/80, p. 259)

It was the same Dov Shilonsky MK (Likud) who, on the following day (30 July 1980), introduced before the Knesset on behalf of the Knesset Constitution, Law and Justice Committee the most notorious piece of the July 1980 legislation, the Amendment to the Prevention of Terrorism Ordinance (1948):

1. Article 4 of the Prevention of Terrorism Ordinance, 1948 (hereafter the Ordinance) following paragraph (f) will read as follows:

(g) [A person who] does any act manifesting identification or sympathy with a terrorist organization in a public place or in such a manner that persons in a public place can see or hear such manifestation of identification or sympathy, either by flying a flag or displaying a symbol or slogan or by causing an anthem or slogan to be heard, or any other similar overt act clearly manifesting such identification or sympathy as aforesaid … shall be guilty of an offence, and shall be liable on conviction to imprisonment for a term not exceeding three years. (*Laws of the State of Israel* [authorized translation from the Hebrew prepared by the Ministry of Justice], Vol. 34, Jerusalem, 1979/80, p. 211 and Vol. I, Ordinances, 1948, p. 77)

Shilonsky's introduction of this Amendment before the House is explicit and illuminating, accurately representing the rabid anti-Arab racism informing the mainstream of political Zionist society:

Mr Chairman, Honourable Knesset. In the Provisional State Council the people who are the spiritual fathers of those who are today in the movement called 'The Alignment' passed the Prevention of Terrorism Ordinance (1948) … Since that time there has arisen in our country terrorism, huge terrorism, terrible and fearful terrorism, the terrorism of bloodthirsty animals … These bloody animals … are the rich of this world, who indulge in debauchery in the most expensive houses of iniquity in the world. US dollars stream into their pockets like water in the Volga. They lack nothing for their comfort were it not for their thirst, their thirst for Jewish blood. They have already drunk too much blood, the blood of women, the blood of old people, the blood of youth. But their thirst for Jewish blood cannot be quenched. Any kind of blood is tasty to their palate without discrimination of clime, be it the hot Mediterranean, or cold European, provided it is Jewish blood. They have declared a war of total annihilation on the entire Jewish people, on every Jew wherever he may live. Against this terror, especially now that times have changed with the advance of science and the means [of terrorism] the law legislated ... in 1948 is not sufficient ... Members of the Knesset. Imagine if anyone here sang the notorious Nazi anthem: 'Und wann Juden-blut vom Messer spritzt, dann geht uns noch mal so gut!' Could we remain silent? Could we give legitimacy to such songs? And I hear that in Arab festivals in Israel and on other occasions, it is sung: 'In blood and spirit we shall liberate the Galilee' ... Experts on the subject tell me that the meaning is the shedding of Jewish blood. Can we remain silent and sit with arms folded in the face of such a thing? Can we sit calmly in the face of such a thing? Can we give legitimacy to the advocacy of this bloodshed? Imagine if anyone raised the Nazi banner in Israel, could we then sit calmly? Could we not then declare that identification with the banner of murderers, or the use of a slogan of the murderers or an emblem of the murderer is a violation of the law? (*Knesset Debates*, Vol. 89, 30 July 1980, pp. 4,325, 4,326)

Two decades later the Knesset resolved to strip the parliamentary immunity of MK Azmi Bishara representing BALAD (the Democratic National Assembly) in order to enable the state to charge him with support for a terrorist organization on the basis of Articles 4(a), 4(b) and 4(g) of the Prevention of Terrorism Ordinance 1948, not only for alleged criminal acts, but also for political utterances delivered in public.

Also, two decades on, the minister of the interior in the Likud-led government coalition, Mr Eli Yishai, chose to apply his authority under the said Article 11(b) of Israel's Nationality Law of 1952 as amended in 1980. On 10 September 2002 he nullified the Israeli citizenship of Nihad Abu Kishk and proceeded with the formal measures required to nullify the citizenship of Qays Ubayd and the permanent residency status of Shadi Sharafa (*Haaretz*, 10 September 2002).[45]

Together with the passage of the 2002 legislation below, these precedents signal a qualitative juncture in the process of the negative transformation of the Israeli body politic and its deterioration towards ever intensifying apartheid and fascism.

The 2002 Knesset legislation

In May 2002 the Knesset passed a bundle of statutes directed to further limit the articulation of democratic solidarity inside the State of Israel with the struggle against Israeli apartheid, such as is carried out in conformity with the standards of international law, including armed struggle. The legislation, passed in one fell swoop in a single session, on 15 May, included:

- Amendment to Basic Law: The Knesset of 1958 (Amendment No. 35) replacing the existing Article 7(a) with an amended Article 7(a);
- Amendment to Political Parties Law of 1992 (Amendment No. 13);
- Amendment to the Penal Law of 1977 (Amendment No. 66); and
- Amendment to the Elections to the Knesset and to the Premiership (Amendment No. 46)

Article 7(a) of the Basic Law: The Knesset of 1958 was first amended in 1985 (Amendment No. 9) which read as follows:

Prevention of participation of candidates' list

7(a) A candidates' list shall not participate in the elections to the Knesset if its objects or actions, expressly or by implication, include one of the following:

(1) negation of the existence of the State of Israel as the state of the Jewish people;

(2) negation of the democratic character of the state;

(3) incitement to racism. (*Laws of the State of Israel* [authorized translation from the Hebrew prepared by the Ministry of Justice], Vol. 39, Jerusalem, 1979/80, p. 216)

Amendment No. 9 was passed by the Knesset in July 1985 with the view to exclude from participation in the political process not only openly racist political formations such as the now illegal *Kakh* Party, founded by the late, openly Nazi Rabbi Meir Kahane (assassinated in New York in 1990), but also democratic political parties and other NGOs challenging the oxymoron of 'a state of the Jewish people' coupled with 'democratic character' and proposing political platforms under banners such as 'A State for All of Its Citizens' (NDA/BALAD: The National Democratic Assembly) or a 'State for All of Its Citizens and 1948 Palestine Refugees' (MAIAP: Movement Against Israeli Apartheid in Palestine).

The duplicity of the formulation of the said Amendment, informing the deliberation of the statutory Central Elections Committee, blocked Rabbi Meir Kahane and his *Kakh* Party from partaking in the elections to the 12th Knesset in 1988 (having made it into the 11th Knesset in 1984) but allowed in an equally rabid apartheid party, *Moledet* (Motherland), founded by General (Reserves) Rehav'am Zeevi (assassinated in Jerusalem in 2001), currently a component of the National Union (*Israel Beitenu*, Our Home Israel) headed by MK Avigdor Lieberman, *Moledet*, headed by MK Benny Alon, and *Tequmah* (Resurrection), headed by MK Tzvi Hendel. Both the now defunct *Kakh* Party and the *Moledet* Party, considered a legitimate partner for government coalition, have been vocal advocates of 'transfer', namely the ethnic cleansing of the native indigenous Palestinian Arab population from the entire territory of British Mandate Palestine, a crime against humanity under international law, as the preferred 'solution' for the Israeli Palestinian conflict.

As the debate in the Knesset relevant to the introduction of the said Amendment No. 35 clearly reveals, the explicit object of the Amendment is to bar from participation in the political process and from membership in the Knesset such political parties as described by MK Ophir Pines, chair of the Knesset Constitution, Law and Justice Committee in his introduction of Amendment No. 35 before the Knesset Plenary:

> When Article 7(a) of Basic Law: The Knesset was passed, the legislators could not conceive of a situation where the Knesset will have [among its members an MK] who would express support for armed struggle against the State of Israel. This was not something that could be conceived at the time. But this is something that to my great regret – and I do not want to suggest that it is happening [in the present] – can for certain happen. (*Knesset Debates*, 15 May 2002)[46]

Ophir Pines was, presumably, referring to statements made by MK Azmi Bishara inside and outside the Knesset, such as:

> Mr Chairman, Members of the Knesset,
>
> The Government of Israel may endeavour to present its withdrawal from Lebanon as compliance with [UN] Security Council Resolution 425. The Lebanese resistance to the Israeli occupation, however, has the right to present this [withdrawal] as a victory over the Israeli occupation. Not in the sense of a regular army [victory] and not in the sense of a classical military victory, but in the sense of a guerrilla war, this was, without doubt, a victory in terms of the threshold of tolerance of the Israeli society in such a case, [namely,] in a war that was not supported by a consensus in the Israeli society, one half of which is opposing the war and Israeli presence [in Lebanon] as well as in the sense of Israel's inability to exercise its full military might. This is how superpowers and large military forces are defeated when they face such people. Also the United States was not able to apply its full military might in Vietnam … The State of Israel was defeated in this war – and it is necessary to fully consider the consequences [of that defeat]. (*Knesset Debates*, Session No. 113 of the 15th Knesset, 31 May 2000. I am indebted to Adalah: Legal Center for Arab Minority Rights in Israel for the reference)

Amendment No. 35 thus reads *inter alia as* follows:

7(a) A candidates' list shall not participate in the elections to the Knesset if its objects or actions, expressly or by implication, include one of the following:

(1) negation of the existence of the State of Israel as a Jewish and a democratic state;[47]

(2) incitement to racism;

(3) support for armed struggle by an enemy state or a terror organization against the State of Israel. (*Laws of the State of Israel, Official Gazette* No. 1845, 22 May 2002, p. 410)

As MK Azmi Bishara pointed out in the plenary debate on Amendment No. 35:

So, what is 'armed struggle', what is 'a terror organization' and what is 'by implication'? Mr Chairman, for now you judge the following putting the Supreme Court of Justice aside. We will no doubt get to argue before the Supreme Court [later]. Is it allowed to utter the statement 'It is the right [of all] peoples to resist occupation' – yes, it is allowed. This is a general, non-specific, abstract and theoretical statement. This is a liberal position. Many people throughout the world subscribe to this statement. There are even international treaties stipulating the right of peoples to resist occupation, adding, by the way, [that they have the right to do so by] utilizing all [available] means. We don't even say: 'by utilizing all means'. Some of us say: 'Look, there are things that are not ethical, there are things that are not legitimate'. Is the utterance of the following sentence: 'The Palestinian people is under occupation' allowed? It is. What, then, is left [that could be said]? This is by implication [support for armed struggle by an enemy state or a terror organization against the State of Israel]. By implication – why so? [Because it follows] Aristo's syllogism. The right of peoples to resist occupation is a legitimate right. The Palestinian people are under occupation. The conclusion is therefore that the Palestinian people have the right to resist the occupation. Is this then support by implication for the right of a terror organization to engage in armed struggle? What is 'by implication'? What is 'armed struggle'? What is 'a terror organization'? What is being debated here? What is debated here is the desire to subject Israeli democracy to [the terms of] Israel's foreign policy. (Sessions of the 15th Knesset, *Stenographic Protocols* [uncorrected version], Fourth Session, 15 May 2002, p. 56)

The stipulation 'support for armed struggle by an enemy state or a terror organization against the State of Israel' was on the same occasion introduced also as Amendment No. 13 to the Political Parties Law of

1992 and underpinned by Amendment No. 46 to the Knesset Elections Law (Consolidated Version) of 1969, introduced into Article 57, after Clause (i) stipulating that a candidates' list shall be submitted to the Central Elections Committee no later than the 35th day before election day, accompanied by the consent of the candidates in writing or by telegram, a new Clause (i1) as follows:

(i1) In the letter of consent as aforementioned in Clause (i) the candidate will make the following declaration: 'I undertake to maintain allegiance to the State of Israel and refrain from acting contrary to Article 7(a) of Basic Law: The Knesset'. (*Laws of the State of Israel, Official Gazette* No. 1845, 22 May 2002, p. 411)

And finally, on the same occasion, 15 May 2002, Amendment No. 66 to the Penal Code of 1977 as follows:

Article 144(d)(2) a) A person who makes public a call for a violent or terror action, or statements of praise, sympathy or encouragement of a violent or terror action, [or] support and identification with [a violent or terror action] (in this Clause – publication of incitement), and subject to the contents of the publication of incitement and the circumstances of its publication, there exists a material possibility that it will cause a violent or a terror action to be committed, shall be sentenced to five years imprisonment;

(b) In this Article 'a violent or terror action' [is defined as] an offence that causes injury to the body of a person, or places a person in danger of death or danger of serious injury. (*Laws of the State of Israel, Official Gazette* No. 1845, 22 May 2002, p. 411)

Needless to say, all those committed to the values of the Universal Declaration of Human Rights without hypocrisy or duplicity would recognize that the first party that ought to be charged under this new legislation is none other than the Government of the State of Israel.

The Knesset did not have to wait too long for an opportunity to rid itself of voices such as that of MK Azmi Bishara above. Some six months later at the request of Prime Minister Ariel Sharon, on 5 November 2002, the president of the State of Israel, Mr Moshe Katzav, issued a written decree dissolving Parliament, the 15th Knesset, and Sharon's administration became a caretaker government, a *de facto* 'transitional government', a government not accountable to parliament and immune against votes of no confidence. The elections for Israel's 16th Knesset were set for 28 January 2003. Before long, the attorney-general, supported by the General Security Services (SHABAK), made the first move. The Election News Update by Adalah (The Legal Center for Arab Minority Rights in Israel) on the subject is instructive:

> Attorney-General, Supported by GSS, Seeks Disqualification of NDA Party from Israeli Elections; Right-Wing MKs Ask to Ban Three Arab MKs and Three Political Parties; Adalah to Represent All Arab MKs and Political Parties

> On 19 December 2002, in an unprecedented move, Attorney-General Elyakim Rubenstein submitted a motion to the Central Elections Committee (CEC) asking to disqualify the National Democratic Assembly (NDA) party from running in the upcoming Israeli elections. The Attorney-General's submission to the CEC relies almost exclusively on previously 'secret' General Security Service (GSS) materials about the activities of MK Dr Azmi Bishara, the head of the NDA.

> As the Attorney-General is an executive branch official and the GSS is directly subordinate to the Prime Minister, the Attorney-General's move amounts to illegal political, governmental intervention in the legislative process.

> The CEC has also been presented with motions filed by other right-wing MKs seeking to disqualify three Arab Members of Knesset (MKs) and three political parties from running in the 28 January 2003 elections in Israel. Challenges against all of the Arab candidates and political parties were submitted pursuant to Section 7(A) of the Basic Law: The Knesset. These motions claim that the goals and activities of the Arab candidates and political parties deny 'the existence of the State of Israel as a Jewish and democratic state' and lend 'support of armed struggle, of an enemy state or of a terrorist organization against the State of Israel'.

> Adalah will represent all of the Arab political leaders and political parties before the CEC, and if necessary, before the Supreme Court of Israel. Adalah's reply briefs to the disqualification motions, including that of the Attorney-General, must be submitted on 25 December 2002 at 10 a.m. The CEC will then schedule and hold hearings on these motions.

> By 3 January 2003, the CEC will vote upon whether or not MKs Dr Azmi Bishara (NDA), Abd el-Malik Dehamshe (United Arab List), and Ahmad Tibi (TA'AL), as individual candidates, may run in the elections. The CEC will also decide upon whether or not to ban three political party lists – the NDA, the joint HADASH-TA'AL list, and the United Arab List – from the parliamentary elections. The CEC, chaired by Supreme Court Justice Michal Cheshin, is composed of 41 representatives of all

political parties in the outgoing 15th Knesset. There are eight representatives of the Labour Party, six Likud, five SHAS, three MERETZ, two Shinui, two Center Party, two National Union, two United Torah Judaism, and one each for all of the remaining parties. Five representatives of the Arab political parties are members of the CEC.

This election marks the first time that the CEC will decide upon the eligibility of individual candidates. This is due to a May 2002 amendment to Section 7(A) of the Basic Law: The Knesset. Section 7(A) is titled, 'Prevention of participation in the elections'. According to this law, the CEC may disqualify a candidate or a political party list from running in the Knesset elections if the goals or actions of the candidate or party (i) deny the existence of the State of Israel as a Jewish and democratic state; (ii) incite to racism; or (iii) [offer] support of armed struggle, of an enemy state or of a terrorist organization against the State of Israel. This latter provision – 'support of armed struggle' – was also added by the 2002 amendment to the list of grounds upon which candidates and political parties may be disqualified from running in the Knesset elections.

If the CEC votes to disqualify an individual candidate from participating in the Knesset elections in accordance with Section 7(A), it must forward its decision and arguments to the Supreme Court for approval. A CEC decision to disqualify a political party list, by contrast, is binding; however, Article 64 of the Elections Law (1969) provides that the list has the right of appeal to the Supreme Court. If the CEC decides to qualify or approve a political party list, the Attorney-General and/or the Chairperson of the CEC and/or one-quarter of the CEC members may also appeal to the Supreme Court. Appeals to the Supreme Court must be filed by 5 January 2003.

The Supreme Court has ruled only once to disqualify an Arab political party from running in the Knesset elections. That ruling, in the Yardor case, was delivered in 1965 against the participation of the El Ard movement, prior to the enactment of Section 7(A). The Supreme Court must deliver final decisions on the qualification of candidates and political party lists for the upcoming elections by 9 January 2003. (*Adalah Elections News Update*, Date: Sat. 21 Dec. 2002 14:32:36, <adalah@adalah.org>)

On Wednesday 1 January 2003, the Central Elections Committee resolved (21 in favour to 20 against) to disqualify MK Azmi Bishara's NDA/BALAD party from running in the next Knesset elections, having the day before disqualified MK Ahmad Tibi (voting 21 in favour to 18 against). On Thursday 9 January, the Supreme Court, sitting in a panel of eleven Justices, headed by Supreme Court President Aharon Barak, overturned the CEC's decisions to disqualify Arab MKs Ahmad Tibi, Azmi Bishara and the NDA party from running in the 28 January election.

The deterioration of the political structures of the State of Israel as reflected in the 2002 Knesset legislation above has been accompanied by manifestations of political corruption and economic deterioration of proportions hitherto unknown in Israel. Thus the going rate for a deal at the Likud Convention, good enough to secure a block of votes sufficient to get a place regarded as a 'safe place' on the list of Likud candidates for the January 2003 elections to the 16th Knesset, is reported to have been US$250,000 (Nahum Barne'a, 'The Season of the [Block Votes] Contractors', *Yediot Aharonot* weekend supplement, 6 December 2002). According to Israel's Central Bureau of Statistics, the discrepancy between the average gross income of the top 10 per cent of households in the State of Israel today (NIS 39,130; approximately US$8,000 per month) is reported to be twelve times higher than the average gross income of the bottom 10 per cent (NIS 3,225; approximately US$650 per month). Over the past two decades, the discrepancies in access to income, property, capital, wage, education and consumption between the top 10 per cent and the bottom 10 per cent in Israel have polarized to a degree that Israel today is second only to the USA in this regard (*Haaretz*, 3 December 2002).

Taken together, against the backdrop of a protracted economic recession and the costly war criminal policies of occupation, the chances are that the tanks of the Israeli army deployed to level down the Jenin refugee camp in the occupied West Bank will be directed to suppress food riots inside Israel, let alone the Supreme Court.

5 · Possibilities for the Struggle Within

The defeat of the PLO in Oslo

As pointed out in the Foreword above, the Declaration of Principles on Interim Self-Government Arrangements (DOP) signed by the PLO on the one part and the Government of the State of Israel on the second part in Washington, DC in September 1993, followed by the so-called 'Oslo peace process', undercut the Palestinian Declaration of Independence of 1988 and the political programmes developed by the Palestine National Councils (PNCs) hitherto. Rather than representing a victory for the Palestinian struggle led by the PLO since its establishment in 1964, the DOP and the subsequent 'Oslo peace process' represent a strategic defeat for the three decades of Palestinian resistance led by the PLO, and cast a serious question as to the potential of the PLO as an alternative to Israeli apartheid.

The first Palestinian Intifada broke out in 1987 inside the 1967 occupied Gaza Strip and the West Bank. Aiming to shake off the 20-year Israeli occupation, it signalled a watershed in the history of the Palestinian resistance. One could reasonably argue that one of the more significant achievements of the first Palestinian Intifada was the convening of the Middle East Peace Conference in Madrid in October 1991, and the appointment, under PLO auspices, of Dr Haydar Abd al-Shafi as head of the Palestinian delegation to the Conference and Dr Hanan Ashrawi as spokesperson.

The prospects of a PLO defeat in the subsequent negotiating process, however, could already be identified in the papers prepared by the PLO in the course of the negotiations, notably Palestinian Interim Self-Governing Authority (PISGA) of January 1992 (see below). The defeat became evident with the DOP.

One important reason for the eventual defeat of the PLO in the negotiations that followed the Madrid Middle East Peace Conference and secret negotiations held in Oslo was the misguided decision of the PLO leadership to overrule Dr Haydar Abd al-Shafi, head of the Palestinian delegation, and proceed with the negotiations despite the refusal of the Israeli delegation, representing the Government of the State of

Israel, to provide cast-iron guarantees that all settlement activities in the 1967 occupied West Bank and Gaza Strip would be suspended without exception for the duration of the negotiations.

A second important reason for the eventual defeat of the PLO was the misguided political assessment, shared by the mainstream of the external PLO leadership and the mainstream of the internal PLO leadership, that it was possible under the prevailing conditions to obtain sovereignty and independence for a Palestinian state that will not be a Palestinian Bantustan alongside an apartheid, Zionist State of Israel.

It is Uri Avnery and the Israeli Council for Israeli Palestinian Peace, as well as the Israeli Communist Party (RAKAH), who bear considerable responsibility for the consolidation inside the PLO mainstream of the misguided political doctrine that it was possible to obtain sovereignty and independence for a Palestinian state, which will not be a Palestinian Bantustan, alongside a State of Israel that remains committed to the values of political Zionist ideology, namely to a political programme that claims that it is a good idea to establish and consolidate in the country of Palestine a sovereign state, a Jewish state, that attempts to guarantee in law (for example, Absentees' Property Law of 1950) and in practice (for example, the mass expulsion of the native indigenous Palestinian Arab people under the cover of the 1948–49 war) a demographic majority of the Jewish tribes (a demographic majority of ethnic Jews) in the territories under its control.

It is Uri Avnery and the Israeli Council for Israeli Palestinian Peace as well as the Israeli Communist Party (RAKAH) who bear considerable responsibility for the progressive demise of the PLO. It is due, *inter alia*, to the persistent advocacy of that camp inside and outside the PLO over many decades that the said misguided political doctrine became progressively more and more influential inside the PLO, resulting in the defeat of the PLO in Oslo.

In the fierce political debate inside and outside the PLO since the mid-1970s between the camp advocating accommodation with political Zionism and the camp advocating resistance on the basis of commitment to anti-Zionist and anti-apartheid values, it is the former camp that won the upper hand, and it is the former camp that is largely responsible for the current defeat. That camp has yet to publish its own self-critical assessment.

It is in this context that Uri Avnery is completely right to insist on his identity as a Zionist Israeli patriot. In 1977 Avnery, together with his colleagues in the Israeli Council for Israeli Palestinian Peace, won a libel case against the Management Committee of the Sephardi Community in Jerusalem for alleging that Avnery and his colleagues were anti-Zionist. Avnery and his colleagues in the Israeli Council for Israeli Palestinian Peace are, to my knowledge, the only Jewish citizens of the State of Israel who can produce a court ruling attesting to their Zionist credentials.

Uri Avnery documents his political intervention *inter alia* in his work *My Friend, the Enemy* (Zed Books, 1986). In this work Uri Avnery both misrepresents and misinterprets the contribution of the principled anti-Zionist Israeli peace camp as well as the work of anti-Zionist individuals who were and remain important to the continuing development of Israeli–Palestinian dialogue.

Uri Avnery spent much of his lifetime lobbying for an Israeli–Palestinian peace that is based on continued Israeli strength as a Zionist state and the recognition of the legality of the State of Israel, within the 1949–67 armistice lines, as a Jewish state in the political Zionist sense of the term, an apartheid state. Since the truth of the Palestinian–Israeli situation is that Israeli–Palestinian peace that is consistent with the values of the Universal Declaration of Human Rights and the standards of international law can be reached primarily on the basis of Israeli Zionist weakness and defeat of Israeli apartheid, Israeli Zionist peace efforts, notably Uri Avnery's, being predicated on a false assumption, bear significant responsibility for the current predicament of Palestine.

And to my knowledge he has yet to account for his activities, possibly war crimes, in the 1948–49 war as a soldier with the Giv'ati battalion commando unit 'Samson's Foxes' directed, as noted above, by such criminal 'orders of the day' as were issued in the daily battle sheets of the political commissar of the Giv'ati battalion, Abba Kobner, a survivor of the Nazi occupation of Europe and the Kobna Ghetto rebellion, who turned to Nazi rhetoric himself, issuing such battle sheets as Battle Sheet dated 12.7.1948 entitled '*Aju al-Yahud* (The Jews Have Come): The Night of Raid and Purge':

> Indeed we broke the spirit of the enemy and also rent their bodies open. But the enemy strength is still there. It is an enemy. It is an army. Though we are confident that the dung of the corpses of the invaders [will fertilize] our fields into blossom …

After all, Uri Avnery is reported to have taken part in the Samson's Foxes operation in the Palestinian Arab village of 'Ibdis, subsequently destroyed and razed to the ground (whose lands have since been transferred for cultivation by *inter alia* Kibbutz Negbah), and to have participated in operations where the Samson's Foxes were ordered to move from Arab village to Arab village and 'shoot at anything that moved, man, woman, child, camel or donkey', as well as to have taken part in operations in the south where the Samson's Foxes commandoes 'raced with their jeeps after all those [Arabs] like hunters hunting rabbits' (Yair Lev, *The Subject: Uri Avnery*, Guerrilla Pictures, 2002).

Uri Avnery does not deny his participation in these operations – but claims that he did not shoot.

But whereas he joined the libel case against the Management Committee of the Sephardi Community in Jerusalem for alleging that he and his colleagues in the Israeli Council for Israeli Palestinian Peace were anti-Zionist, he is not reported to have initiated any move to bring charges of war crimes against Abraham Cohen, Jacob Mali, Ahiyah Shiloni, Meir Levretowsky and Reuben Huber, his comrades in arms in Samson's Foxes, who openly admitted in the documentary picture above to have done so.

The veiling of Israeli apartheid has been critical to the securing of the gains of the political Zionist colonial settlement of Palestine and the cover-up of the war crimes perpetrated by the Israeli army against the Palestinian Arab people in the course of the 1948–49 war. Without this elaborately interwoven veil, it is doubtful that the State of Israel would have been as successful as it was in projecting itself since 1948 as 'the only democracy in the Middle East', the Palestinian 1948–49 *nakba*, a crime against humanity under international law, notwithstanding.

Uri Avnery and *Gush Shalom* are aware that the laws on war crimes are not subject to the statute of limitations and perpetrators can be brought to trial anywhere, anytime. They have joined their voices to those inside Israel and abroad condemning the war crimes perpetrated by the Israeli occupation in the West Bank and the Gaza Strip as well as cautioned against the prospects of Israeli attempts to orchestrate the mass expulsions of Palestinians from the post-1967 occupied territories under the cover of the US-led illegal attack on Iraq.

Yet, given Avnery's own failure and the failure of his camp to engage in self-critical assessment of their political choices in 1948, condemn the war crimes perpetrated by the Israeli army in the course of the 1948–49 war, and motivate prosecution for these war crimes *as well as* for subsequent war crimes, their peace advocacy today is tainted in that it betrays the rights of those most victimized by the political Zionist settler colonial project in Palestine, the 1948 Palestine refugees and their descendants, some four million people today.

Rather than tear away the veil, they collaborate in the perpetuation of the veil.

Yet, in the 15 years since the publication of *My Friend, the Enemy*, alongside the progressive demise of the PLO and its defeat, a parallel process of empowerment of the Palestinian Arab constituency inside Israel has been taking place.

The outbreak of the Palestinian Intifada in 1987 signalled a watershed also for the approximately one million Palestinian Arab citizens of the State of Israel, who became progressively aware that if until 1987 it was largely politically correct to regard the PLO as the sole legitimate representative of the Palestinian Arab people (including the Palestinian citizens of Israel), with the outbreak of the Palestinian Intifada in 1987, that position had to be revised.

It has long been my view that the progressive demise of the PLO is largely due to its moral, emotional, ideological and political failure to take a page from the book of the African National Congress (ANC) and reform itself politically and legally from the sole legitimate representative of the Palestinian Arab people (currently some nine million people) to the democratic alternative for all Palestinians, Arab and non-Arab (currently some 15 million people), and develop a political narrative that encompasses a common future, on an equal footing, for both peoples of Palestine, both the native indigenous Palestinian Arab people and the people that has its origins in the political Zionist colonial project in Palestine.

By the same token, the progressive empowerment of the Palestinian Arab constituency inside Israel is largely due to their having no moral, emotional, ideological or political problem with projecting a common future, on an equal footing, for both peoples; they are largely bilingual (Arabic and Hebrew), often trilingual (Arabic, Hebrew and English); and their political class is today poised to make a significant contribution to the Palestinian resistance and to international Palestine solidarity mobilization on a principled anti-apartheid basis.

There is little doubt in my mind that considerable achievements by the anti-apartheid struggles within the State of Israel notwithstanding (see below), the defeat of Israeli apartheid in Palestine, like the defeat of apartheid in South Africa, cannot be visualized without international solidarity, based on the values of the Universal Declaration of Human Rights.

All consistent solidarity work is rights-based. Since the establishment of the PLO in 1964, and most emphatically since the declaration by the UN General Assembly of Zionism as 'a form of racism and racial discrimination' (UN General Assembly Resolution 3375 of November 1975) the mainstream of Palestine solidarity mobilization has been predicated internationally on the morally, politically and legally correct argument that the values of political Zionism are incompatible with the values of the Universal Declaration of Human Rights and thus with the fundamental internationally recognized rights of the colonized and dispossessed native indigenous Palestinian Arab people, notably their right to return, to self-determination and to an independent state.

It has been on this basis that the mainstream of Palestine solidarity mobilized against political Zionism; for unconditional withdrawal of the Israeli armed forces from the 1967 occupied territories; and for the recognition of the PLO as the sole legitimate representative of the Palestinian people.

Against this backdrop it is hardly surprising that when, in Oslo, the sole legitimate representative of the Palestinian people agreed to internationally binding accords, known as the 'Oslo accords', officially signed in Washington, DC in September 1993, uncritically committing the PLO to recognize 'the right of the State of Israel to exist in peace and security', international Palestine solidarity work was caught in a double bind that is only recently resolved with the patent collapse of the so-called 'Oslo peace process'.

This book, and specifically this chapter, aim to make a contribution to the development of an adequate political anti-apartheid narrative, empowered by the UN World Conference Against Racism (WCAR), Durban, South Africa, 28 August–3 September 2001, for a renewed Palestinian-led resistance to political Zionism and for Palestine solidarity worldwide.

Assessing the danger of Palestinian defeat at the peace negotiations

Assessing the danger of Palestinian defeat at the peace negotiations is not a simple undertaking. It is possible to argue that the agreement of the PLO to authorize a Palestinian negotiating team to embark upon bilateral and multilateral negotiations in the framework of the regional Middle East Peace Conference launched in Madrid in October 1991, on the basis of UN Security Council Resolution 242 and 338 (rather than on the basis of all UN resolutions relevant to the question of Palestine), is itself a defeat, and, therefore, all that could emerge out of the negotiated process cannot, by definition, be anything other than further defeat.

This is not my position and this was not my position.

Against the backdrop of horrific Israeli violations of human rights and international law such as the policy of torture; expulsion; mass administrative arrests; mass demolition of homes; destruction of medical, educational and cultural infrastructure; land confiscations and settlement; and recently the protracted siege of the occupied West Bank and Gaza Strip, is it at all appropriate to consider the danger of Palestinian defeat at the current peace negotiations? I submit that it is not only appropriate, but furthermore, most urgent that this be done. It is my firm belief that it is our duty as people committed wholeheartedly to the defence of human rights and international law everywhere, and specifically in Palestine, to continue an open discussion of the question, if for no other reason than that a Palestinian defeat will inevitably set back our efforts in a serious way. In this respect, a Palestinian victory is not 'their' victory – it is also 'our' victory, and likewise, lest it happen, a Palestinian defeat.

Defeat is not an unproblematic term. There are military defeats that result in political victories. There are defeats in the battle that result in victory in the war. There are defeats that, when identified as defeats, strengthen the resolve of the people to continue the struggle and wrench victory from the depth of adversity. And there are defeats falsely dressed up as victory that demoralize and debilitate the people and set their struggle for freedom back many years. When addressing the question of the danger of Palestinian defeat, it is this last formulation to which I refer.

Assessing the danger of Palestinian defeat in the peace negotiations entails, by definition, informed speculation about the future. Speculation is a contingent exercise. It represents an essential aspect of all human activity, most emphatically political activity. Speculations inform our priorities, underpin our interpretation and illuminate our analysis of current events. They are hypotheses inviting corroboration or falsification by events. But even when falsified, informed speculation, as an important aspect of our intellectual skill, may enlighten our understanding in ways that are unique and valuable and not within the reach of any other mode of political and moral contemplation.

What I have to say is relevant to the future of Palestine. It is therefore speculative by definition.

The PLO is rightly and properly widely acknowledged as the legitimate representative of the Palestinian people. But like any political organization, it is a political instrument created to defend the dignity and promote the welfare of the Palestinian people within the framework of universal morality and international law. The establishment of the PLO in 1964; the admission of the PLO to the United Nations as an Observer Organization in 1974; and the development of the PLO as the State of Palestine in the making culminating in the Palestinian Declaration of Independence of 1988 – these achievements, towards which the heroic efforts of the Palestine solidarity movements in Israel and throughout the world made a significant contribution, also place Palestine solidarity and the supporters of the cause of Palestine in an inevitable predicament. In the final analysis, the decision of the PLO Executive Committee, if and when endorsed by the Palestine National Council (PNC), must be regarded as the responsible decisions of the Palestinian people, and therefore (subject to the qualifications I wish to present below) binding on all Palestine solidarity movements.

But what should individual Palestinians or individual Palestine solidarity persons do if they deem the Palestinian decisions regarding the possible deal on the negotiating table to be not only politically misjudged, but also morally unacceptable? How should they regard the prospective situation when principles conflict with politics? Where does the Palestine solidarity movement turn should it be asked by the PLO to support and rationalize a political programme or a political deal that runs counter to the basic tenets of its conscience and the underlying fountain of its enthusiasm and courage?

Consider, for instance, the question of *de jure* recognition of the State of Israel as a state in the region.

We ought not to confuse the *de jure* diplomatic recognition of any given state as a member state of the United Nations Organization with the recognition of its territorial boundaries, let alone its official ideology and legal system. The USA recognizes the People's Republic of China as a state in the region and has full normal diplomatic relations with the People's Republic of China. This recognition does not in itself entail recognition by the US Congress of the Chinese annexation of Tibet (the US Congress classifies Tibet as occupied territory). Nor does it entail – not legally and not politically – US legitimation of the prevailing state ideology of communism. If anything, I suspect, US recognition of China as a state in the region and US diplomatic relations with China are viewed in Washington, DC as effective vehicles to undermine communism in China.

The same distinctions apply to the case of Israel. PLO recognition of the State of Israel as a state in the region and diplomatic relations between the State of Palestine and the State of Israel do not in themselves entail recognition and legitimation by the PNC of Israeli annexation of any part of Palestine beyond the boundaries of the UN 1947 Partition Plan (UN General Assembly Resolution 181[II]) or of political Zionism and the Israeli apartheid legal system.

What is to be our response, however, if and when the PLO accepted a deal in the permanent status negotiations that is not limited to PLO recognition of the existence of the State of Israel as a state in the region, but surrendered to Israel Palestinian recognition and legitimation of its continued existences as a political Zionist Jewish state: an apartheid state?

In the years following the launch of the regional Middle East Peace Conference under the joint auspices of the USA and the USSR, a malaise has blighted Palestine solidarity work throughout the network of non-governmental organizations in the western world. The malaise was reflected in massive decline of attendance at grassroots meetings, decreasing participation in rallies, poor response to initiatives of protest against violation of human rights by the Israeli occupation authorities and general demoralization. The root cause for the malaise and the decline is, I believe, the feeling that it is no longer inconceivable that the elected leadership of the PLO will deliver, as part of the deal in the permanent status negotiations, recognition and legitimation of the continued existence of Israel as an apartheid state, and, thereby, set back the defence of human rights and international law in Palestine and destroy the gains and the achievements of the Palestinian resistance and the Palestine solidarity movements in Israel and throughout the world in the past forty years.

It was only with the election of Ariel Sharon as prime minister of the State of Israel in February 2001 and the collapse of the so-called Middle East peace process that Palestine solidarity was relaunched throughout the world, now largely on an anti-apartheid basis, with the demand to boycott Israeli produce and leisure tourism to Israel as well as the call for disinvestment in Israel and for international sanctions against the State of Israel.

In NGO and solidarity work conscience takes precedence over reasons of state, and the PLO, like any other political institution, should not expect support and should not be given support if the deal that it endorses violates the basic tenets of conscience. Assuming fundamental commitment to universal values, there is no difference between the individual conscience of a Palestinian freedom fighter, an Israeli Jewish anti-Zionist and a British member of the Palestine Solidarity Campaign. Before the voice of conscience we are all equal, and the first question that, I suggest, is relevant in this connection could be formulated as follows: Does the permanent status political package that is reported as likely to emerge out of the Madrid and Oslo peace negotiations include legitimation by the PLO or by the future State of Palestine of racism, namely, of the continued existence of the State of Israel as a Zionist Jewish state, an apartheid state, a state that predicates its legal structure on discrimination by law between 'Jew' versus 'non-Jew'?

In March 1992, in the framework of the regional Middle East Peace Conference launched in Madrid in October 1991, the Jordanian–Palestinian delegation submitted to the Israeli delegation, after approval by the PLO leadership in Tunis, the Palestinian Interim Self-Governing

Authority (PISGA) plan. PISGA proved to be the precursor of the Palestinian Authority (PA), agreed a year later in the Declaration of Principles
on Interim Self-Government Arrangements (DOP) secretly negotiated in
Oslo and signed in Washington, DC.

A few months later, on 29 June 1993, I delivered an address before the
Council for the Advancement of Arab–British Understanding (CAABU)
at its monthly meeting at the House of Commons, likewise entitled
'Assessing the Dangers of Palestinian Defeat in the Current Peace Negotiations'. Sticking my neck out, I risked a speculative fictitious scenario
assuming, *inter alia*, a permanent status settlement ceding 85 per cent
of British Mandate Palestine to Israeli sovereignty, the remaining 15 per
cent declared as the territory of the independent State of Palestine, to
be federated with the Hashemite Kingdom of Jordan as a United Arab
Kingdom (UAK), and proposing the following conclusion:[48]

> Regarding the documents pertaining to the permanent status, there
> are two subjects that can and should be regarded as our compass in
> this respect:
>
> One, the debate on the question of the Palestinian right to return,
> and,
>
> Two, the question of the international status of Jerusalem.
>
> As the texts relevant to the permanent status negotiations are made
> public, I suggest that we consider them carefully and examine what
> they say regarding the right of the 1948 Palestinian refugees to return
> and resume their residence in any and all parts of Palestine, including
> Israel, and their right to appropriate Israeli citizenship under the terms
> of UN resolutions and international law. Likewise I propose that careful
> attention be given to the textual reference to the question of Jerusalem
> and the status of the city under international law as *corpus separatum*
> under UN administration as per UN General assembly Resolution 181
> of November 1947.
>
> I propose to elaborate the case.
>
> For better or for worse it is within the prerogative of governments
> of sovereign states to cede territories to other sovereign states. It is
> not, however, within the prerogative of governments to compromise
> the individual human and legal rights of such of their citizens who are
> the inhabitants of these ceded territories. If the State of Palestine is
> compelled to cede 75 per cent of its UN 1947 partition plan territory to
> the State of Israel and sanction the surrender of this territory through
> the mechanism of UN resolutions and international law, it is obligated
> by the same token to secure that the rights of its citizens in the ceded
> territories as enshrined in UN resolutions and international law are

respected by the State of Israel – most emphatically, the rights of the Palestinian inhabitants (residents and refugees) to Israeli citizenship.

Whereas it is within the competence of the State of Palestine to surrender Palestinian territory to the State of Israel in the Galilee, the Triangle, the West Bank and the Gaza Strip, it is not within its competence to do so regarding Jerusalem, nor is it within the competence of the State of Israel to annex Jerusalem. Under UN resolutions and international law, Jerusalem is UN territory, and any settlement of the question of Jerusalem that does not respect the international status of the city must be condemned.

In other words, I wish to suggest two key questions relevant to the assessment of the danger of Palestinian defeat at the permanent status negotiations.

One, whether or not the interim agreements stipulate the foundations not only for a Palestinian–Jordanian confederation but also and equally for a Palestinian–Israeli confederation (resulting in a three-way Jordanian–Palestinian–Israeli confederation) where every citizen of the State of Palestine regardless of country of residence is entitled to appropriate by right, by the Constitution of the confederation, underpinned by UN resolutions and international law, not only Jordanian citizenship but also Israeli citizenship, and where the right to vote to Parliament (Jordanian, Palestinian or Israeli) is determined not by citizenship, but by registration of legal domicile, and,

Two, whether the references to al-Quds as the capital of the State of Palestine and to Jerusalem as the capital of the State of Israel in the documents pertaining to the final status of the post-1967 Israeli Occupied Territories stipulate that these two capitals are subject to UN sovereignty and to the international status of the city as determined by UN Resolution 181(II) recommending the partition of Palestine with economic union.

I believe these criteria for the assessment of the danger of Palestinian defeat at the permanent status negotiations remain as valid today as they were a decade or so ago, namely:

If the deal negotiated as a permanent status entails the right of every citizen of Palestine also to dual or triple Palestinian–Israeli or Palestinian–Israeli–Jordanian citizenship, and if the deal confirms rather than undermines the status of Jerusalem as a *corpus separatum* under UN administration, it is my assessment that, however disadvantageous the deal may otherwise be from the Palestinian point of view, the negotiated deal is not a Palestinian defeat falsely dressed up as a victory. Rather, given the enormous power-political imbalance between Israel and the PLO to the detriment of the PLO, a deal that includes these two stipulations is, indeed, truly a Palestinian victory in the negotiation battle: one additional victory in the long struggle for the liberation of Palestine from Zionist apartheid discrimination.

The reader may be aware, however, that these two stipulations are nowhere to be found anywhere in the texts hitherto negotiated since the convening of the Middle East Peace Conference in Madrid in 1991. So long as they remain absent the Palestinian party will be defeated at the negotiation table.

Israel's Zionist society

The Israeli Jewish society identifies itself, and is correctly recognized, as a Zionist society, morally, politically and technically.

Morally, in that the ideological mainstream of the Israeli-Jewish society is predicated upon the preposterous claim that anti-Semitism is not a socially and politically manufactured phenomenon to be understood and combated historically, but rather, that anti-Semitism is an essential aspect of non-Jewish human nature, and as consequence, Jews can never hope to achieve equality of rights as religious or cultural minorities in Gentile societies (see, for instance, the quotation by Leo Pinsker in Chapter 1).

In the framework of political Zionist moral perceptions every Gentile must be classified, cannot but be classified, as a covert or an overt anti-Semite. An enlightened Gentile is a Gentile who is aware of his or her irreducible anti-Semitism, and is thus led to assist the Zionist political organization in the achievement of the Zionist solution to the problem of anti-Semitism on a principled basis. As Hannah Arendt documents in her classical report *Eichmann in Jerusalem*, Adolf Eichmann, for instance, viewed himself as such a principled Gentile supporter of Zionism.

Politically, in that the Zionist political solution to the problem of anti-Semitism is predicated upon two correlative elements: first, the mobilization of Jewish communities throughout the world towards immigration to Palestine, and, second, the establishment of a Jewish state in Palestine, namely the State of Israel, and the mobilization of moral and material support in Jewish communities throughout the world for the continued existence of the State of Israel as a Jewish state in the political Zionist sense of the term, namely, a state that attempts to guarantee in law (e.g., Absentees' Property Law of 1950) and in practice (e.g., the mass expulsion of the native indigenous Palestinian Arab people under the cover of the 1948–49 war) a demographic majority of the Jewish tribes in the territories under its control.

The Zionist movement, since its establishment as a political organization at the first Zionist Congress in Basle in 1897, has been historically divided. The three mainstream Zionist political divisions inside the World Zionist Organization, and since 1948 in parallel inside the State of Israel, are Labour Zionism, Revisionist Zionism and Religious Zionism. In the course of Zionist history profound differences of opinion and judgement developed among those three mainstream Zionist divisions as to the desired scope of the Zionist project in Palestine at any given period of time; the desired strategy for colonization of Palestine and, since 1948, the desired boundaries for the Jewish state; the desired form of social organization for the Jewish society in Palestine; and the desired nature of the political regime of the State of Israel. But, underpinning all mainstream Zionist divisions and political parties, there has been throughout Zionist history a shared political principle formalized in the Jerusalem Programme above.

The claim that it is a good idea to establish and consolidate in the country of Palestine a sovereign state, a Jewish state, that attempts to guarantee in law and in practice a demographic majority of the Jewish tribes in the territories under its control defines the boundary of the Zionist political domain and underpins all World Zionist Organization political programmes. Every Jewish citizen of the State of Israel is aware and at least partially informed of the basic realities underpinning his or her political existence as a Jewish citizen of the Jewish state and the nature of the Palestinian Arab resistance, as evidenced by Moshe Dayan's quote above.

Technically, in that the legal structure and the routine of everyday life of the Israeli Jewish society are determined in every domain by the apartheid distinction of 'Jew' versus 'non-Jew', both through the constitutional framework of the World Zionist Organization and its various executive bodies such as the JA and the JNF, as well as, since 1948, through the legislation of the Knesset, which in the key areas of immigration and settlement is directed to give legal garb in Israeli law to the constitutional principles of the World Zionist Organization.

And thus, through this 'very significant legal innovation' (see Zerah Wahrhaftig, above), of giving legal garb to the Memorandum of Association and the JNF, it was made possible in the State of Israel to prohibit non-Jews, and in the first instance the Palestinian Arab native indigenous population of the country, from purchase or lease of 93 per cent of pre-1967 Israel territory. The same legal structures of apartheid obtain in the domain of access to water resources, as, in fact, to most domains of everyday life under Israeli rule. At all key junctions that determine welfare and housing for the body of the inhabitants under

Israeli rule, the Israeli legislature follows the same pattern of passing laws and contracting covenants that codify as Israeli law enforced by the legislative, the courts, the police and the military machinery of the State of Israel, the constitutional principles of the World Zionist Organization. In order to understand in full the consequences of all this for Israel's internal opposition it is important to recall that under Israeli law, in so far as property rights are concerned, the majority of the Palestinian Arab people do not exist. They are defined out of existence under the Absentees' Property Law of 1950 as 'absentees' (stateless refugees) or 'present absentees' (internally displaced persons inside the State of Israel, third-class citizens). Their rights to the titles of their pre-1948 properties are nullified.

Through the Absentees' Property Law of 1950 the State of Israel guarantees that the overwhelming majority of the Palestinian Arab residents of the territories that fell under Israeli sovereignty as a consequence of the 1948–49 war, both refugees outside the pre-1967 borders of the state and internally displaced persons, citizens inside its pre-1967 borders, are denied their rights to property in Israel.

In other words, the claim that in order to create the physical space for the Jew, the property rights of the Palestinian Arab 'absentee' must be denied is fundamental to political Zionist doctrine. As far as rights to property are concerned the Israeli legislator does not recognize the Palestinian Arab 'absentee' as a Palestinian, nor, for that matter, does he or she recognize him or her as a refugee.

No Israeli political Zionist, in government or in opposition, can accept a 1948 Palestinian Arab refugee presence inside the Jewish state. They can accept Palestinian Arab presence alongside the State of Israel (Peace Now and *Gush Shalom*). But they cannot accept the reconstitution of Palestinian Arab refugees' individual and collective economic, social, cultural, civil, political and national rights inside the State of Israel, since this, it would be correctly argued, would amount to the dismantlement of the State of Israel as a Jewish state in the political Zionist sense of the term, as an apartheid state (though not necessarily of the State of Israel as such). The essence of the Palestinian resistance movement, its driving force and the fountain of its morality, is the struggle to re-establish Palestinian refugee presence in those parts of Palestine from which the Palestinian Arabs have been expelled. The justice of the Palestinian resistance is rooted in its commitment to implement the return of the 1948 Palestine refugees and the rehabilitation of their individual rights and collective national life in all parts of their homeland Palestine from which they are excluded as 'absentees'.

The majority of the Palestinian Arab refugees cannot return to their original homes and lands. These homes no longer exist, and where they do exist they are inhabited by Jewish families. The Palestinian Arab village of Sheikh Muannas is levelled under the car parks and the buildings of the University of Tel Aviv. To the best of my knowledge, the Palestinian struggle for national liberation has not aimed to pull down the University of Tel Aviv and reconstruct the pre-1948 Palestinian Arab village of Sheikh Muannas. The struggle of the 1948 Palestine refugees has, on the other hand, rightly aimed to alter the regional and international balance of power so that the rights of all refugees, for instance the Palestinian Arab refugees of Sheikh Muannas to the titles of their properties inside Israel (destroyed, occupied or otherwise developed) are recognized and that all refugees are able to exercise their legal and legitimate choices under international law with reference to their said properties, including their right to rehabilitate their lives as close as possible to their original homes.

In the case of Sheikh Muannas, 'as close as possible' is likely to be in the very attractive residential quarters of Ramat Aviv, Me'oz Aviv and Afeqah in proximity to Tel Aviv University – and indeed, that is how it should be. In at least one case, the case of the property known as the 'Green House' appropriated by the Tel Aviv University, renovated as the University Club, and named after Marcelle Gordon, there is no reason whatsoever why the Sheikh Muannas families who are the legal inheritors of this property should not repossess the title to the place and, subject to negotiations carried out under the auspices of relevant UN bodies, return to live there.

The Israeli–Palestinian conflict is in its fundamental aspects a conflict between a settler colonial state and the indigenous native resistance. As such it is polarized very much like similar conflicts that have developed since the First World War throughout the colonial periphery of the western world. Given the priorities of settler colonial societies, and given the individual and corporate motivation, which led to their formation in the first instance, all settler colonial societies are structured around, and predicated upon, the necessity to exclude the indigenous native population out of equal participation in the colonial domain.

Since the colonial project is inconsistent with the universal principle of equality of rights for all, the native population as a whole cannot, by the definition of the elementary terms of the colonial project, be given equal rights in the colonial realm. The granting of equality of rights to all, both the settler and the excluded native, must therefore invariably entail, as it has, in fact, historically done, the dismantling of the colonial legal and political structures. In the framework of Zionist political perceptions all political Zionist parties are aligned in their support, either by deliberate design or *post factum*, by way of endorsing the *faits accomplis* established in the course of the 1948–49 war, for the expulsion, evacuation and transfer of the mass of the Palestinian Arab society from the territories of pre-1967 Israel.

This Zionist consensus is expressed lucidly by one of the persons central to the organization of the Zionist colonization project, the late Joseph Weitz, deputy chairman of the Board of Directors of the Jewish National Fund. The entry in his *Diaries*, published in Hebrew in Israel in 1965, of 19 December 1940 ('the only solution is *Eretz Israel* [the Land of Israel], or at least Western *Eretz Israel*, without Arabs. There is no room for compromise on this point ... [T]here is no other way but to transfer the Arabs from here to the neighbouring countries, transfer all of them, not one village or tribe should remain'), was quoted above.

Eight years later, the 1948–49 war gave Weitz and his colleagues at the top echelons of the Zionist and subsequently Israeli political hierarchy the opportunity to put this design into effect. Thus on 18 May 1948 Weitz enters the following report of his conversation with Moshe Shertok (later Sharett), Israel's first minister of foreign affairs:

> Transfer – *post factum*; should we do something so as to transform the exodus of the Arabs from the country into a fact, so that they return no more? ... His [Shertok's] answer: he blesses any initiative in this matter. His opinion is also that we must act in such a way as to transform the exodus of the Arabs into an established fact. (Weitz 1965 Vol. III: 293)

And later that year, he records his reflections following a visit to an Arab village in the process of its being razed to the ground by tractors:

> I went to visit the village of Mi'ar. Three tractors are completing its destruction. I was surprised; nothing in me moved at the sight of the destruction. No regret and no hate, as though this was the way the world goes. So we want to feel good in this world, and not in some world to come. We simply want to live, and the inhabitants of those mud-houses did not want us to exist here. They not only aspire to dominate us, they also wanted to exterminate us. And what is interesting, this is the opinion of all our boys, from one end to the other. (ibid.: 302)[49]

As a consequence of this Zionist consensus, when, following the 1967 war, the remaining parts of Palestine, namely, the West Bank and the Gaza Strip, came under Israeli occupation, the critical discussion inside the World Zionist Organization and among the various Zionist parties inside the State of Israel concentrated on the question of how much, if any, of the newly acquired occupied territories can be incorporated into the Jewish state without jeopardizing its in-built demographic majority of ethnic Jews given the regional and international balance of power at any given stage. The main division in this discussion is familiar and well documented.[50]

The Zionist peace camp

It is important to underline, however, that the critical subject of political Zionist consensus, the area where the idea of the continued existence of the State of Israel as a Jewish state in the political Zionist sense of the term is critically tested, is not the post-1967 occupied territories, but rather the pre-1967 occupied territories conventionally referred to as State of Israel proper.

It cannot be sufficiently emphasized that it is possible to remain inside, though very much at the margin of, the Zionist political realm as opposition calling for unconditional withdrawal from all post-1967 occupied territories, including East Jerusalem. There have been, and there are, political Zionist individuals and political Zionist groupings who argue that, given the regional and the international balance of power, the only rational prospects for the consolidation and continued existence of the State of Israel as a Jewish state in the political Zionist sense of the term, an apartheid state, is on the basis of Israel's pre-1967 borders.

Furthermore, it is possible to remain inside, though very much at the margin of the Zionist realm, as opposition calling for unconditional recognition of the PLO as sole legitimate representative of the Palestinian Arab people and the right of self-determination of the Palestinian Arab people in a sovereign independent PLO-administered state alongside the State of Israel in its pre-1967 borders. In the view of this Zionist opposition, given the regional and international balance of power, including the emergence of the PLO and the mobilization of the Palestinian people in armed resistance against Israel since 1965, such an alternative political programme represents the only long-term guarantee for the continued existence of the State of Israel as a Jewish state in the political Zionist sense of the term, an apartheid state.

Political Zionists claim the right of return for all Jewish communities throughout the world to the biblical Jewish homeland of Palestine after almost two millennia of dispersion and exile, but they cannot recognize the right of the 1948 Palestine refugee communities throughout the world to the implementation of the same right, after less than 60 years of the Israeli-manufactured dispersion of 1948, since if the implementation of their right is recognized, there will be no part of Palestine that could be guaranteed in law and in practice to remain demographically exclusively 'Jewish', not even the greater metropolitan area of Tel Aviv.

The late Golda Meir, as Israel's prime minister at the zenith of Israeli regional and international power political achievement, reflected the logic of the Zionist colonial endeavour in Palestine in her resounding statement to the London *Sunday Times*:

> There was no such thing as Palestinians. It was not as though there was a Palestinian people in Palestine considering itself as a Palestinian people and we came and threw them out and took their country away from them. They did not exist. (*Sunday Times*, 15 June 1969)

Yet, almost a decade later, reflecting the questionable Israeli military performance in the 1973 war and the beginning of the decline of Israel's power position regionally, and internationally, Menachem Begin, as Israel's prime minister, was compelled to concede in the framework of the 1978 US-negotiated Camp David accords recognition of 'The legitimate rights of the Palestinian people and their just requirements' (*Camp David Agreements*, 'West Bank and Gaza', Article C, 17 September 1978).

There is, however, near complete consensus, uniting all political Zionist individuals and parties, that inside the Jewish state, small or large, the universal principle of equality of rights for all, and specifically equality of rights for the Israeli Jewish settler and the Palestinian Arab indigenous native, notably, equal access to the material resources of the state, first and foremost land and water, cannot apply, since if it is applied, the State of Israel will have ended as a Jewish state in the political Zionist sense of the term.

And there still exists a near wall-to-wall political Zionist unanimity on the question of the implementation of the right of the 1948 Palestine refugees to return and to the title of their properties inside Israel. Of the half million people who marched in the streets of Tel Aviv against the Israeli-perpetrated and Falange-executed massacres of Sabra and Shatilah in 1982, only few would support the struggle of the survivors of the massacres and their descendants to reconstitute and rehabilitate their lives and the lives of their families in their neighbourhood in Tel Aviv.

Given the above, it must be clear to all concerned that all political Zionist individuals and organizations will unite and transcend all divisions of value judgement and political programme at one critical point: the point of the demand of the Palestinian Arab refugees of 1948 for return, to the title of their properties inside the State of Israel and to repatriation in all parts of their homeland Palestine including Acre, Haifa, Jaffa, Jerusalem and Beersheba.

Throughout Zionist history, 'moderate' political Zionist individuals and organizations, from Berit Shalom (Covenant of Peace) to Shalom Akhshav (Peace Now), from Martin Buber to Yeshaayahu Leibowitz, were invariably marginalized because of predicating their morality and political programmatic advocacy on a double standard: acceptance of UN Assembly Resolution of November 1947 No. 181(II) recommending the partition of Palestine into two states, a 'Jewish state' and an 'Arab state', with economic union and Jerusalem as *corpus separatum*, on the one hand, and substantive rejection of UN General Assembly Resolution of December 1948 No. 194(III), recalled annually by the General Assembly, urging the return of all Palestinian refugees to their homes, on the other.

Every Jewish citizen of the State of Israel knows, together with the late Moshe Dayan, that there is not one single place built in this country that did not have a former Arab population. Every Jewish citizen of Israel knows, together with the leading Israeli publicist Yeshaayahu Ben-Porat, that 'there is no Zionist settlement, and there is no Jewish state, without displacing Arabs, and without confiscating lands and fencing them off' (*Yediot Aharonot*, 14 July 1972; for full text see note 51).

Every Israeli Jew knows that the Palestinian 'absentee' is at the foundation and the centre of his or her being in Palestine. Every Jewish citizen of Israel knows that so long as the Palestinian 'absentees' are excluded from any part of their homeland they feel like placing a bomb in the place from which they are excluded, and that many, if not most, of the Jewish citizens of the State of Israel had they been in their place, would feel the same. Hence the popular and deep-seated political Zionist conviction that 'one can never trust the Arab'; that the 'Arab will invariably stab his or her benefactor in the back'; that 'given one finger the Arab will grab the entire hand'; that 'the only good Arab is a dead Arab'.

Since the Palestinian Arab 'absentees' have forced their presence on the predominantly political Zionist Israeli Jewish society through the process of armed struggle and the emergence of the PLO as the legitimate representative of the Palestinian people, mainstream political Zionism is committed to attempt at any cost to pound the Palestinian back into the oblivion of 'absentee' existence, or alternatively into a Bantustan existence.

Thus 'moderate' political Zionist opposition inside the World Zionist Organization, inside the Israeli Knesset and inside the Israeli Jewish society as a whole is paralysed by a double bind: as political Zionists they predicate their moral and political programmatic position on cultivated deception regarding the essential moral, political and technical terms of the Zionist colonial enterprise in Palestine. Also, as political Zionists they can never align themselves with the struggle for a joint life of Jews and Arabs on the basis of complete equality of human, namely, economic, social, civil political and national rights. This is the root reason why, in the past three decades, Zionist political opposition, Labour Zionist or otherwise, finds it difficult to unseat the revisionist Zionist governments, notably the present government.

The trappings of settler colonial projects can be refined: note the legal distinctions between 'White', 'Coloured', 'Indian', and 'Black' and the development of the Bantustans and multiple-chamber Parliamentary representation in the now defunct apartheid Republic of South Africa. But by its basic terms of reference, the core of the apartheid project cannot be reformed. As the case of South Africa suggests, an apartheid state can be reformed into a state governed by a democratic constitution only if and when the apartheid legal structures, predicated on institutionalized racism legislated by Acts of Parliament, are dismantled.

Settler colonial societies can develop and consolidate in the face of native popular opposition only if aided and protected by imperial support. At the point when, in the face of native indigenous national resistance, supported by local, regional and international solidarity, the material and political costs of this support are pushed up to levels that are deemed by the imperial power, let alone sections of the apartheid establishment, to be no longer acceptable, the settler society or the settler state will be duly abandoned and the transformation of the disputed territory into an independent state based on the principle of equality of rights to all of its inhabitants, the excluded native indigenous population together with the settler population, will become a possibility favoured by the international community and sanctioned by the UN.

The conclusion of this presentation is that, given the nature of the Israeli polity as an apartheid state as it unfolds in its concrete historical context, internal reform unaided by external intervention is unlikely. The liberal humanist, the communist, the socialist and the anti-Zionist organizations and individuals inside the Israeli Jewish society can rightly credit themselves with heroic achievements over time rather than otherwise. But internal opposition inside the Israeli Jewish society alone cannot and will not constitute a barrier sufficient to put paid to the war crimes and crimes against humanity perpetrated by the governments of the State of Israel against the Palestinian people, let alone construct a leverage sufficient to dismantle the structures of Israeli apartheid.

Ariel Sharon, prime minister of the State of Israel at the time of writing this work, was re-elected not despite but because of his war criminal record, and is likely to be replaced by a worse rather than a better candidate, not to mention the prospects of suspension of the elections and the appointment of a *de facto* transitional government, an emergency government or a military council in an attempt to stabilize a rapidly deteriorating economic and political situation.

The mainstream of the Israeli Jewish population has been systematically debilitated through Hebrew schooling and through the extra-curricular media of political education to the point of outright barbarity. The Israeli Jewish society is subject to a process of escalating Nazification as a result of which the majority of the Israeli Jewish population, both European and Oriental, constitutes a solid base of support for Revisionist Zionist and fundamentalist religious Zionist parties. Opposition and protest that take the values of the Universal Declaration of Human Rights as their point of departure are confined largely to the constituency of the Palestinian Arab citizens of the State of Israel, led by the DFPED/Jabha (Democratic Front for Peace and Equality) and the NDA/BALAD (National Democratic Assembly) at the party-political front and *Ittijah* (Union of Arab Community-Based Associations) together with a range of human rights Arab and Hebrew NGOs at the civil society front.

As to the political Zionist Labour Party, it should be obvious to all that the Labour Zionist tradition is set on the course of irreversible decline and disintegration.

The political situation inside Israel today is completely analogous to the political situation in Germany on the eve of the Second World War. On the one hand, the Palestinian Arab population in the occupied Gaza Strip is now enclosed in what the British Jewish Labour MP for Bethnal Green and Bow, London, Ms Oona King, having visited Gaza, has accurately described as 'hell similar in its nature – though not its extent – to the Warsaw ghetto', concluding sadly that 'given the scale of the atrocities and collective punishment waged by the Israelis against the Palestinians', she had 'no choice but to boycott Israeli products' (*Guardian*, 12 June 2003). On the other hand the humanitarian sensibilities of the Zionist society inside and outside the State of Israel have been progressively eroded by such Zionist civilian and military leadership as Israel's Chief of Staff Moshe Ya'alon referring to the Palestinians as 'cancer' (*Haaretz*, 26 August 2002), echoing the late Prime Minister Menachem Begin twenty years earlier referring to the Palestinians as 'two-legged animals' (and then denying it, *Haaretz*, 16 July 1982); Prime Minister Ariel Sharon in his capacity as Begin's minister of defence instructing army officers on the treatment of Arab 'rioters' to 'tear their balls off' (*Haaretz*, 29 December, 1982); Raphael Eitan in his capacity as chief of staff comparing the future of Palestinians darting forward to pelt stones at targets of the Israeli occupation to the scurrying of 'drugged cockroaches inside a bottle' (*Haaretz*, 13 April 1983); and the late Prime Minister Yitzhak Rabin in his capacity as minister of defence in the Shamir government instructing the army to 'get at them' and 'break the bones' of Palestinian civilians who confront them with stone throwing (*Haaretz*, 20 and 22 January 1988); not to mention religious authorities such as the head and supreme authority of the Jewish fundamentalist SHAS Party, Rabbi Ovadiyah Joseph, who in his address to a mass gathering of his party in March 1993 referred to 'the Arabs' as animals ('There is no animal worse than the Arabs') (quoted in *Haaretz*, 9 August 2000); or the Jewish fundamentalist Rabbi Yitzhak Ginsburg, head of the Jewish seminary 'Joseph Is Still Alive' in occupied Nablus stating that 'the commandment "You shall not commit murder" refers only to the case of a Jew who murders a Jew, but a Jew who kills a non-Jew does not act in transgression of this commandment' (*Haaretz*, 26 April 1996).

None, however, has been prosecuted in Israel for incitement to racism, nor, as yet, outside the State of Israel for war crimes.

Almost three million Palestinian Arab people have lived under Israeli military occupation since 1967 for over thirty-five years. They are denied Israeli citizenship; they are denied their rights to land and property; they are denied their civilian rights; they are subject to mass arrests in Israeli jails; they are deprived of shelter by a systematic policy of mass house demolitions; they are subject to relentless state terrorist attacks, target assassination and bombing of the civilian population; they are crippled by on-going collective punishments, expropriation and destruction of property, agricultural land and crops; they are fragmented by the establishment of illegal Israeli settlements, the mass relocation of Israeli Jewish populations to the illegally expropriated Palestinian land and the development of a permanent and illegal Israeli infrastructure, including by-pass roads and the apartheid wall; they are terrorized by military attacks, torture, arbitrary arrests and detention; they are pauperized by the imposition of severe restrictions on movement (curfews, imprisonment and besiegement of towns and villages), and systematic collective punishment, including economic strangulation and deliberate impoverishment, denial of the right to food and water, the right to adequate medical help, the right to housing, the right to education and the right to work.

Over the 35-odd years of the Israeli occupation of the West Bank and the Gaza Strip, and emphatically since the collapse of the so-called 'Oslo peace process', the political Zionist leadership, notably the Government of the State of Israel, has ideologically prepared Israel's Zionist society to accept the ethnic cleansing, the mass transfer of the Palestinian Arab population in the post-1967 occupied territories, possibly including the one million Palestinian Arab citizens of Israel, expelling millions of people to territories outside the territory of British Mandate Palestine, with all that this might entail, including massacres on a scale unknown in Palestine hitherto.

It is these developments that led the late Professor Yeshaayahu Leibowitz to follow the warning and the condemnation first voiced by one of Israel's leading anti-Zionist and human rights campaigners the late Professor Israel Shahak[52] against the 'Nazification' of the State of Israel, against Israel's 'Judeo-Nazi mentality':

> If we must rule over another people, then it is impossible to avoid the existence of Nazi methods. The [Sabra and Shatila] massacre was done by us. The Phalange are our mercenaries, exactly as the Ukrainians and the Croatians and the Slovakians were the mercenaries of Hitler, who organized them as soldiers to do the work for him. Even so we have organized the assassins in Lebanon in order to murder the Palestinians.
>
> What has happened in Lebanon, the terrible massacre committed in the refugee camps, is an additional step in the process of suicide of the State of Israel. Humanity will have no other choice but to destroy the State of Israel! (*Haolam Hazeh*, 22 September 1982)

Leibowitz's observation were true and accurate in 1982, and more so today.

There are certain conclusions we must draw from our retrospective analysis of the fall of apartheid in the Republic of South Africa. The National Party came to power in the Republic of South Africa in 1948. Had the international community, following the promulgation by the National Party-led apartheid government of the Prohibition of Mixed Marriages Act of 1949 and the Group Areas Act, the Population Registration Act, and the Immorality Amendment Act and the Suppression of Communism Act, all of 1950, promptly enforced the UN Charter and imposed international political and economic sanctions against South Africa, much bloodshed and much suffering would have been avoided.

The call for boycott of Israeli produce, leisure tourism to Israel and disinvestment in Israel is not, however, likely to be raised from inside the mainstream of Israeli Zionist society, nor by the Zionist peace camp, unless the latter critically confronts the consequences of its criminal contribution to the construction of the mainstream political Zionist narrative of the denial of the 1948 Palestinian *nakba*, and, in this context declare the 1948–49 war to have been an unjust war; the ethnic cleansing and the mass expulsion of the native indigenous Palestinian Arab population from the territories that came under the control of the Israeli army in the course of the 1948–49 war and the destruction of some 400 Palestinian rural and urban localities inside Israel a crime against humanity; and the implementation of the rights of the 1948 Palestine refugees *inter alia* to return and to the titles of their properties inside Israel a basic human right.

This is not likely to come from such champions of the Zionist peace camp as Uri Avnery, who, rather than apologize for his role as a member and a combatant, of the Revisionist Zionist paramilitary terrorist organization, the IZL (*Irgun*) and subsequently as a soldier with the Giv'ati battalion commando unit 'Samson's Foxes', takes pride in his Zionist military service, nor from his camp *Gush Shalom* (Bloc of Peace).[53]

The primary aim of *Gush Shalom* is to influence Israeli public opinion and lead it towards peace and conciliation with the Palestinian people, based on the following principles:

- putting an end to the occupation;
- accepting the right of the Palestinian people to establish an independent and sovereign State of Palestine in all the territories occupied by Israel in 1967;
- reinstating the pre-1967 'Green Line' as the border between the State of Israel and the State of Palestine (with possible minor exchanges of territories agreed between the parties); the border will be open for the free movement of people and goods, subject to mutual agreement;
- establishing Jerusalem as the capital of the two states, with East Jerusalem (including the Haram al-Sharif) serving as the capital of Palestine and West Jerusalem (including the Western Wall) serving as the capital of Israel; the city is to be united on the physical and municipal level, based on mutual agreement;
- recognizing in principle the Right of Return of the Palestinian refugees, allowing each refugee to choose freely between compensation and repatriation to Palestine and Israel, and fixing by mutual agreement the number of refugees who will be able to return to Israel in annual quotas, without undermining the foundations of Israel;
- safeguarding the security of both Israel and Palestine by mutual agreement and guarantees; and
- striving for overall peace between Israel and all Arab countries and the creation of a regional union. (based on <http://www.gush-shalom.org/english/intro.html>)

The duplicity of the programme above is breathtaking. There is no way that 'recognizing in principle the Right of Return of the Palestinian refugees' and 'allowing each refugee to choose freely between compensation and repatriation to Palestine and Israel' can be effected and the 'foundations of Israel' as a Jewish state in the political Zionist sense of the term not be undermined. Even if the number of refugees who are able to return to Israel in annual quotas is 'fixed by mutual agreement', so long as each refugee is allowed to choose freely, the attempts of political Zionism to anchor the foundations of Israel in law and in practice in a demographic majority of the Jewish tribes in the territories under its control will inevitably be undermined.

The political Zionist underpinnings of the *Gush Shalom* programme are given additional emphasis in their <http://www.gush-shalom.org/english> web page:

> Both parties can reach a just and agreed upon solution for the tragedy of Palestinian refugees, based on these guidelines: Israel will acknowledge its share of responsibility for this tragedy, and will accept, in principle, the right of return. The refugees will be offered several possible venues of rehabilitation and compensation. One of these venues will allow a limited number of refugees the right to return to the state of Israel, *based on a formula that will maintain the Jewish majority in the state of Israel.* (emphasis added)

The implementation of the Palestinian right of return entails the dismantlement of the Zionist apartheid legal structures of the State of Israel, namely, the foundations of the Jewish state in the political Zionist sense of the term. The refusal to welcome such prospects as the dismantlement of the apartheid 'foundations of Israel' places Uri Avnery and *Gush Shalom* firmly inside the political Zionist camp – though at its margins.

Gush Shalom pioneered the campaign to boycott produce manufactured by the post-1967 Israeli settlements and industrial parks (but not general boycott of Israeli produce) and the demand to research the war criminal record of Israeli officers and pilots (but not including Uri Avnery) with a view to submitting the findings before the International Criminal Court in The Hague.

It would be fair to say that the *Gush Shalom* programme is designated to foster the prevailing political delusion, highlighted by the collapse of the 'Oslo peace process', that an 'independent Palestinian state' could be established alongside an apartheid, Zionist Israel, and not remain part of Israel nor continue to be victimized by Israeli apartheid. Showering local and international awards on Uri Avnery[54] before he apologizes for such of the crimes of Israeli apartheid of which he may have been guilty only fortifies the veil covering up Israeli apartheid and enabling the State of Israel to continue to project itself as 'the only democracy in the Middle East'.

As Ilan Pape perceptively observed, beginning in 1969 with the Rogers Plan, and then with the Kissinger initiatives,

[T]he peace agenda has been an American game. The Americans invented the concept of the peace process, whereby the process is far more important than peace. America has contradictory interests in the Middle East, which include protecting certain regimes in the area that preserve American interests (therefore entailing paying lip service to the Palestinian cause) while it also has a commitment to Israel. In order not to find itself facing these two contradictory agendas, it is best to have an ongoing process which is not war and not peace but something which you can describe as a genuine American effort to reconcile between the two sides – and God forbid if this reconciliation works.

We were playing this game not only because the Americans invented it, but also because the replacement of peace with a 'peace process' became the main strategy of the Israeli peace camp. When the peace camp of the stronger party in the local balance of power accepts this interpretation then the world at large follows suit ...

In 1988 [after the PNC accepted UN 242 in Algiers] and 1993 [at the Oslo Accords] even the Palestinian leadership joined this game. No wonder then that after Oslo, the American policy makers felt that they could round up the whole story. They had Palestinian and Israeli leaderships that accepted the name of the American game. This was the beginning of the process, which culminated with the 'the most generous Israeli offer ever made about peace' in the Camp David summit in the summer of 2000.

Had this process been successful, history would have witnessed not only the expulsion of the Palestinians from their homeland in 1948, but the eradication of the refugees, as well as of the Palestinian minority in Israel, and maybe even Palestine, from our collective memory.

It was a process of elimination that succeeded to a certain extent, were it not for the second uprising. I wonder what would have happened had the second Intifada not broken out. If the Palestinian leadership continued to partake in the ploy to shrink Palestine, physically and morally, it would have succeeded. The second Intifada was trying to stop this. Whether or not it will succeed, we do not know ...

We should be very careful in adopting the American, the Israeli

Peace Now, and I'm sorry to say, the Palestinian Authority discourse about a two-state solution. Because the two-state solution nowadays is not the end of the occupation but continuing it in a different way. It is meant to be the end of the conflict with no solution to the refugee problem and the complete abandonment of the Palestinian minority in Israel. Anybody who has not learned this after the Oslo Accords has a problem of understanding and interpreting reality. We have to make sure that the idea of peace is not hijacked by people who are seeking indirect ways of continuing the present situation in Palestine. This is not easy because the western media has already adopted within its main vocabulary that anyone who wants to present himself as a peacemaker or as a supporter of peace, must talk about a two-state solution. (Ilan Pape, 'The '48 *Nakba* and the Zionist Quest for Its Completion', *Between The Lines*, October 2002, pp. 26–8)

Kibbutz, moshav *and community settlement: the masquerade*

It is conventional in the West to refer to the efforts of the Zionist movement and the State of Israel in the domain of cooperative and trade union organization as one of the outstanding modern contributions to the development of modern socialist or social-democratic achievements. Considered to be most prominent among these achievements are the *Histadrut*, the collective *kibbutz* and the smallholder *moshav*. This conventional reference to the *Histadrut*, the *kibbutz* and the *moshav* as positive Zionist contributions to socialist or social-democratic achievement is plainly wrong. It is predicated on cultivated ignorance of the legal and political structures that inform Zionist and Israeli organization and settlement policies, and is intended to veil the reality of radical legal apartheid masquerading as 'socialist Zionism'.

One of the worst offenders responsible for the obfuscation prevalent in the West with regards to 'socialist Zionism' in general and *kibbutz* 'socialism' in particular is the late Martin Buber. It should perhaps be said at the outset that my own intellectual and moral development was profoundly influenced by Martin Buber's writings. Buber's article 'What is to be Done' in *Pointing the Way* represents a milestone in the process of my ideological radicalization (Davis 1994). This, then, is a personal account of a critical Buber disciple.

Buber did not live to witness the 1967 war and the cruelty and violence of the Israeli occupation of the Golan Heights, the West Bank, the Gaza Strip and the Sinai. However, he did witness the 1948 war and the war crimes of the mass 'ethnic cleansing' of the indigenous Palestinian Arab people perpetrated by the Israeli army under the cover of the hostilities as well as the subsequent razing to the ground of their home localities inside Israel, some 400 rural and urban localities in all.

Like Buber, Leon Roth, Ahad ha-Am professor of philosophy at the Hebrew University in Jerusalem at the time, who married one of my father's cousins, also witnessed the atrocities committed against the Palestinian Arabs in the name of the 'Jewish State'. However, unlike his colleague Buber, he resigned his post and returned to the UK.

Buber, on the other hand, sold out. In 1963 he had this to say:

> I have accepted as mine the State of Israel, the form of the new Jewish community that has arisen from the war. I have nothing in common with those Jews who imagine that they may contest the factual shape which Jewish independence has taken. (Buber 1963: 257)

According to Edward Said, prior to 1948 the Buber family were tenants of the Saids in Jerusalem. They paid rent for their house in the wealthy mixed Arab–Jewish Talbiyya Quarter. Sometime towards 1948, a tenant–landlord dispute erupted between the Saids and Professor Buber, and the case was taken for adjudication before the British Mandate court. Buber lost the case and had to leave the premises. At the door, after returning the keys to Edward Said's father, Buber turned round and said: 'Mr Said, you just wait. I will be back.'

The war that began with the unilateral Israeli declaration of independence in 1948 ended in 1949 with the expulsion of approximately 75 per cent of the indigenous Palestinian Arab populations from the 400-odd Arab localities that came under the control of the Israeli army and with the armistice agreements signed between the newly established State of Israel and its neighbouring Arab states. In the armistice agreements between Israel and the Hashemite Kingdom of Jordan, Jerusalem was partitioned and Talbiyya was ceded to Israel. As a consequence, the Saids were classified under Israeli law as 'absentees', and their rights to their properties in Jerusalem and elsewhere in Israel were nullified and vested with the Israeli Custodian for Absentees' Property. Immediately after the war Buber was as good as his word. He returned to take residence in the Saids' house in Talbiyya, now as tenant of the Custodian. He lived there for the rest of his life (Davis 1994: 54).

Against the backdrop of the cruel Israeli occupation of the West Bank and the Gaza Strip over the past 30-odd years (since 1967) as well as the Israeli denial of the rights of the 1948 Palestine refugees to return to their properties inside Israel over the past 50-odd years, Martin Buber's 'Epilogue' in *Paths in Utopia* makes for almost surreal reading.

Buber's normative support for the cooperative movement in general as an important socialist advance is, in the view of this writer, well placed. But, on the other hand, Buber's assertion that

> As I see history and the present, there is only one all-out effort to create a Full Co-operative which justifies our speaking of success in the socialistic sense, and that is the Jewish Village Commune in its various forms as founded in Palestine. (Buber 1949: 141)

is highly questionable.

This is because Buber simply lies in his account of the cooperative enterprise he refers to as a 'signal non-failure', namely, the Zionist cooperative movement in Palestine and subsequently in Israel. The better-known formations of this cooperative enterprise are the Jewish village communes known as the *kibbutz* (collective) and *moshav* (smallholding cooperative) settlement federation and the more recent development of leafy middle-class suburban localities known as 'community' settlements.

The uniqueness of this Zionist cooperative venture is not, as Buber alleges, that 'it alone has proved its vitality in all three spheres' of 'internal relationships, federation and influence on society at large' (ibid.), or that in establishing the Jewish village commune 'the primary thing was not ideology but work' (ibid.: 142). Nor is the uniqueness of the venture represented in its ability to constantly 'branch off' into new forms and new intermediate forms (ibid.: 145). Rather, the unique feature of the Zionist cooperative enterprise was and remains its utility as a strategic colonial instrument directed to alienate the native indigenous Palestinian Arab population from their lands and its racism: membership in these cooperative village communities was and remains legally open to Jews only.[55]

Buber's *Paths in Utopia* was completed in 1945. The Hebrew edition was published in 1946, the English edition four years later in 1949. Fifty-odd years on, the *kibbutz*, Buber's 'signal non-failure' cooperative venture, is privatizing as rapidly as it can. Very little is left of its mutual aid cooperative structures, except for the Admission Committee, whose primary function is to screen candidates for *kibbutz* membership and ascertain that they are not Arab (and preferably also not gay, lesbian, single parents, elderly, physically and/or mentally challenged, and so on).

To this writer, the Zionist cooperative movement in Palestine has been a primary driving force in the development and consolidation of Israeli apartheid, a role similar to that played by the Dutch Reform

Church in the development and consolidation of South African apartheid.

In recent decades the falsehood of Buber's assessment of the Zionist cooperative venture in Palestine has become progressively transparent. In addition to critical scholarship, including this writer's *Israel: Utopia Incorporated* and *Israel: An Apartheid State*, sons and daughters of the *kibbutz*, and graduates of the *kibbutz* collective educational system (Bruno Bettelheim's 'The Children of the Dream'), have in recent years publicly accused their *kibbutz inter alia* of child and sexual abuse. The *kibbutz* collective dining room has now become a paying cafeteria, and under privatization sections of the *kibbutz* membership (such as the elderly) have been pauperized to the degree that some are not able to afford to pay for a full meal. There have been reports in the Israeli Hebrew press of elderly *kibbutz* members covering their meat portion with a heap of rice in order to save money at the till. A 'signal non-failure', as Buber would have it. (See, for instance, Vered Levy Barzilai's three-part series on the *kibbutz*, 'The Invisible Poor', 'The Charge: A Cruel Experiment with Thousands of Children' and 'The Girls Targeted [for abuse] in the *Kibbutz*', *Haaretz*, 15 September 2000, 29 December 2000 and 19 January 2001 respectively.)

This writer currently lives in an Arab city called Sakhnin in central Galilee, northern Israel. Under the British Mandate (1922–48) the Palestinian Arab people of Sakhnin owned and had access to 70,000 dunums (17,500 acres) of land. In 1948 the State of Israel was established and today the municipal jurisdiction of Sakhnin is less than 10,000 dunums. The balance of 60,000 dunums has been confiscated by the various authorities of the State of Israel for exclusively Jewish settlement, including Zionist cooperative settlement, development and cultivation.

After I get up in my flat in Sakhnin, brush my teeth, shave, comb my balding scalp, dress and go out to the veranda to greet my neighbours, I see my city of Sakhnin surrounded by a circle of rather lovely leafy rural suburban communal cooperative residential localities: Buber's 'new forms and new intermediate forms' of Zionist cooperative village communities. These include Hararit, Yahad, Avtalion, Yodfat, Raqefet, Atzmon, Yuvalim, Eshar, Eshbal and more, mostly perched on the mountain tops around the city and incorporated in the Regional Council of Misgav.

The Misgav Regional Council controls some 185,000 dunums incorporating six Palestinian Arab settlements, classified in Misgav's literature as 'Bedouin', and 28 Jews-only communal settlements around Sakhnin and beyond. The total population of the Misgav Regional Council is less than 15,000 (approximately 12 dunums [3 acres] per person).

Sakhnin City Council municipal jurisdiction is today some 10,000 dunums. Its total population is about 22,000 (approximately 0.5 dunum [0.125 acres] per person).

As I see it, Sakhnin has been victimized by Buber's 'signal non-failure', internally colonized by the 'Full Cooperative' of the 'Jewish Village Commune' and ghettoized by 'new forms and new intermediate forms' of the Zionist cooperative movement.

Buber lied.

The Movement Against Israeli Apartheid in Palestine (MAIAP)

The political awareness that Israel was an apartheid state existed for many years among most anti-Zionists in Israel. But in the wake of the breakdown of the Oslo Accords, before the eruption of the second Intifada, that awareness began to spread beyond the circles of committed anti-Zionist activists and academics to circles that would not necessarily identify themselves as anti-Zionist. By 2000 a loose co-alition of activists based primarily in Jerusalem and Haifa had begun a campaign under the slogan 'No Apartheid'. Although their work was cut short largely due to the Intifada, they left their mark on society and were a catalyst in spreading the understanding of Israel as an apartheid state.

Scholarly interest in the parallels between Israel and South Africa dates back to immediately after the June 1967 war with George Jabbour's seminal work *Settler Colonialism in South Africa and the Middle East* in 1970; followed by Richard Stevens and Abdelwahhab Elmessiri's *Israel and South Africa: The Progression of a Relationship* in 1976; Jane Hunter's *Undercutting Sanctions: Israel, the U.S. and South Africa* in 1986; Benjamin Joseph's *Besieged Bedfellows: Israel and the Land of Apartheid* in 1988, and my *Israel: An Apartheid State* in 2001 (first published in 1987).

Ariel Sharon was elected prime minister of Israel in 2001. By 2002, his government's priorities came into sharp focus with the reoccupation of Palestinian territory in March. Effectively endorsed by the United States, Israeli tanks rolled into almost every Palestinian city and refugee camp in the West Bank and Gaza, wreaking havoc and mass destruction in blatant violation of the Oslo Accords and international law. The main commitment of the Sharon government, its coalition with the Labour Party notwithstanding, is to maintain, expand and defend the illegal Israeli settlements in the post-1967 occupied territories. To this end, a Sharon-led government would smash the Oslo Accords, illegally attempt to dismantle the Palestinian Authority (PA), and would again attempt to perpetrate a mass expulsion of the Palestinian people from the geographical territories of Palestine under the cover of another war – a process referred to in current Israeli political parlance as 'transfer'.

Such a plan, however, is costly. At the time of writing the Sharon government is already burdened with a deficit of 14 billion Shekels, approximately $2.7 billion. In a desperate attempt to plug this fiscal hole, Israeli Finance Minister Sylvan Shalom declared the Israeli economy on the verge of collapse, and the treasury cobbled together a draconian emergency plan that caused a major government crisis. The weakest and already much pauperized sectors of the population in Israel, the Palestinian Arab citizens, would be the first victims of the economic costs of the government's war policies. Impoverished Jewish development towns such as Ofaqim will also suffer. Strikes and mass protests will flare up in Israel. Tyres will be set on fire, roads and key highways will be blocked, and police will be overrun by an angry public unable to meet the basic costs of shelter, clothing, food and education. Faced with this, the government will not hesitate to set itself up as an emergency government or a military council, suspend the Knesset and send in the army.

The deterioration of Israel's party political system and the demise of parliament is already well advanced, as is evidenced by the nullification, for the first time in the history of the Knesset, of the parliamentary immunity of one of its members. His immunity was lifted in order to permit his prosecution for political utterances delivered in the course of the execution of his political work, rather than for alleged criminal actions. It does not matter that the MK in question, Dr Azmi Bishara, NDA/BALAD leader, is a Palestinian Arab citizen of Israel. The demise of the Knesset is further underlined by the recent passage of the government-sponsored laws against incitement to violence or terror, and the law preventing those who support an armed struggle against the occupation from participating in Knesset elections. The proceedings directed against Bishara today will be directed against MK Yossi Sarid, former MERETZ leader, tomorrow. The Israeli sharpshooters brought into Umm al Fahm to shoot civilian protesters in Habbat al-Aqsa in September 2000 will also be brought in to quell disturbances in Ofaqim.

In this context, and underscored by the United Nations World Conference Against Racism (UNWCAR) that celebrated the transformation of South Africa from an apartheid state to a constitutional democratic state, the political awareness that Israel is also an apartheid state, namely, a state that regulates racism in law through Acts of Parliament, is spreading among both Palestinian solidarity constituencies and

Hebrew and Arab democratic constituencies committed to the values of the Universal Declaration of Human Rights.

Against this backdrop, frustrated by the failed attempts to form a coherent anti-apartheid organization in Israel and empowered by the WCAR, the Movement Against Israeli Apartheid in Palestine (MAIAP) was launched on 9 August 2001. Its founding conference was held on 22 March 2002 in Jerusalem at the Qaddumi Building, next to the Ram checkpoint separating Jerusalem from the central and northern West Bank. By then, MAIAP had the WCAR NGO forum declaration as a reference. As difficult as it was to convene the founding conference in the current circumstances, participants believed that their initiative represented a meaningful contribution to the defence of the occupied and dispossessed Palestinian people. MAIAP provided a sound platform to develop the strategies needed to limit the capacity of the Israeli occupation forces further to destroy Palestinian society and polity.

MAIAP's founding document reads as follows:

MAIAP takes as its point of departure the values of the Universal Declaration of Human Rights and their articulation in international law and the struggle of the peoples of South Africa against apartheid and their work for democracy and reconciliation.

MAIAP aims to work towards democratic solutions in geographical Palestine (defined for the British Mandate by the Council of the League of Nations in 1922 as being between the River Jordan and the Mediterranean sea) to ensure the implementation of equal rights for all residents and refugees of this area. MAIAP is committed to work democratically to promote the welfare and the right of self-determination for all people in the area including refugees, internally displaced persons, and residents in opposition to the Bantustanization of Palestine and against Israeli apartheid.

MAIAP intends to expose the legal and other structures of Israeli apartheid within both Israel and the occupied territories; work towards the classification of Israel as an apartheid state in relevant international forums including the UN; work with the public to understand, resist and defeat Israeli apartheid; educate the general, local, regional and international public to appreciate that under the prevailing conditions, alongside an apartheid, Zionist Israel, even an independent Palestinian state will remain part of Israel and will continue to be victimized by Israeli apartheid.

MAIAP's immediate priorities include organizing lecture tours across Palestine for prominent South African anti-apartheid activists. MAIAP will add its voice to campaigns calling for international sanctions and business disinvestment from Israel until the Israeli government complies with UN Security Council resolutions, most notably resolutions 242, 338 and 194.

MAIAP will also lobby for the revocation of the tax-exempt status of Zionist fundraising in the West.

Just as the international anti-apartheid solidarity movement made a critical contribution to the success of the struggle against the apartheid regime in South Africa, MAIAP's goal is to mirror that success against the apartheid regime in Palestine.

Who is a Hebrew?

Assuming the Israeli–Palestinian conflict to be an inter-communal conflict rather than an inter-state conflict, namely, a colonial conflict between the colonized native people and the colonial people originating from the Zionist immigration to Palestine, there are no serious conceptual difficulties in identifying the colonized people, the people dispossessed in the course of the conflict, as the Palestinian Arab people. On the other hand, there remains a persistent conceptual difficulty that haunts the socialist critique of Zionism throughout: the inability of socialist critics of political Zionism to name the said colonial people correctly. Who are the colonial people? The 'Jewish people'? The 'Israeli people'? The 'Israeli Jewish people'?

Added to this difficulty there is the additional problem of laying out a conceptual framework in terms of which a solution to the Israeli–Palestinian conflict can be developed, based on the principles of separation of religion from the state, equality of rights and reciprocity. Reciprocity between which parties? Between Jews on the one part, Christians on the second part and Muslims on the third part? Between Jews on the one part and Arabs on the second part? Between Israelis and Palestinians?

The purpose of this attempt at a reading of the identity construct 'Palestinian Hebrew anti-Zionist Jew of Dual Israeli and British Citizenship' (my own) is to suggest that a possible resolution of these difficulties could be developed by reviving the term 'Hebrew' as an appropriate politically correct name – that is, not a Zionist name – for the designation of the people originating from the Zionist immigration to Palestine. I present this reading as part of an ongoing effort to conceptualize a terminological frame of reference to discuss a solution to the conflict that is not a Zionist solution, but a solution that conforms to the values of the Universal Declaration of Human Rights.

It must be emphasized that the analysis presented below is inspired by the success of the European Economic Community to move via the Maastricht Treaty of 1992 towards greater European Union, and the transformation of the apartheid Republic of South Africa into a democratic South Africa. This is not a descriptive reading. It is normative par excellence and directed at such sections of the intellectual and political elites in the region and beyond as are concerned with the development of a new political narrative that is compatible with democratic values and with their commitment to contribute in thought and action to the transition of the region as a whole, and of individual states in the Middle East separately and together, from confessionalism (the supremacy of the religious community over the state) to democracy (the supremacy of the values of the Universal Declaration of Human Rights over the state).

I propose to begin with an explanation of each term included in the identity construct above in reverse order, beginning with 'citizenship'. Before embarking upon this task, however, I shall outline the normative orientation underpinning my work.

I understand secularism to be the principle of separation between religion (mosque, church, synagogue) and the state. Secularism so understood says nothing about the existence (or otherwise) of God or the origins of human values, but it does say something important about the state: the state, being a human construct, has no value. Its only significance is as a tool, an instrument with which to implement given values, and as such it may or may not deserve various degrees of respect. The proper subjects of human loyalty are values. Loyalty to the state, the worship of a human construct, is the secular equivalent of idolatry. State worship, or loyalty to the state, is represented, *inter alia*, in the violation of the rights of the individual and the abrogation of the principle of equality before the law in the name of the alleged supremacy of reasons of state and in the interests of a putative nation. In contemporary political terminology this is called fascism.

I take my normative point of departure from the United Nations Universal Declaration of Human Rights of 1948 and I declare that my personal and professional loyalties are to the values represented in the said Declaration. I regard the state to be an instrument whose proper use is the enhancement of human welfare in terms of the said values. Whenever there arises a conflict between loyalty to the values of the said Declaration and respect for the law of the state, the values of the Universal Declaration of Human Rights should take precedence. It may be necessary to obey the state. It is never necessary to be loyal to the state.

Citizenship versus identity I suggest that citizenship be conceptualized as a certificate, a datum. Conceptualizing it in this way underlines the distinction between citizenship and identity, notably secularized tribal identity.

As will be discussed below, tribal identity is an emotion, a feeling, a fact of consciousness, whereas citizenship, I suggest, is a datum, a certificate. One can touch and observe one's citizenship: being a certificate it can be held in one's hand. Unlike orthodox religious identity, one cannot touch or observe one's secularized tribal identity. For instance, secular Jews primarily 'feel' their identity to be Jewish, whereas orthodox Jews primarily act out theirs. 'Jewish identity' for secular Jews is primarily a fact of consciousness, while for orthodox Jews it is primarily a matter of observance. Conducting their life in conformity to the precepts of religious law, for orthodox Jews 'Jewish identity' is primarily observable behaviour, not a 'feeling'. They do not have an identity crisis such as the one haunting secular Judaism. For them the question 'Who is a Jew?' does not represent a problem.

The certificate of citizenship regulates the relationship between the individual and the state. In western liberal democratic states, citizenship represents a legal recognition of a basic claim of the individual *vis-à-vis* the state of which he or she is a citizen, namely, a legal recognition by the state of the right of the individual to equal access to the resources of the state: equal access to the civil resources of the state (e.g., standing before courts of law and to property), the power-political resources (e.g., vote and elections), the social services resources (e.g., welfare, education) and the material resources (e.g., land, water).

Citizenship in western liberal democratic states is not a certificate of loyalty to the state or to the regime. It is a certificate of rights. Conceived in this way, dual citizenship or multiple citizenship do not entail dual loyalties or multiple loyalties. All dual or multiple citizenship entails is the recognized status of the individual concerned to the right of abode in two or more states and the right of equal access to the resources of all states where he or she is a citizen. A citizen of a single state has the right of abode in one state. A dual or multiple citizen has the right of abode in two or more states. There is little doubt that dual or multiple citizenships improve the choice of the individual and should be viewed as a good thing. In this context it is remarkable that, rhetorics of Arab unity notwithstanding, the provisions of the League of Arab States (notably, the Agreement of 5 April 1954 on Provisions Regarding Citizenship Among Member States of the League of Arab States) prohibit dual or multiple Arab state–Arab state citizenship.

In the final analysis, while citizenship determines the rights of the individual in the state where he or she is citizen, secular tribal identity determines the ethnic affiliation of the individual. The coupling in law of tribal identity with citizenship results in ethnocracy, not democracy – in apartheid, not nationalism.

Israeli/British In the identity construct above the term 'British' does not designate an identity. It designates a legal relationship to the state of the United Kingdom. Likewise the term 'Israeli' does not designate an identity, but designates a legal relationship, namely, a legal relationship to the State of Israel. The United Kingdom is an old state, founded with the 1066 Norman conquest of the Isles of Albion. The State of Israel is a new state, founded in 1948 with the conquest of the land of Palestine.

'British' does not mean 'English'. Under the sovereignty of the United Kingdom there is one British citizenship but there are at least four nationalities (English, Scottish, Welsh and Irish). In terms of this analysis, any individual who is a citizen of the United Kingdom is British. The United Kingdom is a democratic state in a way that Israel is not because it has one citizenship for all British citizens, regardless of national origin (English, Scottish, Welsh, Irish or other). All British citizens are equal before UK law.

'Israeli' does not mean 'Jewish'. Some 20 per cent of the citizens of the State of Israel are non-Jews, most of them are Palestinian Arabs. Israel is a bi-national state, but under Israeli sovereignty there is not one Israeli citizenship for the two nationalities, rather, there are two unequal citizenships: one for the so-called 'Jewish nation' representing full access to the resources of the state (including land and water) and one for the so-called 'non-Jewish (Gentile) nation(s)' representing access to only some resources of the state (excluding land and water). In fact, under Israeli sovereignty there are at least four classes of citizenship: one for 'Jewish' citizenship; one for 'non-Jewish' citizenship (notably for Arabs); one for 'present-absentee' citizenship (notably for Arab internally displaced persons inside the State of Israel); one for 'nullified' citizenship (notably for some four million 1948 Palestinian refugees and their descendants currently outside the State of Israel).

As repeatedly noted above, under the terms of the UN partition plan for Palestine with economic union of 1947, they are all entitled to the citizenship of the Jewish state. Israel abrogated this right. Before legislating the Law of Return in July 1950, the Knesset passed the Absentees' Property Law in March 1950, stripping away their right to Israeli citizenship and to their massive rural and urban properties (not to speak of bank accounts) inside Israel with the view of making these properties available for new Jewish settlement. It is estimated that at least 70 per cent of the total land area of pre-1967 Israel is Palestine refugee property, classified in Israeli law as 'absentees' property'.

Jew Viewed from an orthodox Jewish point of departure, the answer to the question 'Who is a Jew?' is simple and straightforward: a Jew is any person who submits to the 613 orthodox Jewish precepts, the codex of Jewish orthodox religious law (*Halakhah*) as formulated in the standard text of *Shulhan Arukh*, who is born to a Jewish mother, or who has converted to Judaism according to *Halakhic* religious law.

As noted above, an orthodox Jew has no Jewish identity problem. His or her identity is not primarily a fact of consciousness, but a fact of behaviour; not a feeling, but action. The *Halakhah* determines his or her life from birth to death; from daybreak to sunset; from week to week; month to month; season to season; year by year. It determines how he or she dresses, eats, copulates, celebrates, mourns.

The problems for Jewish identity, as for any other tribal identity, begin with secularization. The only viable answer to the question 'Who is a (secular) Jew?' is: 'anyone who says that he or she is a Jew' or 'anyone who "feels" that he or she is Jewish'. The attempt to formulate a different answer, notably such attempts as were motivated by the legislator of the State of Israel, the Knesset, collapsed into formulations that echo the Nazi definition of 'Who is a Jew?' For the Nazi state and the Nazi occupation authorities a 'Jew' was defined as any person with 'Jewish blood' in their family up to three generations back.

For the Israeli Knesset a 'Jew' for the purpose of the Israeli Law of Return, 1950, is defined as follows:

> 4B For the purpose of this Law, 'Jew' means a person who was born of a Jewish mother or who has become converted to Judaism and who is not a member of another religion.

And, echoing the Nazi definition, the privileges and rights accorded in law to persons recognized by the said Law of Return as 'Jews', notably, the virtually unhindered right of immigration, citizenship and settlement in Israel, are also vested in the children and the grandchildren of Jews, the spouse of a Jew, the spouse of a child of a Jew and the spouse of a grandchild of a Jew, with the exception of a person who was a Jew and willingly changed his or her religion.

In other words, in contradistinction to the orthodox definition of 'Who is a Jew?' the foundation of the secular legal definition of a 'Jew' in the State of Israel for the purpose of the Law of Return, 1950 (the mainstay of Israel's Citizenship Law, 1952) rests neither on observance of religious law, nor on Jewish sentiment, but rather on biology (born to a Jewish mother). The idea of a Jewish state in the Zionist sense of the term is founded on the idea of a state that aims to guarantee in law an ethnic majority of citizens who are recognized, in the first instance, as being biologically Jewish. The Nazi definition of 'Who is a Jew?' has thus been incorporated into Israeli legislation.

Anti-Zionist Zionism is a political programme embodied in the institutions of the Zionist organization, founded at the First Zionist Congress in Basle in 1897. The aims of Zionism, first formulated in the said First Zionist Congress ('establish for the Jewish people a home in Palestine, secured under public law') have since been reformulated by successive Congresses a number of times, the last formulation to date being in the 'Jerusalem Programme'. The executive arms of the Zionist Congress include the World Zionist Organization (WZO), the Jewish Agency (JA) and the Jewish National Fund (JNF). An individual or a political party should be defined as Zionist if they support the aims of Zionism and/or are affiliated to the WZO, the JA, the JNF or any other part of the Zionist organization.

Zionism is not Judaism. Zionism is a negative political and practical programme that until 1948 worked to establish a Jewish state in the land of Palestine, the State of Israel, and since 1948 has worked to consolidate the continued existence of this state, as a Jewish state in the Zionist sense of the term: namely, a state that aims to guarantee in law and in practice an ethnic majority of such people as are identified by the state as 'Jews' (see above). The State of Israel is not a democracy. It is an ethnocracy, an apartheid state. The Zionist idea of a Jewish state is not compatible with the liberal idea of a democratic state.

Judaism is alleged to be a divine religion, not a man-made political programme. There is an important part of orthodox Judaism (*Neturei Karta*) that regards Zionism to be the worst expression of Jewish religious apostasy. They are anti-Zionist Jews. To be anti-Zionist means to be opposed to the political programme of the Zionist organization. To be anti-Jewish means to be a racist. Anti-Zionism is not anti-Semitism, just as in South Africa anti-apartheid is not anti-White.

Notwithstanding its subsequent nullification in December 1991, the UN General Assembly, recalling the UN Declaration on the Elimination of All Forms of Racial Discrimination, was correct to determine that Zionism is a form of racism and racial discrimination (Resolution 3379 of November 1975).

Hebrew For the purpose of this reading of the identity construct above, the term 'Hebrew' designates a language. Hebrew is also the national language of those citizens of the State of Israel whose origin is the Zionist colonial settlement in Palestine. If, for the purpose of this reading, we define the term 'Arab' as any person whose national language is Arabic and 'Hebrew' as any person whose national language is Hebrew, it is possible, as will be shown below, to construct identity equations that are not Zionist and meet the requirement of separation of religion from the state, equality of rights and reciprocity in terms of which it is possible to identify both today's colonized people and today's colonizer people as tomorrow's citizens, on an equal footing, of a future democratic state.

Palestine/Palestinian I take as my point of departure the near consensual modern political definition of the term 'Palestine' as the territory whose political boundaries were defined by the League of Nations in its 1922 Mandate for Palestine granted to Britain. There is no similar consensus regarding the definition of 'Who is a Palestinian?'

For the purpose of this reading the name 'Palestinian' is defined as: (1) any person who has a predecessor born in Palestine as defined above, regardless of the said person's place of birth; (2) any person born in Palestine as defined above; (3) any person married to a Palestinian (man or woman); (4) all the citizens of the State of Israel, including all those identified today by the state as Arab citizens as well as all those identified as Jewish citizens.

In parenthesis it should be noted that collective punishments are illegal under international law and the Universal Declaration of Human Rights. A child born in a Jewish settlement to Jewish settler parents is not guilty of such crimes as may be committed by his or her parents. The right of a Jewish child born in the settlement of Alon Moreh in the West Bank to live in the country of his or her birth is equal to the right of an Arab child born in Balata camp, Nablus, to live there. The Jewish child has an equal right to live there – not to be a settler there; to live there as a citizen on equal footing to the Arab citizen – not to occupy and dispossess. The child of a settler family may choose to leave the country of their birth when it is liberated from Zionist apartheid and is reformed into democracy and Alon Moreh is transformed from a settlement designated 'for Jews only' into a locality open to all citizens, but he or she should be urged to stay. The African National Congress (ANC) won the battle for democracy in South Africa because it saw it to be a matter of principle that the ANC regard itself not as the representative of black South Africans, but the political home for all South Africans, Whites and non-Whites, on an equal footing. The PLO lost the struggle for democracy in Palestine because to date it regards itself to be the sole legitimate representative of the Arab Palestinian people – not of all Palestinians, Arabs and non-Arabs on an equal footing.

Palestinian Hebrew anti-Zionist Jew of dual Israeli and British citizenship In terms of the above reading, it is now possible not only to reject the Zionist designation of the people originating from the Zionist immigration to Palestine, but also to give a politically correct name, that is, not a Zionist name, to the said people. It is also possible to lay out a conceptual framework for a solution to the conflict that is based on the principles of separation of religion from the state, equality of rights and reciprocity – a democratic solution, an anti-Zionist solution.

The Zionist designation of a 'Jewish people' must be rejected on the grounds that Judaism is a term of reference properly designating a religious community, not the collective of citizens of any given state. 'Israeli people' must be rejected on the grounds that Israel does not have one single citizenship for all, but at least four unequal citizenships, one for 'Jewish' citizens, one for 'non-Jewish' citizens and one (nullified citizenship) for 'absentees', namely the Palestine refugees and displaced persons of 1948. The term 'Israeli Jewish people' must also be rejected on the grounds that it represents a blatant violation of the principle of separation of religion from the state in that it weds a political term ('Israeli', namely, pertaining to the State of Israel, with a confessional term, 'Jew').

On the other hand, the name proposed here for the people originating in the Zionist immigration to Palestine, the 'Palestinian Hebrew people' has, I submit, considerable merit. It must be pointed out at the outset that it is not suggested that the proposed name and the classifications detailed below are acceptable today to the mainstream of those citizens of the State of Israel who are classified by the state as 'Jews'. It is, however, suggested that these might be accepted by a future political coalition that will generate and oversee the dismantlement of the Zionist legal structures in Israel and replace them with democratic structures, applying where appropriate the lessons learned from the South African experience.

Under the sovereignty of a future democratic State of Palestine, or a future democratic State of Israel (assuming that the Zionist State of Israel is transformed into a democratic state as apartheid South Africa was transformed under the leadership of Nelson Mandela into democratic South Africa), or a federation or a confederation with dual or triple citizenship, there will reside on an equal footing two peoples, the Palestinian Arab people and the Palestinian Hebrew people – not as

186 · *Apartheid Israel*

colonizer people versus colonized people, but on the basis of an equality before the law and reciprocity of rights. There will be one citizenship: Palestinian or Israeli, or, should the solution of the conflict result in a federal state, dual Palestinian and Israeli citizenship. In such a framework, the identity card of an Arab resident of the State of Palestine would read:

Citizenship (*al-Jinsiyya*)	Palestinian
Peoplehood (*al-Shaab*)	Palestinian Arab
Nationality (*al-Qawmiyya*)	Arab
Religion (*al-Din*)	No-religion / Muslim / Christian / Jewish / Other

The identity card of a Hebrew resident of the State of Palestine would read:

Citizenship (*al-Jinsiyya*)	Palestinian
Peoplehood (*al-Shaab*)	Palestinian Hebrew
Nationality (*al-Qawmiyya*)	Hebrew
Religion (*al-Din*)	No-religion / Muslim / Christian / Jewish / Other

The identity card of an Arab resident of the State of Israel would read:

Citizenship (*al-Jinsiyya*)	Israeli
Peoplehood (*al-Shaab*)	Palestinian Arab
Nationality (*al-Qawmiyya*)	Arab
Religion (*al-Din*)	No-religion / Muslim / Christian / Jewish / Other

The identity card of a Hebrew resident of the State of Israel would read:

Citizenship (*al-Jinsiyya*)	Israeli
Peoplehood (*al-Shaab*)	Palestinian Hebrew
Nationality (*al-Qawmiyya*)	Hebrew
Religion (*al-Din*)	No-religion / Muslim / Christian / Jewish / Other

And the identity label that this author would hope to append to his lapel would read: 'Palestinian Hebrew anti-Zionist Jew of Dual Israeli and British Citizenship'.

It is now possible for us to answer the questions posited above, namely 'Who are the colonial people? the Jewish people? the Israeli people? the Israeli Jewish people?'. It is now also possible for us not only to reject the terms 'Jewish people', 'Israeli people', 'Israeli Jewish people' as inappropriate, but also to point to a positive and constructive alternative and say that the future Democratic State of Palestine or the future Democratic State of Israel or the future Democratic Federal State of Palestine and Israel, after abolishing the Israeli Law of Return, 1950, will recognize the Palestinian Hebrew people, namely, all current citizens of the State of Israel who are classified as 'Jews' and their descendants, not as colonizers, not as settlers, not as occupiers, but as equal citizens under the law on an equal footing with the Palestinian Arab people.

The story of Qatzir

In November 1984 I was invited by Chairman Yasser Arafat to attend the 17th Session of the Palestine National Council (PNC) in Amman and was subsequently nominated Observer-Member of the PNC. With the PLO being classified in Israel as an illegal organization and myself being a dual citizen of Israel and the UK, my agreement to respond to the invitation in the positive entailed that I spend the following decade in exile in the UK. With the *de facto* legalization of the PLO in Israel in the wake of the Oslo Accords I resumed my ordinary residence in Israel in December 1994.

One of the first visits I made after my return was to the city of Umm al-Fahm to meet Advocate Tawfiq Jabarin and his wife Hilana and congratulate them on their great achievement in May 1994 of obliging the Israeli Ministry of Housing (after first threatening to go to the Supreme Court) to recognize their right as a young couple to purchase a prefabricated housing unit in Qatzir, the Central Hill, developed by the Ministry of Housing for priority candidates, notably young couples.

The threat to take the case to the Supreme Court was necessary after the Jabarin family was told that the said Ministry of Housing development in Qatzir, Central Hill, was designated for Jewish families only.

Under the threat of taking the case to the Supreme Court, the Jewish Agency for the Land of Israel (JA), Qatzir: Cooperative Association for Community Settlement in Samaria Ltd and the Ministry of Housing had second thoughts and withdrew their objections, presumably estimating that following the passage of Basic Law: Human Dignity and Liberty by the Israeli Knesset in 1992 it was likely that the Supreme Court would rule in favour of the Jabarin application. After all, the Ministry of Housing is an instrument of the Government of the State of Israel, and the government of Israel is, at least on paper, accountable to all citizens of Israel, Jews as well as Arabs.

The Jabarin family moved to Qatzir in 1995.

I believe the achievement of the Jabarin family represents a milestone in the process of the empowerment of the Palestinian community inside Israel and a turning point in the struggle of the Palestinian citizens of Israel to defend their rights as citizens on an equal footing, notably their basic human right to appropriate housing in all localities in Israel, including localities designated by the Israeli authorities for Jews only.

Needless to say, denying the Palestinian citizens of Israel their right of residence in any locality of their choice, on an equal footing with the Jewish citizen, is a form of apartheid that must be condemned and resisted.

In subsequent meetings Tawfiq Jabarin and I, together with other Arab and Hebrew colleagues and veteran human rights activists, formed a charity named AL-BEIT: Association for the Defence of Human Rights in Israel, which was registered as a charity with the Registrar of Charities in Jerusalem.

AL-BEIT was to be a small innovative non-profit organization established with the view of addressing a hitherto largely neglected area of human rights abuse in Israel, namely, the violation of Article 13 of the Universal Declaration of Human Rights:

1. Everyone has the right of freedom of movement and residence within the borders of each state.
2. Everyone has the right to leave any country, including his own, and to return to his country.

As its first practical priority AL-BEIT aimed to concentrate on the defence of the universal human right to freedom of residence in Israel, first and foremost, the right of Palestinian citizens in Israel to equal housing.

It is in order to point out in this connection that almost all of Israel lands (some 93 per cent of the territory of the State of Israel) are designated in law for exclusive Jewish development, settlement and housing, to the exclusion of non-Jewish citizens of Israel, notably, its Palestinian citizens. As a result the Palestinian community in Israel has been ghettoized in mixed cities (e.g. Acre); overcrowded in under-serviced towns (e.g. Umm al-Fahm) and villages (e.g. 'Ar'ara); and underdeveloped in unrecognized localities (e.g. Kammana), many of the latter totally lacking basic services such as running water, sewerage and electricity, while being threatened with eviction and demolition.

AL-BEIT was founded to raise public awareness of the crippling housing crisis inside the Palestinian community in Israel and embark upon practical programmes, supported by sound applied research. It was also to lobby for and facilitate government-subsidized housing solutions on a non-discriminatory basis for Palestinian families and to provide professional counsel to Palestinian families, citizens of the State of Israel, who wish to establish residence in localities designated by the authorities for Jews only.

Following the Jabarin precedent in Qatzir two other Arab families, the family of Adil and Iman Qaadan of Baqa al-Gharbiyya and Fathi and Nawal Mahamid of Umm al-Fahm approached the Qatzir authorities and applied for residence in Qatzir, this time not at the Ministry of Housing development of prefabricated housing units on the Central Hill, but at the Jewish Agency suburban home development on the Western Hill. They were both told to go away because they were Arabs. When they pointed to the Jabarin precedent they were reminded that the Central Hill was a Ministry of Housing development for all citizens of the State of Israel, including Arab citizens, whereas the Western Hill was a Jewish Agency development, for Jews only.

The Qaadan family turned to the Association for Civil Rights in Israel (ACRI) for professional advice and ACRI took their case to the Supreme Court. The Supreme Court accepted ACRI's application on behalf of the Qaadans.

It is now eight years since the Qaadan application was put before the Supreme Court. The application was first heard before a panel of three Supreme Court justices, which was subsequently enlarged to five. Although the Supreme Court has ruled on the case in the year 2000 in their favour, the Qaadan family are still kept waiting in Baqa al-Gharbiyya and have yet to build their home in Qatzir.

The Mahamid family turned to AL-BEIT for professional counsel. AL-BEIT thought it would not be useful to duplicate the ACRI application and instead opted for a parallel course of action. A contract of delegation drafted by our AL-BEIT legal counsel, Advocate Tawfiq Jabarin, was signed by Fathi Mahamid and myself. The Agency Law (*Hoq ha-Shelihut*) of 1965 makes provisions for undeclared delegation so after the earlier rejection of Fathi Mahamid by Qatzir, I went to Qatzir on his behalf as his undeclared delegate.

The name Uri Davis represents a historical icon in Israel for many citizens aged 40 and above. For many under 40 the name would not ring a bell. Since I was determined to approach Qatzir on a strictly formal basis, I presented myself on my first visit there with my official identity card name, namely, as Dr Uriel Davis. The name did not seem to ring a bell with Ms Tzipi Miller, the Qatzir Coordinator for Population and Absorption. I was not asked about my taste in food, nor about my choice of colours for my clothing, nor about my favourite author, nor about my politics. Had I been asked, I would have declined to answer on the grounds that such questions represent an invasion of privacy.

Neither was I asked if I was 'Jewish'. My identity card said I was.

Having successfully passed the informal interview with Ms Tzipi Miller I was invited for an official interview by the QATZIR: Co-operative Association for Communal Settlement in Samaria Ltd. Having successfully passed that interview I was sent to sign a development contract for plot 1026, 42 Ha-Amirim Avenue, Western Hill, Qatzir, with the Tal-Iron (Qatzir) Economic Company Ltd and deposit the development fee of US$20,000 in reasonable instalments. I was then directed to the Jewish Agency, where I signed yet another agreement entitled 'Agreement of Commitment'. I then signed a development contract with the Israel Lands Administration (ILA), and finally, following the completion of the building, a leasehold contract with the ILA for a period of 49 years (the leasehold being renewable and inheritable).

The successful completion of each of the above steps is a necessary condition for progression on to the next step. Needless to say that all the costs involved (including stamp duties, development fees and construction) were paid by Fathi Mahamid.

Four years later, on Friday 28 May 1999, the house was inaugurated with a housewarming party. The occasion was celebrated in the company of some 70–80 guests, members of the Mahamid and Jabarin families, members and friends of AL-BEIT and one family of Jewish friends from Qatzir. I addressed the gathering as follows:

Dear friends and guests,

I wish to thank you for honouring me and the occasion with your presence here today and apologize for having misled you in that I had incorrectly invited you to the housewarming gathering of my new residence at 42 Ha-Amirim Avenue, Qatzir (Western Hill) today. It is not the inauguration of my home that we are gathered here to celebrate, but the home of Fathi and Nawal Mahamid on whose behalf I had acted.

For a number of months now a rumour has been circulating in Qatzir that this house at 42 Ha-Amirim Avenue is not my house, but the house of the contractor Fathi Mahamid of Umm al-Fahm, who has constructed this splendid building. Some four months ago I was confronted directly by the chief executive officer of the Tal-Iron (Qatzir) Economic Company Ltd, Mr Yoel Mor, who demanded to know when I intended to move into the house and was the said rumour correct.

I assured him that I was moving in towards the end of May this year and managed to evade answering directly his question regarding the correctness or otherwise of the said rumour.

Last week I knocked on the door of the neighbours to inform them that I was moving in that day afternoon and apologized for any inconvenience that might be caused to them because of this housewarming gathering. They were genuinely surprised to learn that I (presumably a Jew) was moving into the house. They were certain that an Arab family was moving in and pleaded with me again and again not to let Arabs into the house. Qatzir, they claimed, was designated as a locality for Jews only. Needless to say that I was not able to give them assurances on this matter. I evaded a direct answer by saying that one thing was sure: I was moving into the house on Friday, 28 May (today). What happens next, I said, was unclear ...

And indeed, a lot of what happens next remains unclear. But not everything is unclear, and I propose to attend below to what is clearly the state of affairs and a little bit to what I hope the state of affairs might be:

- It is clear that racism is a crime and a repugnant obscenity representing a gross violation of the norms of the Universal Declaration of Human Rights. It is the obligation of conscience for each and every decent person to raise their voice against all forms of racism, everywhere and any time, first and foremost everywhere in their proximity and at any time in their adult lifetime, to condemn and resist racism, act to oppose all forms of racial discrimination and strive to have them dismantled and removed.

- It is clear that any distinction, exclusion, restriction or preference based on race, colour, descent or national or ethnic origin that has the purpose or effect of nullifying or impairing the recognition, enjoyment or exercise, on an equal footing, of human rights and fundamental freedoms in the political, economic, social, cultural or any other field of public life (including, needless to say, the right to appropriate housing) is defined as 'racial discrimination' in international law. (See Article 1 of the International Convention on the Elimination of All Forms of Racism and Racial Discrimination of 1966, signed by Israel the same year and ratified in 1979.)

- It is clear that in the identity cards issued by the Israeli Ministry of the Interior to citizens and residents of Israel who are recognized in law as 'Jews' (my own ID included) Jewish religious origin is classified as 'nationality'. In other words, the State of Israel violates the principles and the articles of the said Convention on the Elimination of All Forms of Racism and Racial Discrimination not only in practice but also in its domestic law. The Israeli Knesset crafted a complex legal structure directed to reserve and restrict the right to appropriate housing in all localities of cooperative settlements (including *kibbutz*, *moshav* and community settlements) exclusively to 'Jews', namely to such persons as are recognized in law as 'Jews'. This complex legal structure hinges on the World Zionist Organization/Jewish Agency for the Land of Israel Status Law, 1952, Jewish National Fund Law, 1953, Basic Law: Israel Lands, Israel Lands Law and Israel Lands Administration Law, 1960 and the covenants between the Government of the State of Israel and the WZO/JA and the JNF (1954 and 1961 respectively). It is applied in a way that is plainly racialist by the standards of international law and the norms of enlightened decency acceptable in the West. I would hope that the Supreme Court will find its way to direct the said bodies to reform the manner in which this legal structure is applied, especially at this time, after the passage by the Knesset of the Basic Law: Human Dignity and Liberty, 1992, with the view that it be applied in a way that is consistent with the said norms of enlightened decency.

- It is clear that the Jewish National Fund, QATZIR, the Jewish Agency for the Land of Israel and the Israel Lands Administration have joined hands in Qatzir with the object of denying the Arab citizens of Israel their right to residence in this locality. It is therefore for me a great privilege to hand over today the keys of this house at 42 Ha-Amirim Avenue in Qatzir to the family of Fathi and Nawal Mahamid my friends, on whose behalf I had acted as a delegate beginning with my first visit to the offices of the Tal-Iron (Qatzir) Municipal Council in April 1995 to meet Tzipi Miller, Coordinator of Absorption and Population at the time. I truly hope that the Qaadan family will soon be able to build their home on the plot earmarked for them, pending the ruling of the Supreme Court. And needless to say, I look to the Supreme Court to find its way to direct the said bodies to de-couple their joined hands and allow the transfer of rights in the two specific properties in question to the Qaadan and the Mahamid families respectively, as they did when they found a way to allow the lease of the home of Boris Senior in Kefar Shemaryahu, also built on JNF land, to Sa'ad Murtada, the First Ambassador of Egypt to Israel.

It is Qatzir's good fortune that its name is destined to mark a significant turning point in the law and history of the State of Israel. A day will come when the residents of Qatzir will take pride in the pioneering privilege that has befallen their locality by dint of its proximity to the town of Umm al-Fahm, the village of Baqa al-Gharbiyya and the village of 'Ar'ara. Due to its geographical location, Qatzir has been fortunate to have the remarkable family of Advocate Tawfiq and Hilana Jabarin set up the first Arab home in Qatzir (the Central Hill) and, as of today, the equally remarkable family of Nawal and Fathi Mahamid set up the second Arab home in Qatzir (the Western Hill); to which has been added the admirable contribution of the family of Adil and Iman Qaadan whose application regarding their right to build their home in Qatzir (Western Hill) is still pending before the Supreme Court; as well as the commitment of AL-BEIT Association for the Defence of Human Rights in Israel, under whose auspices this gathering is convened.

I am aware that some among the residents of Qatzir, the majority today, a minority tomorrow, opposed the residence of the Jabarin family in the Central Hill of Qatzir and likewise oppose the residence of the families of the Qaadan and Mahamid family in the Western Hill of Qatzir. But I am also aware that there are some among the residents of Qatzir, a minority today, a majority tomorrow, who welcome the choice of the Jabarins, Qaadans, and Mahamids to make their homes in the locality and accept their presence with open hearts and outstretched arms not because these are 'Arabs' and those are 'Jews', but because both those and these are persons, and as human beings they ought to be granted complete equality of rights.

I should add that in principle it was perhaps possible to accept the idea of the establishment of the State of Israel as a Jewish State as conceived by the United Nations General Assembly in Resolution 181 of November 1947, recommending the partition of geographical Palestine into two bi-national and democratic states, one Jewish and one Arab, joined together by economic union. But this Resolution of the UN General Assembly was not a licence for gross violations of the norms of the Universal Declaration of Human Rights by way of occupation, mass expulsion, dispossession and apartheid discrimination against non-Jews, notably against the Palestinian Arabs as individuals and as a national collective. It was not intended as a licence to establish an ethnocentric state that aims to guarantee in law an ethnic Jewish majority in Qatzir – or any place else, for that matter.

Fathi and Nawal Mahamid and family, it is my privilege to present you on this occasion with the keys to the house at 42 Ha-Amirim Avenue, which I have built in Qatzir acting as your delegate. Until such time as your legal standing in Qatzir is made clear, please be my guests.

I wish to thank you all again for honouring me and the occasion with your presence.

Be blessed

The following week Advocate Tawfiq Jabarin wrote to the Israel Lands Administration (ILA) officially requesting that the rights to the said property at 42 Ha-Amirim Avenue, Western Hill, Qatzir be transferred from my name to the name of Fathi Mahamid. The ILA declined, and the matter has been taken to the Supreme Court for resolution. We expect to win.

For Adil and Iman Qaadan of Baqa al-Gharbiyya, the Judgment of the Israeli Supreme Court, sitting as the High Court of Justice, on Case No. 6698/95, Qaadan vs. Israel Lands Administration (ILA), Ministry of Construction and Housing, Tal-Iron Local Municipal Council, Jewish Agency for the Land of Israel (JA), Qatzir: Cooperative Association for Community Settlement in Samaria Ltd, and the Farmers Association, delivered in Jerusalem on Wednesday 8 March 2000, regrettably represents only one small step forward in their struggle to build their home in Qatzir, the locality of their choice.

The case, considered by a panel of five Supreme Court justices, chaired by the president of the Supreme Court Justice Aharon Barak, ruled, four to one, that

> The State of Israel must consider the petitioners' request to acquire land for themselves in the settlement of Qatzir for the purpose of building their home. The state must make this consideration based on the principle of equality, and considering various relevant factors – including those factors affecting the Jewish Agency and the current residents of Qatzir. The State of Israel must also reconsider the numerous legal issues. Based on these considerations, the State of Israel must determine with deliberate speed whether to allow the petitioners to make a home within the communal settlement of Qatzir.

Given the terms of this judgment, it is likely that the Qaadan family will face long delays, deliberate foot-dragging on the part of the state, notably the ILA, and possibly a number of additional appeals to the Supreme Court before they are able to dig the foundation of their home on a plot of land registered to their name in the community settlement of Qatzir. For them, the judgment, I fear, represents just one small step forward.

For the anti-Zionist struggle, however, the judgment represents a giant leap forward in the right direction towards the democratization of the State of Israel.

While the Declaration of the Establishment of the State of Israel, the so-called 'Proclamation of Independence', claims that the State of

Israel 'will ensure complete equality of social and political rights to all its inhabitants irrespective of religion, race or sex', omitting reference to discrimination on the basis of nationality, the Supreme Court in its said judgment establishes that:

> As a general rule, the principle of equality prohibits the state from distinguishing between citizens on the basis of religion or nationality. The principle also applies to the allocation of state land. (*Judgments of the Supreme Court of Israel* [PADI], Case No. 6698/95, Vol. 54 [I], 2000, pp. 258–88)

The inclusion of the term 'nationality' in the stipulations of the said judgment prohibiting discrimination in Israel is indeed a giant leap forward along the road to the democratization of the State of Israel and the defence of the national as well as individual rights of the Palestinian Arab citizens of Israel.

Also, while the so-called Israeli 'Proclamation of Independence' has, strictly speaking, no legal status in Israeli law (it is a relevant interpretative instrument, not law), the said judgment has constitutional status and will impact on all future Israeli Parliament legislation as well as state practices.

Of further profound significance is the Supreme Court ruling that:

> This conclusion is derived both from the values of Israel as a democratic state and from the values of Israel as a Jewish state. The Jewish character of the state does not permit Israel to discriminate between its citizens. In Israel Jews and non-Jews are citizens with equal rights and responsibilities. (ibid.)

This ruling marks a watershed in the definition of Israel as a Jewish state.

Until the publication of this judgment, the State of Israel was able to roll back its sovereignty and allocate in law important state responsibilities to bodies that are obligated by the basic terms of their incorporation to discriminate on the basis of religion and/or nationality. Thus, for instance, the state vested with the religious (Rabbinical, Muslim and Christian) courts the sole authority, *inter alia*, of registration of marriage and divorce, subject to the norms of religious law (Jewish *Halakhah*, Muslim Shari'a and Christian Ecclesiastic). In a similar way, the state vested with the Jewish Agency the primary responsibility, *inter alia*, for settlement.

As of the publication of this judgment a new constitutional norm has been established to the effect that:

If the State, through its own actions may not discriminate on the basis of religion or nationality, it may not facilitate such discrimination by a third party. It does not change matters that the third party is the Jewish Agency. Even if the Jewish Agency may distinguish between Jews and non-Jews, it may not do so in the allocation of state lands. (ibid.)

Since 1948 the principle of discrimination in law in the State of Israel was 'Jew' versus 'non-Jew', first and foremost 'Jew' versus 'Arab', with the state conceding that the trademark of 'Jewish identity' was the inherently retrograde Jewish orthodox *Halakhic* definition. The definition of 'who is a Jew' in Israeli law echoes this orthodox *Halakhic* definition (the 'Jewish State' being the 'State of the Jewish people', and a 'Jew' for the purpose of the Law of Return, for instance, being a person 'who was born to a Jewish mother or who has become converted to Judaism and who is not a member of another religion').

With this judgment, the Supreme Court altered the definition of the 'Jewish State' (though not necessarily of 'who is a Jew' in Israeli law) at the constitutional normative level. If 'the Jewish character of the state does not permit Israel to discriminate between its citizens', then only such values of the Jewish heritage as are consistent with the values of the Universal Declaration of Human Rights can be deemed relevant to the definition of Israel as a Jewish state. As of this judgment, even if the 'Jewish State' remains the 'State of the Jewish people' it is constitutionally prohibited to discriminate on the basis, *inter alia*, of religion or nationality – let alone race or sex.

Since 1948 the State of Israel has done exactly the opposite. In the name of the so-called 'Jewish State' all instruments of the state have acted in concert to expel, exclude, dispossess, suppress and in all manner discriminate against the Palestinian Arab people, beginning with the mass ethnic cleansing of the 1948 Palestine refugees. For over fifty years the Israeli Supreme Court remained silent in the face of the perpetration of war crimes and crimes of apartheid by Israel against the Palestinian people, just as for fifty years it had remained silent in the face of the systematic torture practised in Israeli jails and detention centres against Palestinian political prisoners and detainees, as well as other prisoners. Now that the Supreme Court had spoken on both issues, one could cry at the atrocity of this silence.

But once the Supreme Court has spoken on both issues, the impact of its judgment in both cases will have been dramatic. Just as the practice of torture in Israeli jails and detention centres had to change following the Supreme Court Judgment on torture in September 1999 (and, as the Public Committee Against Torture in Israel reports, torture has, in most cases, ceased), so, following the judgment on the Qaadan case, discriminating state practices in matters pertaining to future Israeli land policies will also have to change. Thus, following the said judgment, the notorious deal considered by Ariel Sharon and Avraham Burg, respectively minister of infrastructure and chairman of the Jewish Agency for the Land of Israel at the time, for the mass transfer of Israeli state lands to the ownership of the Jewish Agency, primarily in the Negev, will now probably have been made void.

In my understanding, this is the closest the Supreme Court could get to the application of the fundamental principle of the enlightenment: the principle of separation of religion from the state. After all, the two Basic Laws (Basic Law: Human Dignity and Liberty of 1992 and Basic Law: Freedom of Occupation also of 1992, and amended 1994) that, according to the president of the Supreme Court, Justice Aharon Barak, represent a constitutional revolution in Israel, blatantly violate the said fundamental principle, the principle of separation of religion from the state, in that they define the State of Israel 'as a Jewish and democratic state'. Given this constraint it seems that the closest to the said principle within reach of the Supreme Court is represented in this judgment. It is, indeed, the Israeli equivalent to the US Supreme Court judgment of Brown *vs.* Board of Education of Topeka, Kansas.

As noted above, in my reading, the Qaadan family has still a long wait before it moves its residence to Qatzir. The case of the Mahamid family, on the other hand, will perhaps take a different and less prolonged course. Like the Qaadans of Baqa al-Gharbiyya, the Mahamid family of Umm al-Fahm approached the Qatzir authorities with the view to establish a home there, and, like the Qaadans, they were refused because they were Arabs. But while the Qaadan family turned to the Association of Civil Rights in Israel (ACRI) and to the Supreme Court, the Mahamid family turned to Advocate Tawfiq Jabarin and to AL-BEIT.

Following consultation, the Mahamids were advised to engage this writer as their delegate for the purpose of building their home in Qatzir under the terms of Israel's Agency Law of 1965. After signing all the required legal paperwork and passing the interview by the Absorption Committee of the Qatzir Cooperative Association, I began building. All costs of the project, including the costs of purchase of the leasehold for the plot of land from the ILA, were covered by Fathi Mahamid. By 1999 the house was finished, and the Mahamids moved to inhabit their second home at 42 Ha-Amirim Avenue in Qatzir.

Following the celebration of the move of the Mahamid family to their home in Qatzir in May 1999, Advocate Tawfiq Jabarin wrote to the Israel Lands Administration (ILA) requesting that the rights to the said property hitherto registered in my name be registered in the name of Fathi Mahamid. The ILA wrote back to say that their agreement to the transfer of the registration of the rights to the property at 42 Ha-Amirim Avenue from my name to the name of Fathi Mahamid was conditional on the prior agreement of the Jewish Agency and the Qatzir Cooperative Association.

As of the said Supreme Court judgment on the case of Qaadan, this, to my reading, is no longer the case.

However, although the said judgment ruled on the case of the Qaadan family, not the Mahamid family, it is regrettably my belief that the said property at 42 Ha-Amirim Avenue will be registered in the name of Fathi Mahamid long before the Qaadan family is given a plot of land to build their home in Qatzir, the Western Hill.

Still, when considering the important constitutional precedent and the giant step towards the democratization of the State of Israel that the judgment of the Supreme Court on the Qaadan case undoubtedly represents, we should remember that the State of Israel will not be transformed into a democratic state when it becomes the state of all its citizens, Arabs and non-Arabs alike – rather, it will become democratic when it is transformed into a state of all its citizens as well as its 'absentees', the 1948 Palestine refugees.

The Mahamid home at 42 Ha-Amirim Avenue is built on 'absentee' land.

As noted above, at the time of writing, two years after winning the Supreme Court ruling on their behalf, the Qaadan family are still in Baqa al-Gharbiyya and denied access to Qatzir. Their case, though, is not unique. In 1951, the internally displaced persons of Bir'im and Iqrith won a Supreme Court ruling to the effect that no legal barrier existed to their return (see Kimmerling 1977). Fifty years later, they are still denied their right to return.

The country of Palestine still awaits its Mandela, and the State of Israel its De Klerk.

Appendix 1 Vladimir Jabotinsky, 'The Iron Wall' (Excerpts)

The author of these lines is considered to be an enemy of the Arabs, a proponent of their expulsion, etc. This is not true. My emotional relationship to the Arabs is the same as it is to all other peoples – polite indifference. My political relationship is characterized by two principles. First: the expulsion of the Arabs from Palestine is absolutely impossible in any form. There will always be two peoples in Palestine.

Second: I am proud to have been a member of that group which formulated the Helsingfors (Helsinki) Programme. We formulated it, not only for Jews, but for all peoples, and its basis is the equality of all nations. I am prepared to swear, for us and for our descendants, that we will never destroy this equality and we will never attempt to expel or oppress the Arabs. Our credo, as the reader can see, is completely peaceful. But it is absolutely another matter if it will be possible to achieve our peaceful aims through peaceful means. This depends, not on our relationship with the Arabs, but exclusively on the Arabs' relationship to Zionism ...

Any native people – it's all the same whether they are civilized or savage – view their country as their national home, of which they will always be the complete masters. They will not voluntarily allow, not only a new master, but even a new partner. And so it is for the Arabs. Compromisers in our midst attempt to convince us that the Arabs are some kind of fools who can be tricked by a softened formulation of our goals, or a tribe of money grubbers who will abandon their birthright to Palestine for cultural and economic gains. I flatly reject this assessment of the Palestinian Arabs. Culturally they are 500 years behind us, spiritually they do not have our endurance or our strength of will, but this exhausts all of the internal differences ... They look upon Palestine with the same instinctive love and true fervour that any Aztec looked upon his Mexico or any Sioux looked upon his prairie ... This childish fantasy of our 'Arabo-philes' comes from some kind of contempt for the Arab people, of some kind of unfounded view of this race as a rabble ready to be bribed in order to sell out their homeland for a railroad network ...

Colonization itself has it own explanation, integral and inescapable, and understood by every Jew and Arab with his wits about him. Colonization can have only one goal. For the Palestinian Arabs this goal is inadmissible. This is in the nature of things. To change that nature is impossible ...

If it were possible (and I doubt this) to discuss Palestine with the Arabs of Baghdad and Mecca as if it were only some kind of small, immaterial borderland, then Palestine would still remain for the Palestinians not a borderland, but their birthplace, the centre and basis of their own national existence. Therefore it would be necessary to carry on colonization against the will of the Palestinian Arabs, which is the same condition that exists now ...

Zionist colonization, even the most restricted, must either be terminated or carried out in defiance of the will of the native population. This colonization can, therefore, continue and develop only under the protection of a force independent of the local population – an iron wall which the native population cannot break through. This is, *in toto*, our policy towards the Arabs. To formulate it any other way would only be hypocrisy ...

In this sense, there are no meaningful differences between our 'militarists' and our 'vegetarians'. One prefers an iron wall of Jewish bayonets, the other proposes an iron wall of British bayonets, the third proposes an agreement with Baghdad, and appears to be satisfied with Baghdad's bayonets – a strange and somewhat risky taste – but we all applaud, day and night, the iron wall ...

All this does not mean that any kind of agreement is impossible, only a voluntary agreement is impossible. As long as there is a spark of hope that they can get rid of us, they will not sell these hopes, not for any kind of sweet words or tasty morsels, because they are not a rabble but a nation, perhaps somewhat tattered, but still living. A living people makes such enormous concessions on such fateful questions only when there is no hope left. Only when not a single breach is visible in the iron wall, only then do extreme groups lose their sway, and influence transfers to moderate groups. Only then would these moderate groups come to us with proposals for mutual concessions ... on practical questions like a guarantee against expulsion, or equality and national autonomy ... But the only path to such an agreement is the iron wall, that is to say the strengthening in Palestine of a government without any kind of Arab influence, that is to say one against which the Arabs will fight. In other words, for us the only path to an agreement in the future is an absolute refusal of any attempts at an agreement now. ...

Appendix 2 David Ben-Gurion: Statement of Introduction of the Law of Return Before the Knesset (Excerpts)

Mr Chairman, members of the Knesset ... The Law of Return and the Citizenship Law placed before you have a mutual relation and a common ideological source which stems from the historical uniqueness of the State of Israel, a uniqueness in relation to the past and in relation to the future, in relation to the interior and in relation to the exterior. These two laws determine the character and the special mission of the State of Israel as a state bearing the vision of redemption of the Jewish people.

The State of Israel is a state like all other states, and all general features existing in other states also exist in the State of Israel. It stands on a certain territory, on a population existing within it, on its internal and external sovereignty, and its rule does not extend beyond its boundaries. The State of Israel rules only over its inhabitants. The diaspora Jews, who are citizens of their countries, have no legal and civil relation to the State of Israel, and the State of Israel does not represent them in any legal sense. But the State of Israel differs from other states both in the causes of its revival and in the purpose of its existence. It rose only two years ago but its roots are in the distant past and it feeds on ancient sources; its rule is limited to its inhabitants but its gates are open to every Jew wherever he may be. This is not a Jewish state merely because Jews are the majority of its population, it is a state for Jews everywhere, and for every Jew who wants it.

On 14 May 1948 this new state was not established as something out of nothing, it was a return to a former glory, 1,813 years after the destruction of Jewish independence, seemingly forever, in the days of Bar-Kochva and Rabbi Akiva. The causes of the creation of Israel were not just the immediate, direct acts which preceded the Declaration of Independence ...

It is impossible to understand the revival of the Jewish state without knowledge of the new settlement in the last three generations of the movement of *Hibat Zion* (Love of Zion), of Zionism, the Enlightenment and Hebrew literature, of the national and revolutionary movements in Europe in the nineteenth century, the resurrection of Hungary, Italy, the Balkan nations, and more – without the results of the First and Second World Wars, the formation of the League of Nations and the United Nations. But it is also impossible to understand the resurrection of the Jewish state without the knowledge of the Jewish people from its beginning, its history in the days of the first and second Temples, the history of prophecy, spirit, and vision in the Jewish people, the history of the Jewish diaspora, the idea of Messianism and its many manifestations throughout the generations, the incessant efforts of the wandering nation to return to its homeland throughout the generations, under all circumstances since the destruction, and without knowledge of the eternal culture created in this land and its influence on Israel and other nations.

The resurrection of Israel was not an event limited to its place and moment of occurrence, it was a world event, in terms of both time and place, an event terminating a long historical development, re-ordering constellations and serving as a source of changes beyond its era and location.

It may be too early, and not necessarily relevant to the laws before you, to define the role of the State of Israel in the system of global forces and its contribution to the reshaping of humanity. But from the day the state was established it was clear, not only to the Jews within it, that something had happened to the Jews, the greatest event in Jewish history, affecting every Jew wherever he be.

Not by accident did the Declaration of Independence start with short statements on the continuous bond between the Jewish people and its ancient homeland, and as the first and main axiom about the path of the state it was declared, before anything else, that 'The State of Israel will be open to the immigration of Jews from all countries of their dispersion', and a call was voiced 'to the Jewish people all over the world to rally to our side in the task of immigration and construction, and to stand by our side in the great struggle for the fulfilment of the dream of generations for the redemption of Israel'.

Just as it was obvious that the renewal of the State of Israel was not a beginning, but a continuation, a continuation of the ancient past, so was it understood that it was not a completion and an end, but another step on the long road to total Jewish redemption. ...

The Law of Return is one of the fundamental laws of the State of Israel. It embodies a central purpose of our state, the purpose of the ingathering of exiles. This law states that it is not this state which grants Jews from abroad the right to settle in it, but that this right is inherent by virtue of one's being a Jew, if one wishes to settle in the country.

In the State of Israel Jews do not have privileges denied to non-Jewish citizens. The State of Israel is based on the full equality of the rights and duties of all its citizens. This principle too is stated in the Declaration of Independence: 'The State of Israel will uphold the full social and political equality of all its citizens without distinction of religion, race, or sex'. But it is not the state which grants the diaspora Jews the right to return. This right preceded the State of Israel, and it was this right which built the State of Israel. This right originates from the historical bond between the fatherland and the nation, which was never severed. The law of nations has recognized this bond in practice.

The Law of Return differs from immigration laws which determine the conditions under which the state will accept immigrants, and their type. Such laws exist in many countries and they change from time to time according to internal and external changes.

The Law of Return has nothing to do with immigration laws. It is the law of perpetuity of Jewish history; this law asserts the principle of sovereignty by force of which the State of Israel was established.

It is the historical right of any Jew, wherever he may be, to return and settle in Israel, whether because he is deprived of rights in exile, or is insecure in his existence, or is expelled and expropriated, or cannot live a Jewish life as he wishes, or loves the ancient tradition, the Hebrew culture and Jewish independence.

The Citizenship Law completes the Law of Return and states that by force of the fact of immigration to Israel the Jew becomes a citizen in the fatherland, and has no need of any further act or formality, or any condition apart from the will to settle in the country and live in it.

These two laws, the Law of Return and the Citizenship Law, constitute the Bill of Rights, the Charter, guaranteed to all Jews in the diaspora by the State of Israel. (*Knesset Debates*, Vol. 6 [3 July–10 August 1950], pp. 2,035–37)

Appendix 3 Naim Khader: The Democratic State and Armed Struggle (Excerpts)

The democratic state

I personally believe that the establishment of a democratic state over the entirety of Palestinian soil is the development that will secure to all the residents, Christians, Jews and Muslims, equality of rights and duties. And the democratic state in the final analysis is the only lasting, just and acceptable solution that will secure a comprehensive solution of the problem of the Palestinian Arab people and likewise the problem of the Israeli Jews.

Indeed, I am convinced that any solution achieved before the implementation of this strategic objective will remain a temporary and transitional preparation of the way towards the comprehensive democratic solution. There is no doubt that any transitional solution that is not a step along the road towards the establishment of the democratic state clearly constitutes a danger to the progressive and revolutionary elements in the Palestinian revolution or at least contributes to their containment. This in turn entails the weakening of the progressive movement in the region of the Middle East and even in the Arab world as a whole, because any such solution fortifies the existence of the Zionist doctrine in Palestine. This doctrine is of its nature an expansionist, imperialist and reactionary enemy doctrine that will not hesitate to strike any progressive movement that will emerge in the region as it has indeed continually done since its penetration into Palestine, the heart of the Arab world. There will not be peace in the Middle East except through the liquidation of the Zionist doctrine in its present formulation and practice. The democratic solution, namely, the establishment of a democratic state, is the only solution that can secure the dismantling of the Zionist movement and the advancement of an acceptable alternative both for the Jews who are currently resident in Palestine and for a just solution for the exiled Palestinian-Arab people as well as for those who live under the occupation.

The democratic state is a revolutionary thesis advocated by all the groups constituting the Palestinian revolution and specifically by the

Palestine Liberation Organization, the sole legitimate representative of the Palestinian people. It is a thesis that indicates the steadfastness of the Palestinian revolution and its civilized spirit, its depth of thinking and its strong commitment to the value of the human being. This thesis transcends the Zionist enemy as an enemy that must be fought, in order to reach out to the Israeli Jewish person with whom it is incumbent upon us to live together in brotherhood and peace. This thesis overcomes the idea of war and destruction and killing because it is consistent with the course of history and it looks towards the building and construction after the war.

This thesis indicates that the Palestinians do not fight for the love of war or for revenge, but rather for the liberation of land and man whatever their religion might be, because vengeance is negative and destructive whereas liberation is positive and constructive. We do not fight the Jews because they are Jews in order to kill them or expel them or throw them into the sea. We fight the occupier viciously whatever his religion, race or country of origin might be. We have in the past fought against the occupying Catholic Crusaders and we have fought the occupying Muslim Ottomans and we have fought the occupying Protestant British and we are currently fighting the Jewish Zionist in his capacity as occupier. We are fighting the occupier and the colonizer irrespective of the religion to which he happens to subscribe.

The thesis of the democratic state is a humanist revolutionary thesis. Liberation under the conditions of colonialism customarily involves the expulsion of the foreign occupying colonizer and the return of the exiled people to its home and land. Yet given our understanding of the problem of the Jewish people and given our belief that the revolution must entail the liberation of the land and the human person, we therefore submitted the project of a democratic state that affords the opportunity for every human being who currently resides in Palestine including the foreigner who came to Palestine, as invader, an occupier and a colonizer to remain in Palestine and to live with us in peace and to assist us and to be assisted by us in the building of a democratic society that will secure equal rights to all its inhabitants and equal duties by all its inhabitants without any reference to sex, colour or religion. When we submit this project in sincerity we do not wish to deceive anyone through this project, nor do we submit this project as mere propaganda.

There is no doubt that the state will be a republic and will carry the name of Palestine because this is the historical name that this land has always carried throughout the centuries. We therefore say the Democratic Republic of Palestine. We avoid the word secular in order not to be mistakenly understood that we intend to abolish religion. We do not wish to abolish religion, but we do say that religion is a personal question relevant to the individual and his belief and that it is impermissible to establish religion as an element that adds to the rights or subtracts from the rights and the duties of any inhabitant. Had we proposed a secular republic of Palestine we could have effectively been understood in Western contexts as defining a state with a specific confessional nature, since secularism has itself almost become a religious tradition in the West. And we do not say a multi-religious state because we do not wish to impose religion on anybody, and we obviously do not say an apostate state, but we say a democratic state where religion will remain a personal question and where religious tradition will be respected, but where religion will not play any role relevant to government or national responsibilities determining rights and duties. We do not say a progressive state because a democratic state, of its nature, must be progressive since otherwise its democracy is bound to be false and superficial. True democracy entails in our view also progress. And we do not say a popular state because the word republic in itself contains the concept of participation of the people, the entire people, in government subject to agreed procedures. And we do not say a socialist state first because the word 'socialism' has been much distorted in our time. How many parties and groups or regimes claim socialism and in reality are completely devoid of socialism? We understand socialism to mean the just distribution of wealth, privileges and responsibilities at all levels and to mean also the supremacy of principle over power and free popular elections.

Is democracy anything else (than socialism thus defined)? We mean true democracy, obviously. I do not believe that a democratic republic will permit the powerful to oppress the weak, the rich to exploit the poor and the minority to determine the destiny of the majority. We believe that socialism will not be assessed on the basis of words and slogans but rather on the basis of action and application. We prefer a democratic state that will apply socialism without carrying the name over a state which is named socialist but the name is its only share in socialism and social justice. We are therefore content to say: 'The Democratic Republic of Palestine'. Here I disagree with the choice of the title of the booklet and I believe that the correct one ought to be: *Towards a Democratic Republic of Palestine*.

Armed struggle

I do not have the least doubt that so long as the Zionist doctrine remains dominant in the minds of the Israeli leaders and dictates their racialist expansionist and oppressive practice, armed struggle will remain the only way and has no substitute. There is no doubt that those who have lived under Zionism and who have suffered from Zionism throughout the long years in the past have reached the same conclusion, even though certain specific conditions could conceivably compel them to avoid the expression of this conclusion publicly, even had they wished to do so because of their desire to remain inside the boundaries of legality imposed upon them by Zionism itself without challenging it by voicing such statements. So long as Zionism continues to govern the minds of the Israeli leadership as well as individual Israelis in this way the problem as far as the Palestine Revolution and the patriotic forces are concerned will remain a problem of life and death and not a problem of occupation and withdrawal. I do not say this in order to outbid anyone. This is my conviction. It is consistent with the Palestine National Covenant and the resolutions of the Palestine National Councils.

This does not mean that I will not be satisfied except with a military solution that will enable me to dismantle the Zionist doctrine and practice in one single blow and in one single battle. I believe in a protracted war of popular liberation and hard continuous daily struggle. But I similarly believe in stages and I believe that every step forward that we take as a result of our struggle and our efforts is a step backwards imposed on our enemy and that every victory we achieve in reality is naturally a defeat for the enemy. But it is necessary to be on guard in order that the step forward should not lead us into a trap and in order that what we believe to be a defeat inflicted upon the enemy be not turned into a diversion that will permit the enemy to collect its forces to launch an even more vicious attack and achieve a greater victory.

My conviction in the necessity of armed struggle against Zionism is consistent with my strong belief in political struggle. I consider political struggle to be necessary, furthermore, to be a fundamental condition with other conditions for victory. And the armed struggle will lose much of its importance and significance if it is not accompanied by the political struggle, and it is here that the supreme importance of the political and diplomatic gains achieved by the Palestine Liberation Organization, especially in the past few years, is rooted. These gains were not achieved, allegations by some notwithstanding, on account of the armed resistance that the Palestine Liberation Organization has undertaken to intensify.

There is no doubt that the political struggle that inevitably must accompany military pressure compels a large number of the Jews subject to the Zionist doctrine to review and to develop the conviction that this doctrine constitutes a political and national danger, even physical danger, not only for the Palestinian Arabs but also for the Jews themselves, since they are in reality its victims. And there is no doubt that a number of those Jews and Israelis will gradually begin to participate in the struggle alongside the Palestinians. And there is nothing to prevent some of them from participation even in armed struggle against Zionism and the reaction and exploitation and imperialism which it represents. ... There are a number of Israeli Jews who stand with us in the same trench in our struggle, as well as some who carry arms with us. What is there to prevent their number increasing? Nothing except the fears of those who do not wish that there emerge on the scene anyone who is more committed and more patriotic than themselves.

The Palestinian people have carried the gun and proclaimed the armed revolution and have not ceased to do so, and have embarked upon the political struggle and will necessarily undertake to intensify it. There are Jews and Israelis who struggle politically and with complete devotion alongside us as well as those who have carried arms in solidarity with us and those who are prepared to carry arms at the appropriate time. This is a very encouraging phenomenon because the liberation of Palestine and the establishment of the democratic state is a joint responsibility for all the progressive forces in the region. No doubt the greatest share of this responsibility falls in the main and in the first instance upon the shoulders of the Palestinian Revolution not because we eliminate the Jews out of our consideration ... but because the Palestinian Arabs are oppressed and dispossessed and they have come to understand the nature of Zionism, its aspirations, its thinking and its dangers; it can no longer deceive any one of them. On the other hand are the Jews who are still being deceived by Zionist doctrine and practice – their participation in our struggle will be gradual. In addition every group among the Jews that becomes convinced of the justice, seriousness and importance of our cause for the future of the Palestinians and the Israelis simultaneously will be incorporated into our struggle.

It is very difficult to conceive that all the Israelis will transform their Zionist political beliefs in one fell swoop but, as in the Soviet Union during the glorious October Revolution and in France at the time of the French Revolution, there are always vanguard forces that lead the revolution whereas the majority of the people join the struggle only after the launching of the revolution and participate in it or adopt its principles after its victory. I say this not because we eliminate the Jews from our consideration in the determination of armed struggle but because we take reality, the possible and the likely as our point of departure and we do not believe in miracles.

Is it not the case that the October Revolution and the existence of the socialist state constitute a basic condition for the political and the social transformation of hundreds of thousands of the Russian people? And who can claim that the Russian people in its entirety was socialist or communist before the start of the revolution? It is true that we cannot impose the revolution against the will of all the Jews in the country, but we shall succeed if there develops in Israel a vanguard progressive force ready to join in the realization of the revolution. ...

It is true that there have been liberation movements that have resorted to armed struggle and it is true that other liberation movements were not compelled to adopt this course. To the Palestinian people, history has confirmed irrefutably that the enemy and its allies will not permit it any route other than armed struggle and military combat. Had the Fateh not shot the first bullet in 1965 and had the Palestinian people limited itself to political struggle and peaceful means, there would not have been today a Palestinian revolution and it would not have succeeded in forcing recognition from the world and there would not be today anyone who would discuss the question of our inalienable national rights and our right of self-determination and the establishment of an independent Palestinian state under the leadership of the Palestine Liberation Organization. I can even say that had the armed revolution not been developed we would not have read in *Al-Ittihad* what we read by way of articles on the national rights of the Palestinian people and their inevitable recognition.

(Naim Khader, PLO representative to Belgium and the European Economic Community [EEC], was assassinated in Brussels, probably by the Israeli MOSSAD, on 1 June 1981)

Appendix 4 AL-BEIT: Association for the Defence of Human Rights in Israel

Background

In May 1994 Palestinian lawyer Tawfiq Jabarin, a resident of Umm al-Fahm, made legal history when he contested and overcame the racial bylaws of community settlement Qatzir, located on the outskirts of his town, and became the first Palestinian citizen of Israel to directly purchase a government-subsidized home there (government-subsidized, as distinct from Jewish Agency-subsidized).

Following Jabarin's successful exploitation of legal loopholes in the case of Qatzir, he was approached by veteran human rights activist Dr Uri Davis, and together they initiated the establishment of AL-BEIT: Association for the Defence of Human Rights in Israel with the aim of building on this experience.

AL-BEIT was founded in March 1995 by a group of veteran human rights activists as a non-profit organization with the view to address a hitherto largely neglected area of human rights abuse in Israel, namely, the violation of Article 13 of the Universal Declaration of Human Rights:

(1) Everyone has the right to freedom of movement and residence within the borders of each state.

(2) Everyone has the right to leave any country, including his own, and to return to his country.

In the context of defence of Article 13 above, the first practical priority of AL-BEIT is the defence of the right to freedom of residence in Israel, first and foremost, the right of Palestinian citizens in Israel to equal housing. AL-BEIT aims to advance the access of the Palestinians (citizens and non-citizens) to Israel state lands on an equal footing to all the citizens of the state with a view to promoting housing solutions for families and communities on a non-discriminatory basis.

The problem AL-BEIT aims to address

The housing crisis in the Arab sector in Israel is the result, in the first instance, of the Palestinian *nakba* and the consequent long-term government policies and strategic housing priorities discriminating against the non-Jewish citizens of Israel, first and foremost against the Palestinian citizens of Israel. It is further exacerbated by the high natural growth rate of the Palestinian community (over 3 per cent per annum), compared with the Jewish community (averaging under 2 per cent per annum); the limited social mobility of the Palestinian community, enforced by Israel's official housing policy; and the further limitation of available land for construction through zoning policies based on discriminatory political and demographic considerations.

An additional obstacle affecting young couples in the Palestinian community inside Israel is the fact that government-subsidized mortgages for purchasing homes are at least 33 per cent lower for most non-Jewish citizens.

As a result the Palestinian community in Israel has been ghettoized in mixed cities (e.g. Acre), overcrowded and underserviced towns (e.g. Umm al-Fahm), villages (e.g. 'Ar'ara) and unrecognized localities (e.g. Kammana), many of the latter totally lacking basic services such as running water, sewerage and electricity, while being threatened with eviction and demolition.

Added to these structural disadvantages, the authorities present obstacles in all matters pertaining to the issue of building licences in Arab localities and regional planning on behalf of Arab localities, amounting to a calculated policy directed against the Arab population. As a result Arab families in Israel must choose between two vicious options: not to build, or otherwise to build without licence. Should families opt for the latter possibility, they face serious danger of demolition of their home.

Less than 10 per cent of the land under Israeli sovereignty is privately owned. Some 15 per cent is owned by the Jewish National Fund (JNF), incorporated in 1907 as a company limited by guarantee in England, and in 1953 in Israel by Knesset legislation, which is constitutionally bound to develop and lease its lands only to Jews. The remaining 75 per cent, legally state domain, is administered under Basic Law, Israel Lands Law, and Israel Lands Administration Law, all three legislated in 1960, and under the covenant signed between the government of the State of Israel and the JNF in 1961. As noted above, the aim of AL-BEIT is to advance the access of the Palestinians (citizens and non-citizens) to Israel state lands on an equal footing with all the citizens of the state.

Appendix 5 *Palestine National Council: Palestinian Declaration of Independence, Algiers, 15 November 1988*

In the name of God, the Compassionate, the Merciful.

Palestine, the land of the three monotheistic faiths, is where the Palestinian Arab people was born, on which it grew, developed, and excelled. The Palestinian people was never separated from or diminished in its integral bonds with Palestine. Thus the Palestinian Arab people ensured for itself an everlasting union between itself, its land and its history.

Resolute throughout that history, the Palestinian Arab people forged its national identity, rising even to unimagined levels in its defence as invasion, the design of others, and the appeal special to Palestine's ancient and luminous place on that eminence where powers and civilizations are joined ... All this intervened thereby to deprive the people of its political independence. Yet the undying connection between Palestine and its people secured for the land its character and for the people its national genius.

Nourished by an unfolding series of civilizations and cultures, inspired by a heritage rich in variety and kind, the Palestinian Arab people added to its stature by consolidating a union between itself and its patrimonial land. The call went out from temple, church and mosque to praise the Creator, to celebrate compassion, and peace was indeed the message of Palestine. And in generation after generation, the Palestinian Arab people gave of itself unsparingly in the valiant battle for liberation and homeland. For what has been the unbroken chain of our people's rebellions but the heroic embodiment of our will for national independence? And so the people were sustained in the struggle to stay and to prevail.

When in the course of modern times a new order of values was declared with norms and values fair for all, it was the Palestinian Arab people that had been excluded from the destiny of all other peoples by a hostile array of local and foreign powers. Yet again had unaided justice been revealed as insufficient to drive the world's history along its preferred course.

And it was the Palestinian people, already wounded in its body, that was submitted to yet another type of occupation over which floated the falsehood that 'Palestine was a land without people'. This notion was foisted upon some in the world, whereas in Article 22 of the Covenant of the League of Nations (1919) and in the Treaty of Lausanne (1923), the community of nations had recognized that all the Arab territories, including Palestine, of the formerly Ottoman provinces were to have granted to them their freedom as provisionally independent nations.

Despite the historical injustice inflicted on the Palestinian Arab people resulting in their dispersion and depriving them of their right to self-determination, following upon UN General Assembly Resolution 181 (1947), which partitioned Palestine into two states, one Arab, one Jewish, this resolution still provides those conditions of international legitimacy that ensure the right of the Palestinian Arab people to sovereignty and national independence.

By stages, the occupation of Palestine and parts of other Arab territories by Israeli forces and the willed dispossession and expulsion from their ancestral homes of the majority of Palestine's civilian inhabitants were achieved by organized terror; those Palestinians who remained, as a vestige subjugated in its homeland, were persecuted and forced to endure the destruction of their national life.

Thus were principles of international legitimacy violated. Thus were the Charter of the United Nations and its resolutions disfigured, for they had recognized the Palestinian Arab people's national rights, including the Right of Return, the Right to Independence, the Right to Sovereignty over territory and homeland.

In Palestine and on its perimeters, in exile distant and near, the Palestinian Arab people never faltered and never abandoned their belief in their rights of return and independence. Occupation, massacres and dispersion achieved no gain in the unabated Palestinian consciousness of self and political identity, as Palestinians went forward with their destiny, undeterred and unbowed. And from the long years of trial in ever mounting struggle, the Palestinian political identity emerged further consolidated and confirmed. And the collective Palestinian national will forged itself in a political embodiment, the Palestine Liberation Organization, its sole, legitimate representative, recognized by the world community as a whole, as well as by related regional and international institutions. Standing on the very rock of belief in the Palestinian people's inalienable rights, and on the ground of Arab national consensus and of international legitimacy, the PLO led the campaigns of its great people, moulded into unity and powerful resolve, one and indivisible in the triumphs, even as it suffered massacres and confinement within and without its home. And so Palestinian resistance was clarified and raised into the forefront of Arab and world awareness, as the struggle of the Palestinian Arab people achieved unique prominence among the world's liberation movements in the modern era.

The massive national uprising, the Intifada, now intensifying in cumulative scope and power on occupied Palestinian territories, as well as the unflinching resistance of the refugee camps outside the homeland, have elevated consciousness of the Palestinian truth and right into still higher realms of comprehension and actuality. Now at last the curtain has been dropped around a whole epoch of prevarication and negation. The Intifada has set siege to the mind of official Israel, which has for too long relied exclusively upon myth and terror to deny Palestinian existence altogether. Because of the Intifada and its revolutionary irreversible impulse, the history of Palestine has therefore arrived at a decisive juncture.

Whereas the Palestinian people reaffirms most definitely its inalienable rights in the land of its patrimony:

- now by virtue of natural, historical, and legal rights and the sacrifices of successive generations who gave of themselves in defence of the freedom and independence of their homeland;
- In pursuance of resolutions adopted by Arab summit conferences and relying on the authority bestowed by international legitimacy as embodied in the resolutions of the United Nations Organization since 1947;
- And in exercise by the Palestinian Arab people of its rights to self-determination, political independence, and sovereignty over its territory;
- The Palestine National Council, in the name of God, and in the name of the Palestinian Arab people, hereby proclaims the establishment of the State of Palestine on our Palestinian territory with its capital Jerusalem (Al-Quds Ash-Sharif).

The State of Palestine is the state of Palestinians wherever they may be. The state is for them to enjoy in it their collective national and cultural identity, to pursue in it a complete equality of rights. In it will be safeguarded their political and religious convictions and their human dignity by means of a parliamentary democratic system of governance, itself based on freedom of expression and the freedom to form parties. The rights of minorities will duly be respected by the majority, as minorities must abide by decisions of the majority. Governance will be based on principles of social justice, equality and non-discrimination in public rights on grounds of race, religion, colour or sex under the aegis of a constitution that ensures the role of law and an independent judiciary. Thus shall these principles allow no departure from Palestine's age-old spiritual and civilizational heritage of tolerance and religious co-existence.

The State of Palestine is an Arab state, an integral and indivisible part of the Arab nation, at one with that nation in heritage and civilization, with it also in its aspiration for liberation, progress, democracy and unity. The State of Palestine affirms its obligation to abide by the Charter of the League of Arab States, whereby the cooperation of the Arab states with each other shall be strengthened. It calls upon Arab compatriots to consolidate and enhance the emergence in reality of our state, to mobilize potential, and to intensify efforts whose goal is to end Israeli occupation.

The State of Palestine proclaims its commitment to the principles and purposes of the United Nations, and to the Universal Declaration of Human Rights. It proclaims its commitment as well to the principles and policies of the Non-Aligned Movement.

It further announces itself to be a peace-loving state, in adherence to the principles of peaceful co-existence. It will join with all states and peoples in order to assure a permanent peace based upon justice and the respect of rights so that humanity's potential for well-being may be assured, an earnest competition for excellence be maintained, and in which confidence in the future will eliminate fear for those who are just and for whom justice is the only recourse.

In the context of its struggle for peace in the land of love and peace, the State of Palestine calls upon the United Nations to bear special responsibility for the Palestinian Arab people and its homeland. It calls upon all peace- and freedom-loving peoples and states to assist it in the attainment of its objectives, to provide it with security, to alleviate the tragedy of its people, and to help to terminate Israel's occupation of the Palestinian territories.

The State of Palestine herewith declares that it believes in the settlement of regional and international disputes by peaceful means, in accordance with the UN Charter and resolutions. Without prejudice to its natural right to defend its territorial integrity and independence, it therefore rejects the threat or use of force, violence and terrorism against its territorial integrity, or political independence, as it also rejects their use against the territorial integrity of other states.

Therefore, on this day unlike all others, 15 November 1988, as we stand at the threshold of a new dawn, in all honour and modesty we humbly bow to the sacred spirits of our fallen ones, Palestinian and Arab, by the purity of whose sacrifice for the homeland our sky has been illuminated and our land given life. Our hearts are lifted up and irradiated by the light emanating from the much blessed Intifada, from those who have endured and have fought the fight of the camps, of dispersion, of exile, from those who have borne the standard of freedom, our children, our aged, our youth, our prisoners, detainees and wounded, all those whose ties to our sacred soil are confirmed in camp, village and town.

We render special tribute to that brave Palestinian woman, guardian of sustenance and life, keeper of our people's perennial flame. To the souls of our sainted martyrs, to the whole of our Palestinian Arab people, to all free and honourable peoples everywhere, we pledge that our struggle shall be continued until the occupation ends, and the foundation of our sovereignty and independence shall be fortified accordingly.

Therefore, we call upon our great people to rally to the banner of Palestine, to cherish and defend it, so that it may forever be the symbol of our freedom and dignity in that homeland, which is a homeland for the free, now and always.

In the name of God, the Compassionate, the Merciful.

'Say: "O God, Master of the Kingdom, Thou givest the Kingdom to whom Thou wilt, and seizest the Kingdom from whom Thou wilt. Thou exaltest whom Thou wilt, and Thou abasest whom Thou wilt; in Thy hand is the good; Thou art powerful over everything."'

Sadaqa Allahu al-'Azim

Notes

1. I am indebted to the late Professor Israel Shahak, Chairman of the Israeli League for Human and Civil Rights, for the reference. The late Rabbi Joachim Prinz (1902–88) was an influential Jewish leader in his day. He was a member of the executive board, vice-president and chairman of the governing board of the World Jewish Congress (WJC); president of the American Jewish Congress (1958–66); chairman of the Conference of Presidents of Major American Jewish Organizations (1965–67); director of the Conference on Jewish Material Claims Against Germany; chairman of the World Conference of Jewish Organizations and the Commission on International Affairs of the American Jewish Congress. Presumably his views on a Jewish state based on the Nazi principle of the purity of the nation and the race enhanced his career as a rabbi and an American Jewish community leader, rather than otherwise.

2. See, for instance, Flapan 1987; Kimmerling and Migdal 1993; Masalha 1992; Morris 1987; Pape 1992; Shlaim 1988.

3. The reference in Brenner has a typographical error. It is Vol. XIII of *Yad Vashem Studies* (not Vol. XII).

4. The complete sentence reads as follows: 'Thus it [the Zionist Organization] would build up gradually a nationality, and so make Palestine as Jewish as America is American or England English' (as quoted by Gilbert 1978: 117).

5. Joseph Weitz was born in Wolhynia (Russia) in 1890 and immigrated to Palestine in 1908. He became head of the Plant and Afforestation Department of the JNF (1918–32); director of the Land Development Division of the JNF (1932–59); chairman of the Subcommittee for Naming Agricultural Settlements and chairman of the Land Development Council of the JNF (1960–67). He was a former chairman of the Israel Land Authority and a prolific publicist and author of books on land, colonization and afforestation. He published his memoirs in six volumes.

6. For additional quotes from Weitz's *Diary* on the subject of 'transfer' see Chapter 5.

7. Testimony by Meir Pa'il, Israeli army storm-troop (*Palmah*) commando at the time, and subsequently Israeli army general, MK and lecturer in military history at Tel Aviv University. The testimony was recorded on 9 April 1948 and presented to his army superior the late Israel Galili, subsequently minister of state. Meir Pa'il published the document 24 years later in *Yediot Aharonot*, 4 April 1972.

8. I am indebted to the late Professor Israel Shahak, chairman of the Israeli League for Human and Civil Rights, for the reference.

9. In order to expand the circles of political and financial support for the Zionist colonial project inside Jewish communities worldwide, notably in the USA, the 16th Zionist Congress meeting in Zurich in 1929 resolved to establish the 'Enlarged Jewish Agency' on the basis of parity between Zionists and 'non-Zionists', namely, such Jewish organizations and leaders who supported the establishment of a 'Jew-

ish national home' in Palestine, but took exception to the political ambitions of political Zionism aiming to establish a sovereign Jewish state there.

10. The equivalent title of the official Hebrew text reads: 'Agreement for the Reconstitution of the Jewish Agency for the Land of Israel'. The term 'Israel' rather than 'Land of Israel' in the official English-language text could be read to mean the 'State of Israel', veiling the political Zionist ideological term of the 'Land of Israel' (*Eretz Israel*) that characterizes the official name of the Jewish Agency (the Jewish Agency for the Land of Israel). Such and similar veils of ambiguity were and remain essential not only to protect Zionist fundraising in the West from too close a scrutiny by the tax authorities (see below), but also to protect the entire political Zionist project from international sanctions. This consideration applies not only to the question of Israel's illegal apartheid policies, but equally to the question of Israel's nuclear policies. The State of Israel would not have been able to project itself as 'the only democracy in the Middle East' and evade international sanctions directed against its apartheid policies had it not at least partly succeeded in covering its apartheid legislation by veils of legal ambiguity. By the same token, Israel would not have been able to protect itself from international sanctions against its illegal nuclear policies had it not been at least partly successful in covering its arsenal of illegal weapons of mass destruction by veils of political ambiguity ('Israel shall not be the first state in the Middle East to introduce weapons of mass destruction').

It was the nuclear technician Mordechai Vanunu who blew the whistle on Israel's illegal nuclear policies and illegal production facilities in Dimonah and brought his evidence for publication in the *Sunday Times* (5 October 1986). He was consequently kidnapped from London by the Israeli security services and sentenced in Israel to 18 years' imprisonment on charges of espionage (of which he spent nearly 12 years in solitary confinement). Vanunu was charged with espionage, but this was not his crime. His 'crime' was that he seriously jeopardized Israel's elaborate veil of ambiguity covering up its illegal nuclear policies, thereby exposing Israel to international sanctions and the suspension of the massive aid packages from the USA.

11. For further reading see Khalidi 1988, 1992; Palumbo 1987; Rogan and Shlaim 2001.

12. According to three field surveys, which the Association of Forty undertook in 1988, 1994 and 2000, there are 32 villages and neighbourhoods in the north and the centre of the State of Israel and 117 villages in the south where some 100,000 inhabitants reside (of whom 70 per cent reside in the south and 30 per cent in the north). For further information see Association of Forty 1996, 2001.

13. For a review of the legal status of 'absentee property' under international law, see Cattan 1969: 157–74; Hadawi 1957.

14. See also Hadawi 1957; Cattan 1969; Said 1980; Kretzmer 1990; Yiftahel 1992; Kedar 2001.

15. See Mazzawi 1997: 129. As Mazzawi points out in his seminal study of Palestine and the law, an important point to note is 'the repeated reference on behalf of Israel to the United Nations General Assembly's partition resolution and Israel's insistence on it as the sole basis of the legitimacy of Israel ... And if the partition resolution was then valid it remains so today, since its maker – the United Nations General Assembly – has not in any way undone it' (ibid.: 140; see also ibid.: 148). It is, however, sobering to remember that a resolution that impinges equally critically on the question of Palestine, UN General Assembly Resolution 3379 of November 1975, determining that 'Zionism is a form of racism and racial discrimination',

was rescinded by the UN in December 1991. Although UN resolutions and the standards of international law represent one of the most weighty defences of the rights of the Palestinian people, the justice of the Palestinian struggle is anchored in the values of the Universal Declaration of Human Rights.

16. The Law of Return of 1950 is not the only piece of legislation passed by the Knesset where the apartheid distinction between 'Jew' and 'non-Jew' is rendered explicitly. Other such laws are the Religious Jewish Services Law of 1971 and the Chief Rabbinate Law of 1980. For an overview of Israeli legislation in this regard see Adalah: The Legal Center for Arab Minority Rights in Israel 1998.

17. In matrimonial matters pertaining to custody, alimony and property, parallel civil and religious court jurisdiction obtains.

18. The World Zionist Organization/Jewish Agency for the Land of Israel Law Proposal was brought by the government to the Knesset. David Ben-Gurion, the first prime minister of the State of Israel, introduced the Law Proposal in the name of the government. The Knesset debated the WZO/JA Law Proposal at its Sessions on 5 and 6 May 1952 (First Reading) and then in its Sessions on 11 August 1952 (Second and Third Readings). In the latter Session the opposition defeated the government in the debate on the government-proposed formulation of Article 4 of the Law Proposal and an amendment proposed by MK Yizhar Harari (Progressive Party) and MK Israel Bar-Yehudah (MAPAM) won a majority vote (31 in favour, 27 against). As a consequence, the government pulled its Law Proposal after the Second Reading (but before the final Third Reading) and reintroduced its Law Proposal for a new First Reading for debate in the Knesset at its Sessions on 4, 5 and 24 November 1952. Also on this occasion it was David Ben-Gurion who introduced the Law Proposal to the Knesset. Ben-Gurion's quote is taken from his address to the Knesset introducing the said Law Proposal at the second First Reading.

Needless to say, the legality of the procedure was challenged in the course of the debate, but the government got away with the manoeuvre, and the said joint Harari Amendment was defeated this time round.

19. For a detailed discussion of UN Security Council Resolution 242 see, *inter alia*, Mallison and Mallison 1986; Cattan 1988; Mazzawi 1997.

20. The question of what are the international borders of the State of Israel is a moot point. Taking as point of departure the UN General Assembly Resolution 181(II), Plan of Partition with Economic Union of November 1947, the successor government to His Majesty's Britannic Government of Palestine was not to be that of a 'Jewish state', but both the government of the 'Jewish state' and the government of the 'Arab state' joined together in economic union with Jerusalem as a *corpus separatum* under international UN administration. Thus the borders of the Mandate territory of Palestine as defined by the League of Nations for the Mandatory power, His Britannic Majesty's Government, are the international borders for both 'Jewish' and 'Arab' states joined together in economic union, in other words, the borders of the economic union.

Until 1979, strictly speaking the State of Israel had no international borders. The 1948–49 war was concluded with a series of armistice agreements between the State of Israel and the neighbouring Arab states (Egypt, February 1949; Lebanon, March 1949; Jordan, April 1949; Syria, July 1949). References to 'Israel's pre-1967 borders' (the 'Green Line') are erroneous in that they refer to what ought to be properly named Israel's armistice lines.

In 1979 the Government of the State of Israel and the Government of the Arab

Republic of Egypt signed the Israel–Egypt Peace Treaty agreeing an Israeli staged withdrawal from all the territories occupied by Israel in the Egyptian Sinai Peninsula. And indeed, by 1982 Israel had withdrawn to the international border line that obtained between Egypt and British Mandate Palestine – except that under UN resolutions, notably, UN General Assembly Resolution 181(II), and the standards of international law, this border was designated to be the border between Egypt and *two* states: the 'Jewish state' (Israel) and the 'Arab state' (Palestine).

The international borders agreed between Egypt and Israel in the framework of the Israel–Egypt Peace Treaty of March 1979 are the legitimate borders of the Arab Republic of Egypt – but not of the State of Israel. The same applies to the Treaty of Peace Between the State of Israel and the Hashemite Kingdom of Jordan of October 1994.

By signing the separate peace treaties with Israel, both the Arab Republic of Egypt and the Hashemite Kingdom of Jordan endowed legitimacy to the blatant and war criminal violation by Israel of all UN resolutions relevant to the question of Palestine, notably UN General Assembly Resolution 181(II).

21. For a detailed study of Israeli policies regarding non-Jewish specifically Muslim *waqf*, religious properties, see Dumper 1993; also Islamic Cultural Centre 1978; Khalifa 1994.

22. Transkei, Bophuthatswana, Ciskei, Lebowa, Venda, Gazankulu, QwaQwa, KwaZulu, KwaNdebele and KaNgwane.

23. See John Dugard, 'The Denationalization of Black South Africans in Pursuance of Apartheid', in *The Review*, No. 33, December 1984. I am indebted to Dr Anis al-Qasim, secretary-general of the International Organization for the Elimination of All Forms of Racial Discrimination (EAFORD) for the reference and the insight and to Steven Goldblatt for the clarification of this reference.

24. Currently, the population within Israel's 1948–49 boundaries stands at approximately 5.2 million Jewish citizens and 1.2 million Palestinian Arab citizens. In other words, through a natural growth rate of close to 3–4 per cent per annum, the Palestinian Arab population under Israeli rule and occupation since 1948 is eight times larger than it was, from 150,000 to 1,200,000 million in less than 60 years (*Statistical Abstracts of Israel* 2002, No. 53, Table 2.1, pp. 2–9).

With a negligible margin, the non-Jewish population of the State of Israel is Palestinian Arab. It is worth noting that the Israeli government Central Bureau of Statistics no longer renders separate citations for East Jerusalem (annexed in 1967) and the Golan Heights (annexed in 1981). The figures for the population within Israel's 1948–49 boundaries therefore include the population of these two areas.

25. After the Russian conquest of Circassia from the Ottomans in 1878, many Circassian clans and families loyal to the Ottoman regime emigrated to various countries throughout the Ottoman empire. The Ottoman Sultan Abd al-Hamid extended his support to the Circassian resettlement and made lands available to them in Palestine, *inter alia*, where there are two Circassian villages, Kufr Qama in Lower Galilee and Rihaniyya in Upper Galilee. The attempt to settle Circassians in the Northern Sharon, in the northern coastal plain, where they established the village of Sarkas, failed, and the original Circassian inhabitants were gradually replaced by native Palestinian Arabs. In 1947 the village population totalled 400 inhabitants.

26. I am indebted to Steven Goldblatt for the reference.

27. Palestinian Arab citizens of the State of Israel have equal standing before

the courts of law in principle only. In practice the courts tend to mete out different sentences for similar offences committed in similar contexts for 'Jewish' offenders and 'non-Jewish' offenders, namely offenders who are Palestinian Arab citizens of Israel. Research of the judicial criminal process leading to convictions (or otherwise) in the Israeli courts in 1980–92 conducted by the Centre for the Study of Crime, Law and Society at the University of Haifa, revealed systematic differences between Jews and Arabs. The study suggests, *inter alia*, that the likelihood for 'Arab' offenders to be found guilty and sentenced to prison terms is up to twice as high as the likelihood for 'Jewish' offenders of comparable 'case profiles' convicted (or otherwise) for similar offences committed in comparable contexts (see Rattner and Fishman 1998).

28. Yeshaayahu Leibowitz, iconoclast, scientist, philosopher and man of letters (1903–94). Born in Riga, Yeshaayahu Leibowitz was educated in Germany and Switzerland and immigrated to Palestine in 1935. He joined the Hebrew University and taught chemistry, physiology, and history and philosophy of science. He wrote many books and articles, lectured publicly, and was an editor of several volumes of the *Encyclopaedia Hebraica*. One of Israel's foremost renaissance intellectuals, outspoken in his views on Judaism and Israel, he aroused a great deal of debate among religious and non-religious circles. The decision in 1992 to award him the Israel Prize sparked much controversy, and Leibowitz declined it. He died in Jerusalem in 1994. An orthodox Jew, Leibowitz argued fiercely for the separation of religion from the state, pointing out that the failure to do so prostitutes both religion and the state. He was also a consistent and staunch opponent of the Israeli occupation of the territories conquered in the 1967 war and supported conscientious objection to serving in the post-1967 occupied territories and in Lebanon. It was he who in 1983 coined the term 'Judeo-Nazi mentality' with reference to fundamentalist right-wing terrorism in Israel (based on, *inter alia*, <http://www.jajz-ed.org.il/100/people/bios/yleib.html>).

29. A further complication is introduced in the classification of categories on Israeli identity cards, which each permanent and temporary resident of the State of Israel – Jew and non-Jew – must carry at all times from the age of 16, under penalty of the law. In the first decades following the establishment of the State of Israel in 1948, identity cards did not register citizenship, only nationality and religion. The reference to 'nationality', however, was rendered in Hebrew as *leom* but in Arabic as *milla* (not *qawmiyya*). *Milla* is the Ottoman legal term for confession; sections of the Ottoman law (*Majalla*) apply in Israel up to the present. Subsequently, the classification of categories on Israeli identity cards was reformed. The reference to 'nationality' in Arabic in the main body of the document (now a laminated computerized card) was now correctly translated as *qawmiyya* and the reference to citizenship included in a non-laminated computerized supplement slip, listing the additional categories of: street address, flat, name of locality, postal code, military personal number, personal status, identity card number of spouse, name of spouse, citizenship, family name prior to marriage, previous family name if altered in the past seven years, previous first name if altered in the past seven years, children until the age of 18. Given the contradictions underpinning the definition of who is a Jew in the 'Jewish state', however (see above), and faced with the reality of a growing constituency of hundreds of thousands of citizens of the State of Israel who are not Arab and not classified as 'Jews' under the Population Registry Law of 1965, notably immigrants from the former Soviet Union, the classification of categories on Israeli identity cards was once again reformed in 2002, now removing reference to nationality altogether.

30. The term 'Hebrew' as a national classification also appears in the official

Israeli Ministry of Interior Table of Nationalities as a designation for nationality. The term was introduced into the official Table of Nationalities consequent to the ruling of the Israeli Supreme Court in 1970 in the case of Jonathan Ratosh *vs.* Israeli Ministry of the Interior (quoted in Johanna Shelah *vs.* The State of Israel, Judgments of the Supreme Court of Israel [PADI], Case No. 653/75, Vol. 31[II], 1977, p. 423). I am indebted to Professor Uzzi Ornan, brother of the late Jonathan Ratosh, for the reference.

31. *Oleh* (the one who ascends) is a legal term in Israel, designated to classify Jewish immigrants only. Non-Jewish immigrants into Israel are not entitled to this designation under Israeli law. Non-Jewish immigration to Israel does not, presumably, entail ascent. The status of *oleh* entitles the person so classified not only to 'automatic' immigration, settlement and citizenship in Israel, but also to a substantial and comprehensive set of material benefits with regards to housing, tax exemptions, import of household equipment, employment, university tuition, and so on. These benefits are allocated in law to Jewish immigrants (*olim*) only. Under the 1970 Amendment to the Law of Return, non-Jewish members of mixed marriage families (namely, mixed marriages of Jews, children and grandchildren of Jews and their spouses) are regarded, for the purpose of the Law of Return, as Jewish immigrants.

32. The relevant Articles of the Entry into Israel Law and the Israel Nationality Law (both passed by the Knesset in 1952) read as follows:

Entry into Israel Law:

The entry of a person, other than an Israel national or an *oleh* under the Law of Return (1950), into Israel shall be by visa and his residence in Israel shall be by permit of residence under this law (Article 1). The granting of a residence permit under this law is at the exclusive discretion of the Minister of the Interior.

Nationality (Amendment No. 4) Law, 5740-1980:

Extension of nationality by residence to additional categories of persons

3A. (a) A person born before the establishment of the State shall be an Israel national by residence in Israel from the date of the coming into force of the Nationality (Amendment No. 4) Law, 5740-1980 (hereinafter referred to as 'the date of the 5740 amendment') if he meets the following requirements:

(1) He is not a resident of Israel by virtue of any other provision of this Law;

(2) he was a Palestinian citizen immediately before the establishment of the State;

(3) on the 21st Tammuz, 5712 (14th July, 1952), he was a resident of Israel and was registered in the Register of Inhabitants under the Registration of Inhabitants Ordinance, 5709-1949;

(4) on the date of the 5740 amendment, he was a resident of Israel and was registered in the Population Register;

(5) he is not a national of one of the states mentioned in section 2A of the Prevention of Infiltration (Offences and Jurisdiction) Law, 5714 1954.

(b) A person born after the establishment of the State shall be an Israel national by residence in Israel from the date of the 5740 amendment if he meets the following requirements:

(1) He is not an Israel national by virtue of any other provision of this Law;

(2) on the date of the 5740 amendment, he was a resident of Israel and was registered in the Population Register;

(3) he is a descendant of a person who meets the requirements of paragraph (1) to (3) of subsection (a).

33. The period defined in the law is effectively the period between UN Resolution No. 181(II) Recommending the Partition Plan for Palestine (29 November 1947) and the unilateral declaration of the establishment of the State of Israel on 15 May 1948.

34. See for instance Jiryis 1976; el-Asmar 1975; Lustick 1980; Rabinowitz and Baker 2002.

35. Halabi 1991; Kretzmer 1990.

36. The Israel Workers' List (RAFI) was founded in 1965 following the Ben-Gurion split from the Land of Israel Workers' Party (MAPAI). In 1968 it merged again with MAPAI and *Ahdut ha-Avodah* (Labour Union) to form the Israel Labour Party.

37. For details, see Emmanuel Farjoun, 'Palestinian Workers in Israel: A Reserve Army of Labour', *Khamsin: Journal of Revolutionary Socialists of the Middle East*, 7 (Ithaca Press, London, 1980) and the *Jerusalem al-Fajr*, I (17–19) August 1980; Sarah Graham-Brown, *Palestinian Workers and Trade Unions* (Middle East Research and Action Group [MERAG] in conjunction with UK Palestine Coordination, London, undated [c. 1980]; Israeli League for Human and Civil Rights, *The Market of Arab Children in Israel* (preface by Mordechai Avi-Shaul, President) (Tel Aviv, 1978); Salim Tamari, 'Building Other People's Homes: The Palestinian Peasant Household and Work in Israel', *Journal of Palestine Studies* 11(1), 1981, pp. 31–66; Michael Shalev, 'Jewish Organised Labor and the Palestinians: A Study of State/Society Relations in Israel', in Barukh Kimmerling (ed.) *The Israeli State and Society: Boundaries and Frontiers*, Albany: State University of New York Press, 1989, pp. 93–133; Moshe Semyonov and Noah Lewin-Epstein, *Hewers of Wood, Drawers of Water: Non-Citizen Arabs in the Israeli Labour Market*, Ithaca, NY: ILR Press, 1987; Leila Farsakh, *Palestinian Workers in Israel: 1967–1997*, MAS, Ramallah, 1988; Yehezkel Lein, *Builders of Zion: The Human Rights Violations of Palestinians from the Occupied Territories Working in Israel and the Settlements*, B'Tselem, Jerusalem, 1999; Mervat Rishmawi and Rhys Johnson, *Right to Work: Economic Rights Under Military Occupation*, LAW, Ramallah, 1999; Avram Bornstein, *Crossing the Green Line Between the West Bank and Israel*, Philadelphia: University of Pennsylvania, 2002; and Tobias Kelly, 'Illusions of State: Law, Citizenship and Labour in the West Bank', PhD thesis submitted to the London School of Economics (LSE), 2003. I am indebted to Tobias Kelly for his assistance in compiling the above bibliography.

38. It is officially estimated that the MAHAL comprised 3,000 volunteers. Of these, about 1,500 were from the USA and Canada, 500 from South Africa and 1,000 from Britain. The majority of the MAHAL volunteers returned to their countries of origin after the 1948–49 war, but 300 former MAHAL volunteers remained in Israel or returned later to settle there (based on information in the *Encyclopaedia Judaica*, Vol. 11, pp. 722–3).

39. Following an interview with Boris Senior at his home, 73 Hasadot Street, Kefar Shemaryahu, Boris Senior instructed his solicitor, Advocate Uriel Genihar of 12 King Davis Avenue, Tel Aviv, to allow me to copy the entire Sa'ad Murtada file for my reference. I visited the office of Advocate Genihar on 7 November 2002. His staff were kind enough to search the office archives for the file. Israeli law obligates solicitors to keep files in their archives for up to seven years. Having gone out of her way to locate it, Uriel Genihar's secretary informed me that the Boris Senior/Sa'ad Murtada file was logged as having been shredded.

40. The Defence (Emergency) Regulations of 1945 is a series of extreme measures originally made law in Palestine by the British Mandate authorities in their attempt to curb and contain both Palestinian Arab armed insurrection aiming to replace British Mandatory rule with an independent Palestine, and Zionist military operations aiming to establish in Palestine a state that would be 'as Jewish as England is English'.

41. The relevant text, Law and Administration Ordinance (Amendment No. 11) Law of 1967, reads as follows:

1. In the Law and Administration Ordinance, 1948, the following section shall be inserted after section 11A: (Addition of section 11B.)

Application of law.

11B. The law, jurisdiction and administration of the State shall extend to any area of Eretz Israel designed by the Government by order.

2. This Law shall come into force on the date of its adoption by the Knesset. (Commencement.)

Levi Eshkol, Prime Minister; Jacob S. Shapiro, Minister of Justice
Shneur Zalman Shazar, President of the State
(*Laws of the State of Israel*, Vol. 21, 1966/67).

42. The act of official annexation entails the declaration by the government of the State of Israel in the *Official Gazette* that the corpus of Israeli civilian legislation is applied to the territory annexed.

43. It is appropriate to note here that until the dismantlement of the separate military administration for the Palestinian Arab population of Israel in 1966, Palestinian Arabs resident in pre-1967 Israel were conventionally prosecuted in military courts under the Defence (Emergency) Regulations of 1945. The legal situation in the West Bank and the Gaza Strip is technically complex given that pre-1967 Jordanian civilian legislation is applied in the West Bank, and pre-1967 Egyptian military legislation – under the same Defence (Emergency) Regulations of 1945 – is applied in the Gaza Strip. For a detailed exposition of this subject, see Shehadeh and Kuttab 1980; Shehadeh 1988, 1997.

44. For the period prior to the current extensively available digital information see for example: Adnan Amad (ed.), *The Israeli League for Human and Civil Rights. The Shahak Papers*, Near East Ecumenical Bureau for Information and Interpretation (NEEBII), Beirut, undated (c. 1973); Israel Shahak, *The Non-Jew in the Jewish State: A Collection of Documents*, Jerusalem, 1975; Felicia Langer, *With My Own Eyes: Israel and the Occupied Territories, 1967–1973* (foreword by Israel Shahak), Ithaca Press, London, 1975; Insight Team, 'Israel and Torture', *Sunday Times*, London, 19 June 1977; Felicia Langer, *These are My Brothers: Israel and the Occupied Territories, Part II*, Ithaca Press, London, 1979; Reports of the United Nations General Assembly Special Committee to Investigate Israeli Practices Affecting Human Rights of the Population of the Occupied Territories (Established by Resolution No. 2443 [XXIII] of 19 December 1968); Law in the Service of Man, *A Report on the Treatment of Security Prisoners at the West Bank Prison of al-Faraa*, Ramallah, 1984.

For digital information see, for instance, Jerusalem Media & Communication Center (JMCC) Palestine Report (Palestinian news in English) <www.jmcc.org/media/reportonline>; LAW: The Palestinian Society for the Protection of Human Rights & the Environment <http://www.lawsociety.org>; Adalah: The Legal Center for Arab Minority Rights in Israel <http://www.adalah.org>; BADIL: Resource Center for Palestinian Residency & Refugee Rights <http://www.badil.org>; Public Committee Against Torture in Israel <http://www.stoptorture.org.il>; Israeli

Committee Against House Demolitions (ICAHD) <http://www.icahd.org>; Physicians for Human Rights <http://www.phr.org.il>; Alternative Information Center (AIC) <http://www.alternativenews.org>; The Other Israel <http://members.tripod.com/~other_Israel>; Between the Lines <http://www.between-lines.org>; OMCT: World Organization Against Torture <http://www.omct.org>; Amnesty International <http://www.amnesty.org>

45. It should be pointed out here that at the time of writing the three Palestinian Arabs in question (two citizens, Nihad Abu Kishk and Qays Ubayd) and one permanent resident (Shadi Sharafa) have yet to be found guilty in court of the charges presented to the court by the state alleging contact with the military arms of the Hamas, Hizbullah and the Popular Front for the Liberation of Palestine respectively, and direct involvement in hostile terrorist activities. The minister of the interior, Eli Yishai, chose to apply his authority under the said Article 11(b) of Israel's Nationality Law of 1952 as amended in 1980 to initiate proceedings towards the nullification of their Israeli citizenship and permanent residency status on the basis of the charges as presented by the state to the court. These measures represent a blatant violation of Article 11 of the Universal Declaration of Human Rights to the effect that everyone charged with a penal offence has the right to be presumed innocent until proved guilty according to law in a public trial at which he has had all the guarantees necessary for his defence.

It should also be noted that whereas the minister of the interior chose to apply his authority under the said Article 11(b) of Israel's Nationality Law of 1952 (as amended in 1980) against two Palestinian Arab citizens and one permanent resident of the State of Israel on the grounds of committing 'an act constituting a breach of allegiance to the State of Israel', he refrained from doing likewise in the case of convicted Jewish terrorists, notably Yigal Amir, the fundamentalist Jewish assassin who murdered the late Prime Minister Yitzhak Rabin.

Finally, in the press debate that followed the decision of the minister of the interior to nullify the Israeli citizenship of Nihad Abu Kishk and initiate formal proceedings to nullify the citizenship of Qays Ubayd and the permanent residency status of Shadi Sharafa, it transpired that in the view of the legal advisers to the Ministry of Interior, the fact that the State of Israel signed the UN Convention on the Reduction of Statelessness of 1961 is not legally binding on the government since the Convention was not ratified by the government (*Haaretz*, 1 September 2002).

46. At the time of researching this book, the *Knesset Debates* for the year 2002 have not as yet been bound. The text quoted has been downloaded from the digital database of the Law Library, University of Haifa.

47. A comparative reading of the text of Amendment No. 9 to the Basic Law: The Knesset, 'Clause 7(a)(1) A candidates' list shall not participate in the elections to the Knesset if its objects or actions, expressly or by implication, include one of the following: (1) negation of the existence of the State of Israel as the state of the Jewish people) of 1985 to the text of Amendment No. 35, 'Clause 7(a)(1) A candidates' list shall not participate in the elections to the Knesset if its objects or actions, expressly or by implication, include one of the following: (1) negation of the existence of the State of Israel as a Jewish and a democratic state' of 2002 reveals a significant change, namely, that the reference to 'the state of the Jewish people' was replaced with the reference to 'a Jewish and a democratic state'.

Read in and of itself, this change represents an advance towards liberalizing the idea of the 'Jewish state'. However, such advances as are gained by the said liberalizing advance are immediately nullified by Clause 7(a)(3) disqualifying a candidates' list on the grounds of 'support for armed struggle by an enemy state or a terror organization against the State of Israel'. I am indebted to Advocate Marwan Dalal, staff attorney at Adalah: Legal Centre for Arab Minority Rights in Israel, for the insight.

48. In the quote below the terms 'final status' and 'peace process' (or 'current peace negotiations') have been changed to 'permanent status' and 'permanent status negotiations' respectively.

49. For details of the overall Israeli military evacuation plan see, in Walid Khalidi (ed.), *From Haven to Conquest*, 'Plan Dalet' by Netanel Lorch, and 'Appendix VII: Zionist Military Operations 1 April 1949–15 May 1948, within the Framework of Plan Dalet', Institute of Palestine Studies, Beirut, 1971, pp. 755–60, 856–7.

50. See, for instance, Rael Jean Isaac, *Israel Divided: Ideological Politics in the Jewish State*, Johns Hopkins University Press, Baltimore, MD, 1976; Michael Brecher, *Decision in Crisis: Israel 1967 and 1973*, University of California Press, Berkeley and Los Angeles, 1980; and Rael Jean Isaac, *Party and Politics in Israel: Three Visions of a Jewish State*, Longman, New York, 1981.

51. 'The Mistake, the naivety and the hypocrisy', by Yeshaayahu Ben-Porat, *Yediot Aharonot*, 14 July 1972.

The affair of the Rafah Approaches is essentially the fencing of lands in that area by a military authority for the consideration of needs described as being of 'security'. Security, in the language of the Israeli establishment, and of the establishment in the Land of Israel since way back, meant, and still means, not only to erect an artillery position or a gun in a given spot so as to defend it, but also – and at particular times perhaps essentially – the creation of Jewish territorial continuity in order to establish a pure Zionist fact. In other words: the redemption of the country by way of land appropriation by various means, Jewish settlement on the same lands, and its fortification by military and security means.

This is what took place in the Rafah Approaches, and this is not different in essence from what has taken place in other locations in the Land of Israel and the State of Israel since the day Zionism started to established itself. This includes displacing Arab residents, in this case Bedouin, from the areas that were fenced, and preventing them from returning to their lands. When Katyusha shells land on Kiryat Shmoneh or in its surroundings, isn't there almost always an announcement made by the IDF spokesman, saying that 'our forces shot back in the direction of the sources of fire'? And what does it mean, if not counter-shelling, almost automatic, directed at the Lebanese village nearest to the 'sources of fire' and in which – in the shelled village – there may be saboteurs, but there are certainly peaceful toilers of the land.

One certain truth is that there is no Zionist settlement and there is no Jewish State without displacing Arabs and without confiscating lands and fencing them off. A second truth is that in the war against the Arabs, including the terrorists, Israel never committed itself and cannot commit itself to harm only regular or irregular warriors. And a third truth is that within the framework of the assumptions developed above, Israel has tried in the past and will try in the future to do its best not to kill innocent civilians and not to displace Arab inhabitants by methods not approved of and sanctioned by law and order.

Overt and courageous talk, and clarification of the Zionist conception of the world upon which the state was founded may indeed expose the government to strong criticism at home and to vicious attacks in the world. In spite of that, open-heartedness, both at home and abroad, will dissipate misunderstandings and tear apart the envelope of hypocrisy which covers many of our actions and failures … (Quoted in Uri Davis and Norton Mezvinsky, *Documents from Israel 1967–1973: Readings for a Critique of Zionism*, Ithaca Press, London, 1975, pp. 74–5).

52. Professor Israel Shahak (1933–2002), teacher of organic chemistry at the Hebrew University of Jerusalem and chairman of the Israeli League for Human and Civil Rights. Born the youngest child of a prosperous and highly cultured Polish Jewish family. During the wartime Nazi occupation of Poland, the family was forced into the Warsaw ghetto. Shahak was a starving 12-year-old when he was liberated by American soldiers. Soon afterwards, he immigrated to what was still Palestine. He became a model citizen. Service in an elite regiment was followed by a job as assistant to Professor Ernest David Bergmann, the chair of Israel's Atomic Energy Commission. Israel Shahak underwent two major conversions in his life. At the age of thirteen, he scientifically examined the evidence for the existence of a Jewish god and found it wanting. The second conversion occurred shortly after the 1967 war, when he concluded from observation that Israel was not yet a democracy, after all: it could not be, because it was treating the newly occupied Palestinians with shocking brutality. For the next three decades, he spent all his spare time on attempts to change this, and not just as chairman of the Israeli League for Human and Civil Rights. From his small, bare, West Jerusalem flat, which lacked all creature comforts, Shahak poured forth reports with titles like 'Torture in Israel' or 'Collective Punishment in the West Bank'. Based exclusively on mainstream Israeli sources, all were painstakingly translated into Shahak's fourth language, English. Soon, though, Shahak became concerned with the cause of these human rights incidents: this, he came to believe, was Israel's religious interpretation of Jewish history, which led it to ignore centuries of Arab life in the country, and to disregard non-Jewish rights. Confiscation, every schoolchild was told, was simply 'the redemption of the land' from those who did not belong there. To Shahak, this was straightforward racism, damaging both sides.

Jewish History, Jewish Religion, a detailed study of the attitudes to non-Jews held by Israel's religious establishment, was published by Pluto Press in 1994. Shahak also emphasized the fate decreed for Jewish heretics: this fate was death, and, shortly after the book appeared, Israeli Premier Yitzhak Rabin was assassinated by an orthodox student. *Jewish Fundamentalism in Israel* (Pluto Press, 1999) written with Norton Mezvinsky, looked at the growing power of right-wing orthodox groups in Israeli political life. Typically, Shahak made clear that this was not just an altruistic concern: 'A fundamentalist Jewish regime, if it came to power in Israel,' he warned, 'would treat Israeli Jews who did not accept its tenets worse than it would treat Palestinians.' (Based on Elfi Pallis's obituary, *Guardian*, 6 July 2002.)

53. A political biographical outline of Uri Avnery's career in this context is in order. Uri Avnery was born in 1923 in Beckum, Germany, as Helmut Ostermann. With the rise of Adolf Hitler to government power in 1933, his family left Germany and settled in Palestine and in the period 1938–41 he was a member of the IZL (*Irgun*) under the command of Menachem Begin, who in 1977 became Israel's fifth prime minister. Between 1941 and 1946 Uri Avnery was a regular contributor to the fascist Hebrew periodicals *Ha-Hevrah* ('Society') and *Bamaavak* ('In the Struggle'). In the 1948–49 war he was a company commander of the motorized commando unit known as 'Samson's Foxes', whose political commissar was the writer and the poet Abba Kobner. In 1951 together with Shalom Cohen he took over the photographic news weekly *Haloam Hazeh* ('This World'), of which he was editor-in-chief until he sold the paper in 1990 to one of Ariel Sharon's closer collaborators, and, at the time of writing, his prime

minister's emissary to the White House, the businessman Arye Genger. In 1958 Avnery was a founding member of the anti-French Israel Committee for Free Algeria; in the mid-1960s, a founding member of the League Against Religious Coercion and the Committee Against the Military Government; in the period 1965–1973, Member of Knesset for the Haolam Hazeh – New Force movement, and 1979–1980, Member of Knesset for Sheli (acronym for Semol Yisraeli, Israeli Left). Throughout his life, Uri Avnery presented his membership in the IZL and in the Giv'ati brigade commando unit 'Samson's Foxes' as positive credentials testifying to his credibility as an Israeli patriot. The implications of this have affected Avnery's political career throughout. *Haolam Hazeh* weekly under Avnery's and Cohen's leadership quickly became Israel's best muckraking independent Israeli newspaper, exposing corruption and attacking both foreign and home policies of the Israeli government. Throughout the 1950s and 1960s the paper led the struggle against the violation of human and political rights of Arabs under Israeli Jewish rule, against the notorious Defence (Emergency) Regulations of 1945, against the military regime, religious coercion, corruption, etc.

Yet, during the 1967 war, as editor-in-chief of *Haolam Hazeh*, he issued a daily news sheet *Daf* ('Page') which came out with an issue carrying a huge headline 'On Damascus!' advocating the Israeli occupation of the Syrian capital. When the annexation of East Jerusalem came to a vote in the Israeli Parliament shortly after the war (27 June 1967) Uri Avnery joined the national coalition government and voted for the annexation of the city. To the best knowledge of this writer, this is the only political act he publicly regretted throughout his entire political career. (Quoted in Fouzi el-Asmar, Uri Davis and Naim Khader [eds], *Debate on Palestine*, Ithaca Press, London, 1981, pp. 145–9.)

54. Honorary citizenship of Abu-Ghosh near Jerusalem, for his part in preventing the eviction of the village (notorious for the collaboration of a significant section of its population with the Revisionist Zionist paramilitary and terrorist organization the *Irgun* or IZL), 1953; honorary citizenship of Kafr Qasim, Israel 1996, on the occasion of the fortieth anniversary of the war crime, for his principal role in exposing it (the Kafr Qasim massacre was, in fact, first exposed by the Advocate Mordechai Stein, publisher of *The Democratic Newspaper*); Aachen Peace Prize for 'Gush Shalom with Uri Avnery', 1997; Kreisky Prize for human rights, Vienna, 1997; Lower Saxony Prize for human rights, 1998; Palestinian Award for human rights, awarded by LAW, Palestinian Society for Human Rights, Jerusalem, 1998; and the Right Livelihood Award for 'Gush Shalom and Uri Avnery together with Rachel Avnery', 2001 on the likes of Uri Avnery.

55. The total area of the State of Israel in its pre-1967 armistice lines boundaries is 20,600,000 dunums (including lakes), 20,100,000 dunums (excluding lakes), of which some 4,200,000 are classified by the Israel Lands Administration (ILA) as agricultural land. Of the said 20-odd million dunums, 93 per cent are under the ownership of the state (some 73 per cent), the Jewish National Fund (JNF; some 14 per cent) and the Development Authority (some 13 per cent). (Based on Israel Lands Administration 2001: 65.)

The Israeli Jewish *kibbutz* population, constituting approximately 2 per cent of the total Israeli population, controls some 35 per cent (1.5 million dunums) of the total of agricultural lands inside pre-1967 Israel. The Israeli Jewish *moshav* population, constituting approximately 3.3 per cent of the total Israeli population, controls 26 per cent (1.1 million dunums) of the total of agricultural lands. (Based on *Statistical Abstract of Israel*, No. 53, Table 2.9, pp. 2–26 and 2–27; Kedar and Yiftahel 1999: 11; and Lehn in association with Davis 1988: 114.)

Bibliography

Abu Lughod, Janet (1971) 'The demographic transformation of Palestine', in Ibrahim Abu Lughod (ed.), *The Transformation of Palestine*, Northwestern University Press, Evanston, IL.

Abu Sitta, Salman (1998) *The Palestinian Nakba, 1948*, Palestinian Return Centre, London.

— (1999) *Palestinian Right to Return: Sacred, Legal and Possible*, Palestinian Return Centre, London.

— (2001) *The End of the Palestinian–Israeli Conflict: From Refugees to Citizens at Home*, Palestine Land Society and Palestinian Return Centre, London.

Adalah: The Legal Center for Arab Minority Rights in Israel (1998) *Legal Violations of Arab Minority Rights in Israel: A Report on Israel's Implementation of the International Convention on the Elimination of All Forms of Racial Discrimination*, Shfaram.

Allen, Jim (1987) *Perdition: A Play in Two Acts*, Ithaca Press, London.

Aloni, Shulmith (1971) *Ha-Hesder [The Arrangement]: From the Rule of Secular Law to the Rule of Religious Law*, Otpaz, Tel Aviv (Hebrew).

— (n.d., *c.* 1970) *Israel Has No Constitution – Why?*, pamphlet (Hebrew).

Arendt, Hannah (1963) *Eichmann in Jerusalem: A Report on the Banality of Evil*, Faber & Faber, London.

Asmar, Fouzi el- (1975) *To be an Arab in Israel*, Frances Pinter, London.

Association of Forty (1996) *Memorandom*, Ein Hod.

— (2001) *The Unrecognized Arab Villages*, Ein Hod.

Avnery, Uri (1986) *My Friend, the Enemy*, Zed Books, London.

Bartal, Gabriel (1991) *The General Federation: Structure and Activities*, Executive Committee, General Federation of Workers in the Land of Israel, Tel Aviv, 1991 (updated edn) (Hebrew).

Brenner, Lenni (1983) *Zionism in the Age of the Dictators: A Reappraisal*, Croom Helm, London, 1983.

— (1987) 'Zionism and rescue', in Jim Allen, *Perdition: A Play in Two Acts*, Ithaca Press.

— (ed.) (2002) *51 Documents: Zionist Collaboration with the Nazis*, Barricade Books, Fort Lee, NJ.

Buber, Martin (1949) *Paths in Utopia* (trans. R. F. C. Hull), Routledge & Kegan Paul, London.

— (1963) *Israel and the World*, Stockmen Books, New York.

— (1963) *Pointing the Way* (ed. and trans. with introduction by Maurice Friedman), Harper Torchbooks, Harper & Row, New York and Evanston, IL.

Cattan, Henry (1969) *Palestine, the Arabs and Israel*, Longman, London.

— (1988) *The Palestine Question*, Croom Helm, London.

Center for Policy Analysis on Palestine (1992) *Facts and Figures About the Palestinians*, Information Paper No. 1, Center for Policy Analysis on Palestine, Washington, DC.

Davis, Uri (1977) *Israel: Utopia Incorporated – A Study of Class, State, and Corporate Kin Control*, Zed Books, London.

— (1994) *Crossing the Border* (autobiography), Breirot Publishers (Hebrew), Tel Aviv (English trans. 1995, Books & Books, London).

— (1996) *Citizenship for Palestine Refugees and the Peace Process*, Shaml: Palestinian Diaspora and Refugee Centre, Monograph Series No. 1, Ramallah.

— (1997) *Citizenship and the State: Comparative Study of Citizenship Legislation in Israel, Jordan, Palestine, Syria and Lebanon*, Ithaca Press, Reading.

— (2000a) *Citizenship and the State in the Middle East* (co-ed. with Nils Butenschon and Manuel Hassassian), Syracuse University Press, New York.

— (2000b) 'Who is a Hebrew: a reading of an identity construction: Palestinian Hebrew anti-Zionist Jew of dual Israeli and British citizenship', *SAIS Review: A Journal of International Affairs*, Paul H. Nitze School of Advanced International Studies, Johns Hopkins University, XX (1): 107–16.

— (2001) *Israel: An Apartheid State*, Zed Books, London.

Davis, Uri and Norton Mezvinsky (eds) (1975) *Documents from Israel 1967–1973*, Ithaca Press, London.

Dowty, Alan (2000) 'Much ado about little: Ahad Ha'am's "truth from Eretz Yisrael", Zionism, and the Arabs', *Israel Studies*, 5 (2), Fall.

Dumper, Michael (1993) *Islam and Israel: Muslim Religious Endowments and the Jewish State*, Institute for Palestine Studies, Washington, DC.

Encyclopaedia Hebraica (1976) Encyclopaedia Publishing Company, Jerusalem.

Encyclopaedia Judaica (1971) Keter Publishing House, Jerusalem.

Finkelstein, Norman (2000) *The Holocaust Industry*, Verso, London.

Flapan, Simha (1979) *Zionism and the Palestinians*, Croom Helm, London.

— (1987) *The Birth of Israel: Myths and Realities*, Croom Helm, London.

Gabbay, Rony E. (1959) *A Political Study of the Arab–Jewish Conflict: The Arab Refugee Problem (A Case Study)*, Librairie E. Droz, Geneva and Librairie Minard, Paris.

Gilbert, Martin (1978) *Exile and Return, the Emergence of Jewish Statehood*, Weidenfeld and Nicolson, London.

Ginsberg, Asher (Ahad ha-Am) (1930), 'Truth from *Eretz Israel*', Judischer Verlag, Berlin, 1921 (new edn).

Goldstein, Jacob (ed.) (1976) *The Eretz Israel Workers' Movement in the Second [Zionist] Immigration*, Department for Eretz Israel Studies, University of Haifa.

Gruenbaum, Yitzhaq (1946) *Bi-Yemei Hurban ve-Shoah* (In the Days of Destruction and Holocaust), Haverim, Tel Aviv.

Hadawi, Sami (1957) *Land Ownership in Palestine*, Palestine Arab Refugee Office, New York.

Halabi, Usama (1991) 'Arab citizens' rights and their status in Israel', *Majallat al-Dirasat al-Filastiniyya*, No. 5, Winter: 127–48 (Arabic).

Hecht, Ben (*c.* 1962) *Perfidy*, Julian Messner, New York.

Hertzberg, Arthur (1973) *The Zionist Idea*, Temple Book, Atheneum, New York.

Hirst, David (1977) *The Gun and the Olive Branch*, Faber & Faber, London (Futura Publications 1978).

Hunter, Jane (1987) *Undercutting Sanctions: Israel, the U.S. and South Africa* (revised edn), Washington Middle East Associates, Washington, DC.

Islamic Cultural Centre (1978) *Islamic Pious Foundations in Jerusalem: Origins, History and Usurpation by Israel*, London.

Israel, Central Bureau of Statistics (2001) *List of Localities*, Technical Publication Series No. 72, Jerusalem.

— (2002) *Statistical Abstracts of Israel 2002*, No. 53, Jerusalem.

Israel Lands Administration (2001) *Report on the Activities of the Administration for the Financial Year 2000*, No. 40, ILA, Jerusalem (Hebrew).

Issa, Mahmoud (1997) *Lubya: A Palestinian Village in the Middle East – Historiography, Culture and Identity* (sponsored by Danish Research Council for the Humanities, published by Carsten Niebuhr Institute of Near Eastern Studies), University of Copenhagen.

Jabbour, George (1970) *Settler Colonialism in South Africa and the Middle East*, Palestine Books No. 30, University of Khartoum and PLO Research Center, Beirut.

Jabotinsky, Vladimir (1984) 'The Iron Wall', first published in Russian under the title 'O Zheleznoi Stene' in *Rassvyet*, 4 November 1923; published in English in *Jewish Herald* (South Africa), 26 November 1937; reprinted here from Lenni Brenner, *The Iron Wall: Zionist Revisionism from Jabotinsky to Shamir*, Zed Books, London, pp. 73–5.

Jewish National Fund (1949) 'Jewish villages in Israel', unpublished document, Jerusalem.

Jiryis, Sabri (1976) *The Arabs in Israel* (foreword by Noam Chomsky), Monthly Review Press, New York.

Joseph, Benjamin (1988) *Besieged Bedfellows: Israel and the Land of Apartheid*, Greenwood Press, New York.

Judgments of the Supreme Court of the State of Israel (PADI) (1962) Case No. 72162, Vol. 16 (IV) (Hebrew).

— (1969) Case No. 58/68, Vol. 23 (II).

— (1972) Case No. 18/72, Vol. 26 (I).

— (1977) Case No. 653/75, Vol. 31 (II).

— (2000) Case No. 6698/95, Vol. 54 (I).

Kedar, Alexander (Sandy) (2001) 'The legal transformation of ethnic geography: Israeli law and the Palestinian landholder 1948–1967', *New York University Journal of International Law and Politics*, 33 (4), Summer.

Kedar, Alexander (Sandy) and Oren Yiftahel (1999) *Agricultural Lands in Israel Towards the End of the Millennium: Historical, Legal and Social Aspects*, Research Report No. 4, Centre for the Study of Crime, Law and Society, University of Haifa (Hebrew).

Khader, Naim, 'An Initial Response to Dr Emil Tuma and His Comments on the Socialist Republic of Palestine', in Fouzi el-Asmar, Uri Davis and Naim Khader, *Debate on Palestine*, Ithaca Press, London.

Khalidi, Walid (1988) 'Plan Dalet: master plan for the conquest of Palestine', *Journal of Palestine Studies*, 18 (69), Autumn: 4–20.

— (1992) *All That Remains*, Institute for Palestine Studies, Washington, DC.

Khalifa, Ahmed Fathi (1994) *The Muslim Tourist Guide*, Al-Aqsa Society for the Preservation of the Muslim Awqaf, Umm al-Fahm (Arabic).

Kimmerling, Baruch (1977) 'Sovereignty, ownership and presence in the Jewish–Arab territorial conflict: the case of Bir'im and Ikrit', *Comparative Political Studies*, 10 (2).

— (1983) *Zionism and Economy*, Schenkman Publishing, Cambridge, MA.

Kimmerling, Baruch and Joel Migdal (1993) *Palestinians: The Making of a People*, Free Press, New York.

Kretzmer, David (1990) *The Legal Status of the Arabs in Israel*, Westview Special Studies on the Middle East in cooperation with the International Center for Peace in the Middle East, Tel Aviv, Westview Press, Boulder, CO.

Kuttab, Jonathan and Raja Shehadeh (1982) *Civilian Administration in the Occupied West Bank: An Analysis of Israeli Military Government Order No. 947*, Law in the Service of Man, Ramallah.

Laqueur, Walter (1972) *A History of Zionism*, Weidenfeld & Nicolson, London.

Lehn, Walter (1974) 'Zionist land: the Jewish National Fund', *Journal of Palestine Studies*, Summer.

Lehn, Walter in association with Uri Davis (1988) *The Jewish National Fund*, Kegan Paul International, London.

Lustick, Ian (1980) *Arabs in the Jewish State: Israel's Control of a National Minority*, University of Texas Press, Austin.

Mallison, Thomas and Sally Mallison (1986) *The Palestine Problem in International Law and World Order*, Longman, Harlow.

Masalha, Nur (1992) *Expulsion of the Palestinians: The Concept of 'Transfer' in Zionist Political Thought, 1882–1948*, Institute for Palestine Studies, Washington, DC.

— (1997) *A Land without a People: Israel, Transfer and the Palestinians 1949–96*, Faber and Faber, London.

Mazzawi, Musa (1997) *Palestine and the Law: Guidelines for the Resolution of the Arab–Israel Conflict*, Ithaca Press, Reading.

Morris, Benny (1987) *The Birth of the Palestine Refugee Problem*, Cambridge University Press, Cambridge.

Orni, Ephraim (1974) *Agrarian Reform and Social Progress in Israel*, Jewish National Fund, Jerusalem.

Orr, Akiva (1983) *The UnJewish State: The Politics of Jewish Identity in Israel*, Ithaca Press, London.

— (1994) *Israel: Politics, Myths and Identity Crisis*, Pluto Press, London.

Oz, Amos (1983) 'About the soft and the delicate', *Davar*, 17 December 1982, reprinted in *Here and There in Eretz Israel in the Autumn of 1982*, Am Oved, pp. 70–82 (Hebrew).

Palestine Liberation Organization/Department of Refugee Affairs (2000) *The Palestinian Refugees Factfile*, PLO/Department of Refugee Affairs, Ramallah, April.

Palumbo, Michael (1987) *The Palestinian Catastrophe: The 1948 Expulsion of a People from Their Homeland*, Faber & Faber, London.

Pape, Ilan (1992) *The Making of the Arab–Israeli Conflict: 1947–1951*, I.B. Tauris, London.

Peretz, Don (1958) *Israel and the Palestinian Arabs*, Middle East Institute, Washington, DC.

Prinz, Joachim (1934) *Wir Juden*, Erich Reiss, Berlin.

Rabinowitz, Danny and Khawla Abu Baker (2002) *The Stand Tall Generation: The Palestinian Citizens of Israel Today*, Keter, Jerusalem (Hebrew).

Rattner, Arye and Gideon Fishman (1998) *Justice for All? Jews and Arabs in the Israeli Criminal Justice System*, Research Report No. 1, Center for the Study of Crime, Law and Society, University of Haifa (Hebrew).

Reinhart, Tanya (2002) *Israel/Palestine: How to End the War of 1948*, Seven Stories Press, New York.

Rogan, Eugene and Avi Shlaim (eds) (2001) *The War for Palestine: Rewriting the History of 1948*, Cambridge University Press, Cambridge.

Rosen-Zvi, Ariel (1990) *Israeli Family Law: The Sacred and the Secular*, Papyrus Publishing House, Tel Aviv University, Tel Aviv (Hebrew).

Said, Edward (1980) *The Question of Palestine*, Routledge & Kegan Paul.

Sartre, Jean-Paul (1965) *Anti-Semite and Jew*, Schocken Books, New York.

Shahak, Israel (1994) *Jewish History, Jewish Religion: The Weight of Three Thousand Years* (foreword by Gore Vidal), Pluto Press, London.

Shava, Menashe (1991) *The Personal Law in Israel* (3rd expanded edn), Publications of the Faculty of Law, No. 13, Tel Aviv University, Massadah, Tel Aviv (Hebrew).

Shehadeh, Raja (1988) *Occupier's Law: Israel and the West Bank*, prepared for Al-Haq/Law in the Service of Man, the West Bank Affiliate of the International Commission of Jurists (rev. edn, Institute of Palestine Studies, Washington, DC).

— (1997) *From Occupation to Interim Accords: Israel and the Palestinian Territories* (Cimel Book Series, No. 4), School of Oriental and African Studies and Kluwer Law International, The Hague, 1997.

Shehadeh, Raja and Jonathan Kuttab (1980) *The West Bank and the Rule of Law*, International Commission of Jurists and Law in the Service of Man, Geneva and Ramallah.

Shlaim, Avi (1988) *Collution Across the Jordan: King Abdullah, the Zionist Movement and the Partition of Palestine*, Clarendon Press, Oxford.

Smuts, J. C. (n.d.) 'ADDRESS Delivered by J.C. SMUTS P.C. M.L.A. Prime Minister of the Union of South Africa On MONDAY, NOVEMBER 3rd 1919 In the TOWN HALL, JOHANNESBURG AT A RECEPTION Given in his Honour by the JEWISH COMMUNITY OF SOUTH AFRICA Under the Auspices of the South African Zionist Federation and the South African Jewish Board of Deputies' (pamphlet).

State of Israel People's Council, *Protocols of Debates*.

— *Knesset Debates*.

— *Stenographic Protocols*.

— *Law of the State of Israel*.

— Central Bureau of Statistics (2001) *List of Localities, Their Population and Codes*, Technical Publications Series No. 72, Jerusalem.

— (2002) *Statistical Abstracts of Israel*, No. 53, Jerusalem.

Stevens, Richard (1975) *Weizmann and Smuts: A Study in Zionist–South African Cooperation*, Institute for Palestine Studies, Beirut.

Stevens, Richard and Abdalwahab Elmessiri (1977) *Israel and South Africa: The Progression of a Relationship* (rev. edn), New Brunswick, NJ.

United Nations (1947) *Plan of Partition with Economic Union*, UN General Assembly Resolution 181(II) of 29 November 1947, quoted in Institute of Palestine Studies, *United Nations Resolutions on Palestine and the Arab–Israeli Conflict, 1947–1998*, Institute for Palestine Studies, Washington, DC, 1975, pp. 4–14.

— (1988) 40th Anniversary of the Universal Declaration of Human Rights 1948–1988, *The International Bill of Human Rights* (Universal Declaration of Human Rights, International Convenant on Economic, Social and Economic Rights, International Covenant on Civil and Political Rights and Optional Protocol), United Nations, New York.

Weissmandel, Rabbi Michael Dov (1960) *Min ha-Metzar* (From the Depth of Distress), Emunah Press, New York, 1960 (Hebrew).

Weitz, Joseph 91965) *My Diary and Letters to the Children*, Massadah, Tel Aviv (Hebrew).

World Zionist Organization (1992) *The Constitution of the World Zionist Organization and Regulations for Its Implementation*, Organization Department, WZO, Jerusalem.

Yiftahel, Oren (1992) *Planning a Mixed Region in Israel: The Political Geography of Arab–Jewish Relations in the Galilee*, Avebury, Gower Publishing, Aldershot.

Yizraeli, David (1974) *The Palestine Problem in German Politics, 1889–1945*, Bar Ilan University, Ramat Gan.

Index